'Disability concerns us all – and this nuanced, rigorous, timely account charts for the first time the politics of disability advocacy and new media. Essential reading.'

Gerard Goggin, *University of Sydney, Australia*

'Trevisan has produced a persuasive, empirically-rich study that makes an important contribution to how we understand the contemporary disability rights movement, not just in the UK, but around the world. This study illuminates the role of social media in formulating and advancing a rights-based policy agenda, and how the Internet can be used to combat the stigma sometimes still surrounding persons with disabilities. The result is a fascinating read for disability experts, but also more broadly for scholars of progressive political movements.'

Derrick L. Cogburn, *School of International Service,*
American University, USA

D1732854

Disability Rights Advocacy Online

Disability rights advocates in the United Kingdom and the United States recently embraced new media technologies in unexpected and innovative ways. This book sheds light on this process of renewal and asks whether the digitalisation of disability rights advocacy can help re-configure political participation into a more inclusive experience for disabled Internet users, enhancing their stakes in democratic citizenship. Through the examination of social media content, Web link analysis, and interviews with leading figures in grassroots groups on both sides of the Atlantic, Filippo Trevisan reveals the profound impact that the Internet has had on disability advocacy in the wake of the austerity agenda that followed the 2008 global financial crisis. In Britain, a new, tech-savvy generation of young disabled self-advocates has emerged from this process. The role of social media platforms such as Facebook in helping politically inexperienced users make sense of complex policy changes through the use of personal stories is discussed also. In addition, this book explains why British disability advocates adopted more innovative and participatory strategies compared to their American counterparts when faced with similar policy crises. This book reviews the implications of this unexpected digital transformation for the structure of the disability rights movement, its leadership, and the opportunity for disabled citizens to participate fully in democratic politics *vis-à-vis* persisting Web access and accessibility barriers. An original perspective on the relationship between disability and the Internet, and an indispensable read for scholars wishing to contextualize and enrich their knowledge on digital disability rights campaigns in the broader ecology of policy-making.

Filippo Trevisan is Assistant Professor in the School of Communication at American University in Washington, DC, where he is also Deputy Director of the Institute on Disability and Public Policy. His research interests include new media technologies, political participation, grassroots advocacy, disability and inequality.

Routledge Studies in Global Information, Politics and Society
Edited by Kenneth Rogerson, Duke University and Laura Roselle, Elon University

International communication encompasses everything from one-to-one cross-cultural interactions to the global reach of a broad range of information and communications technologies and processes. *Routledge Studies in Global Information, Politics and Society* celebrates – and embraces – this depth and breadth. To completely understand communication, it must be studied in concert with many factors, since, most often, it is the foundational principle on which other subjects rest. This series provides a publishing space for scholarship in the expansive, yet intersecting, categories of communication and information processes and other disciplines.

The Power of Information Networks
New Directions for Agenda Setting
Edited by Lei Guo and Maxwell McCombs

Television News and Human Rights in the US & UK
The Violations Will Not Be Televised
Shawna M. Brandle

Beyond the Internet
Unplugging the Protest Movement Wave
Edited by Rita Figueiras and Paula do Espírito Santo

Twitter and Elections Around the World
Campaigning in 140 Characters or Less
Edited by Richard Davis, Christina Holtz-Bacha, and Marion Just

Political Communication in Real Time
Theoretical and Applied Research Approaches
Edited by Dan Schill, Rita Kirk, and Amy Jasperson

Disability Rights Advocacy Online
Voice, Empowerment and Global Connectivity
Filippo Trevisan

Disability Rights Advocacy Online

Voice, Empowerment and Global Connectivity

Filippo Trevisan

Routledge
Taylor & Francis Group

NEW YORK AND LONDON

First published 2017
by Routledge
711 Third Avenue, New York, NY 10017

and by Routledge
2 Park Square, Milton Park, Abingdon, Oxon, OX14 4RN

First issued in paperback 2018

Routledge is an imprint of the Taylor & Francis Group, an informa business

Library of Congress Cataloging in Publication Data
Names: Trevisan, Filippo, author.
Title: Disability rights advocacy online: voice, empowerment and global connectivity / Filippo Trevisan.
Description: New York, NY : Routledge, 2017. | Series: Routledge studies in global information, politics and society; 13 | Includes bibliographical references and index.
Identifiers: LCCN 2016018726 | ISBN 9781138847828 (hbk) | ISBN 9781315726489 (ebk)
Subjects: LCSH: People with disabilities–Civil rights–Great Britain. | People with disabilities–Civil rights–United States. | Social advocacy–Great Britain. | Social advocacy–United States. | Internet and activism–Great Britain. | Internet and activism–United States.
Classification: LCC HV1559.G6 T74 2017 | DDC 323.3–dc23
LC record available at https://lccn.loc.gov/2016018726

ISBN 13: 978-0-367-00027-1 (pbk)
ISBN 13: 978-1-138-84782-8 (hbk)

Typeset in Sabon
by Sunrise Setting Ltd., Brixham, UK

For my parents,
Anna and Milvio

Contents

Figures

Tables

Series Editor's Foreword

This book series is interested in the broad range of works that seek to understand the relationship between media technology, politics and society. We are proud to include Trevisan's work on disability advocacy and Internet-based media. This work focuses on citizenship, highlighting the agency of those who overcome barriers to media use. The reaction to welfare reform in the U.K. (2010–12) serves as an important case to understand the strengths and limitations of disability advocacy online. The comparison to the U.S. provides a broader context. Overall, through this work we learn more about access to technology and the political process.

Laura Roselle

Acknowledgements

Obviously this book could never have been possible without the help, support and encouragement of a great number of people with whom I shared different parts of this journey. First of all, I want to thank Sarah Oates and Charlotte Pearson who provided incredible mentorship in the complex task of bringing together the fields of Internet politics and disability studies. I was very fortunate to be able to benefit from their expert advice and look forward to our future collaborations. I am extremely grateful also to Diana Owen and the American Studies program at Georgetown University for supporting me during my fieldwork trip to Washington, DC in the summer of 2011, as well as to Verenda Camire for helping to make that visit stress-free and wonderfully enjoyable. More heartfelt thanks go out to Paul Reilly for the many inspiring conversations we had about this project in recent years and Mariana Leyton Escobar for our chats about the literature. I also want to acknowledge the activists, advocates and campaigners who took the time to be interviewed for this project in the U.K. and the U.S. This book simply would not have been the same without their generous contribution.

I am indebted also to the book series editors, Laura Roselle and Ken Rogerson, for believing in this project from when I first told them about my idea for this book and providing wonderful encouragement through the writing process. Thank you also to the editorial team at Routledge, in particular Natalja Mortensen and Lillian Rand, who were always on hand to answer my queries, no matter how last minute these were. As this is my first monograph, I could not have asked for more expert and patient guidance. In addition, I wish to thank my colleagues in the School of Communication and the Institute on Disability and Public Policy at American University. Completing this book during my first year in a new job, at a new institution and having just moved to a new country was never going to be simple. It was truly humbling to be able to count on the support of so many great new colleagues who supported me during this transition and with whom I immediately felt at home.

A final set of thanks goes out nearer to home. First to my family back in Italy, in particular my parents Anna and Milvio, to whom this book is dedicated, and my brother Giacomo. Despite the time difference, they have always been there when I needed them, most recently experimenting with mobile technology to reduce distance. Finally, I wish to say a massive thank you to my wife Lotta for her love and encouragement, for lifting my spirits with the occasional Finnish home bake and for generously lending her skills as a formatting and reference software wizard – I cannot cease to be amazed by her knowledge and patience. Any mistakes or omissions are of course my own.

Funding

The research carried out for this book was funded by the Economic and Social Research Council, grant number ES/G01213X/1: *Disabled People, the Internet and Participation: Building a Better Society?*

Abbreviations

ADA	Americans with Disabilities Act
CRPD	Convention on the Rights of Persons with Disabilities
DDA	Disability Discrimination Act
DLA	Disability Living Allowance
DPOs	Disabled People's Organisations
DWP	Department for Work and Pensions
ESA	Employment and Support Allowance
ILF	Independent Living Fund
PIP(s)	Personal Independence Payment(s)
TUC	Trades Union Congress
WCA	Work Capability Assessment
WRB	Welfare Reform Bill

Disability Organisations and Groups

United Kingdom

	Action for ME
	Ambitious About Autism
	Disability Alliance
DBC	Disability Benefits Consortium
	Disability Rights U.K.
DPAC	Disabled People Against Cuts
	Inclusion London
LCD	Leonard Cheshire Disability
	Mencap
	Mind
NAS	National Autistic Society
NCIL	National Centre for Independent Living
RADAR	Royal Association for Disability Rights

RNIB   Royal National Institute of Blind People
        Scope
        Spartacus Network
        The Broken of Britain
        The Hardest Hit
        The MS Society
UKDPC   United Kingdom Disabled People's Council

United States

        Access Living
        ADAPT
AAPD   American Association of People with Disabilities
        The ARC
        Autism Speaks/Autism Votes
CCD   Consortium for Citizens with Disabilities
        Easter Seals
LDA   Learning Disabilities Association of America
NCIL   National Council on Independent Living
NDRN   National Disability Rights Network
NFB   National Federation of the Blind
MHA   Mental Health America
        National MS Society
UCP   United Cerebral Palsy

Introduction

In January 2016, the toy company Lego unveiled its first ever wheelchair-using figure. Lego's decision to include this new figure in its product range followed repeated requests from disability rights advocates that toys should represent disabled children better. In particular, a U.K.-based grassroots campaign called 'Toy Like Me' was a key driver behind Lego's decision. Toy Like Me communicated mainly through its Facebook page and did not have a website. To demonstrate public support for its Lego campaign, it launched an online petition using the popular platform Change.org. Eventually, about 20,000 people worldwide signed the petition. The Lego campaign may look fairly straightforward, but it certainly shows that disability rights e-advocacy has potential. Despite being relative latecomers to the digital arena compared to advocacy organisations in other areas, a growing number of grassroots disability groups have employed new media technologies to influence public decision-making in recent years, sometimes successfully and others less so. This book explores the interaction between disability rights advocacy and Internet-based media, considering its implications for the levels of citizenship of disabled people in the United Kingdom and the United States.

The United Nations Convention on the Rights of Persons with Disabilities (CRPD) states that disabled people have a right to participate fully in political and public life (art. 29). However, several barriers remain that prevent disabled citizens from having the opportunity to exercise their political rights fully, including in advanced democratic nations such as the U.K. and the U.S. (Equality and Human Rights Commission 2010; Schur et al. 2013). This is a particularly important issue at a time when the financial instability that followed the global economic crisis of 2008 and the austerity measures that were devised in response to it threaten to cut the support that many disabled people need in order to be able to lead an independent life. Given these circumstances, it is extremely important that disabled citizens have access to opportunities to influence public decision-making effectively. Policy measures such as drastic government budget cuts, the downsizing of welfare programmes and reductions in public services appear to have touched a special chord with citizens in several countries. This has led to the emergence of resistance networks that in recent years have made extensive use of online media to mobilise supporters, organise them and spread their messages across different social groups and beyond national borders. Prime examples of this 'activist revival' have included the Spanish *Indignados* and the transnational Occupy movement, both of which rose to prominence in 2011 (Castells 2012; Gerbaudo 2012).

Although each of these phenomena took place in different contexts, their emergence raises the issue of whether new media technologies and the ways in which citizens use them have entered a new phase of maturity in which mass mobilisation and sweeping political change are reflected and accelerated – if not ignited – by online platforms. This could be interpreted as a consequence of the growing tendency for citizens not only to benefit from augmented and facilitated access to information online (Howard & Chadwick 2009), but also to be capable and expectant of an especially active role in both established and emergent political organisations (Bimber et al. 2012). Undoubtedly, these are very broad issues that reach beyond the agenda of any individual scholar and are likely to dominate Internet/politics research for several years to come. However, at this time of activist ferment, it is particularly important to ask what the growing centrality of Internet-based media to the dynamics of grassroots organising means for those who traditionally have been excluded from the civic arena. As the politics of austerity carries on and a protracted period of uncertainty looms following Britain's decision to leave the European Union in June 2016, the rights of marginalised social groups are at a severe risk of being eroded even further due to the lack of equal opportunities and effective ways for them to express dissent. Are traditionally disadvantaged groups also going to benefit from the digitalisation of advocacy and protest in these times of crisis, or will online organising constitute a source of additional inequality and exclusion instead?

Most of the studies that investigated the relationship between disadvantaged groups and the Internet so far reported negative conclusions, suggesting a rather bleak outlook for those who are already politically marginalised. Typically, this work has associated people experiencing disadvantage with the raw end of digital divide theories, emphasising the tendency for those on low incomes and/or with modest educational attainments to benefit less than others from online media or be completely unconnected (Norris 2001; Warschauer 2003). Among these groups, disabled people have occupied an especially prominent position. In particular, the existing literature on disability and new media focuses overwhelmingly on access and accessibility issues, stressing how socially constructed technology is bound to reproduce exclusionary barriers and generate disability discrimination in the online sphere (see, for instance, Goggin & Newell 2003; Ellis & Kent 2011). Intuitively, these issues should worry both researchers and activists as they highlight some important barriers that could prevent disabled citizens from becoming fully involved in the changing landscape of grassroots politics at a time in which welfare reforms and other austerity measures threaten some of their most fundamental socio-economic rights. Nevertheless, one also has to ask whether such a strong focus on the digital divide can truly nurture a comprehensive understanding of the complex relationship between disability and the Internet. Scratching beneath the surface of accessibility literature offers a different picture. This is one in which new media technologies may afford disabled Internet users opportunities to re-negotiate some disabling barriers (Roulstone 1998, p. 129), but where alternative research strands have been side-lined in favour of a dominant narrative that fits with both the digital divide paradigm and the barrier-centred social model of disability.

Recent work in Internet studies has defied common wisdom by showing that online media can indeed foster social cohesion and civic engagement among those experiencing socio-economic disadvantage (Gad et al. 2012). In addition, the last few years have been characterised by some substantial advancements in Internet accessibility (Ellcessor 2016) and the cost of connection has been falling at a staggeringly fast pace (International Telecommunication Union 2012), making access not only more affordable but at the same time also more relevant to disabled people. As a result, a majority of disabled respondents in recent survey studies on Internet use in both the U.K. (Dutton & Blank 2013) and the U.S. (Fox 2011) defined themselves as regular users. This, coupled with on-going political and economic uncertainty, makes widening the scope of disability and new media research both timely and worthwhile. This is not an attempt to underplay the importance of access and accessibility issues, which ought to remain top priorities for researchers, technology developers and policy-makers alike. Instead, it is intended as a contribution towards a fuller and more nuanced understanding of the complex relationship between disability and the Internet, as well as a way of determining the position of disabled people in today's fast-changing techno-political environment. In other words, this book responds to the need to illuminate under-researched aspects of the relationship between disability and online media by shifting the investigative focus from that sizeable proportion of disabled people who are unconnected to the majority that, despite accessibility issues, regularly uses the Internet.

Moving from the idea that disruptive events can push otherwise disengaged and disenfranchised citizens towards political action (Woliver 1993), this book maps and discusses the online opposition to the disability welfare reform introduced by the U.K. Conservative-led government between 2010 and 2012. By pursuing this approach and adopting the idea of inclusive citizenship (Lister 2007) as the overarching framework, the arguments presented in this book avoid the trap of technological determinism and are shaped consistently by empirical evidence. Inevitably, this also means that opportunities to generalise findings are somewhat restricted by the limitations usually associated with case study research. Undoubtedly, this book represents but a starting point in the complex task of reaching beyond the restrictive access/accessibility framework applied so far in disability and new media studies. Nevertheless, as the first extensive contribution in this area, the fieldwork carried out for this study revealed some unexpected elements that it is hoped would spur further research and reflection among both scholars and activists. In particular, several empirical findings are discussed that actively contravened theory-based assumptions, highlighting both positive and negative aspects of the digitalisation of disability rights advocacy that surrounded the U.K. welfare reform controversy. In addition, the British experience is contextualised by comparing it to parallel developments in digital disability rights advocacy in the U.S. This provides innovative insights on the intersection of online campaigning, democratic political systems and circumstantial crisis factors more broadly.

The first two chapters trace the contours of the issues explored in this book by reviewing existing work in the fields of disability and citizenship, and online political participation respectively. In particular, Chapter 1 explores the origins of disabled people's political exclusion. After discussing the relationship between socio-economic and political rights in citizenship theory, this chapter exposes the reasons for the enduring confinement of disabled people to a condition of 'second class' citizenship, reflecting on relevant policy measures and the recent history of British disability activism, its organisational forms and key players. The chapter then reviews the work on disability and the Internet that has been carried out to date and argues in favour of a substantial expansion in this area, asking whether online media can help re-configure democratic politics into a more inclusive environment for disabled Internet users.

Chapter 2 builds on this by discussing key trends in the study of e-democracy and the conceptualisation of collective action in the twenty-first century. Most importantly, this chapter identifies online non-political 'third spaces', the practice of sharing personal narratives on social media, and digital interaction more generally as enablers of political participation for users otherwise unfamiliar with public debate and disenfranchised from representative democracy. While these channels and practices are explored as potential opportunities to overcome the organisational barriers that led to stagnation in disability activism in recent years, the role of disruptive events as triggers of participation is discussed also. This chapter then concludes by identifying the radical reform of disability welfare introduced by the U.K. government between 2010–12 and the contested plans for drastic reductions in federal Medicaid funding presented by the American Republican Party in 2011 as suitable catalysts for mobilisation among disabled citizens in Britain and America respectively.

Chapters 3 through to 6 present and discuss empirical data including the analysis of Facebook conversation threads, a detailed inventory of the online media used by high-profile disability rights groups in both countries, in-depth interviews with their core organisers and Web link analysis. In particular, Chapter 3 focuses on the role of the U.K. welfare reform controversy as a catalyst for digital renewal in British disability advocacy. Three main group types are uncovered that relied heavily on online media to oppose government plans for an overhaul of disability welfare provisions. These include: pre-existing, formal disability organisations (both 'professionalised' non-profits and member-led self-advocacy groups); groups of experienced self-advocates that embraced e-advocacy for the first time; and emerging digital networks born out of the efforts of young disabled bloggers-cum-activists that operated exclusively online. Three emblematic case studies (The Hardest Hit; Disabled People Against Cuts; and The Broken of Britain) are then selected for in-depth analysis. This first stage of the analysis uncovers a very vibrant e-advocacy scene, capable of providing disabled Internet users with a range of opportunities for participation. However, it also raises some important questions with regard to the structure of these groups and their inclination to promoting truly meaningful participation for their online supporters. These questions are then tackled through the analysis of discussion threads drawn from each group's Facebook page in Chapters 4 and 5.

In particular, Chapter 4 provides a detailed analysis of the general trends that span the use of Facebook in all three case studies. These include: the role played by core organisers in nurturing – or at times hindering – the transition of their supporters from mere observers to active participants in online conversations; the tendency for discussion to cluster around specific policy issues rather than quintessentially political or ideological topics; and the use of personal narratives as vehicles for users unfamiliar with political discussion to understand and articulate complex policy issues. While it would be premature to claim that a sense of community was 'manufactured' in these groups, this chapter discusses why the most innovative among them succeeded in creating vibrant – but not self-sustaining – collectives, while the others found it more challenging to integrate Facebook with their broader advocacy plans. In particular, this chapter draws on the tendency for each case study to (not) use Facebook as a vehicle to promote both online and in-person collective action. Overall, three different perspectives on the role of social media in disability rights advocacy emerged, which in turn underpinned different action repertoires and user-experiences, ranging from 'contentious politics as usual' to seemingly participatory campaigning.

Following on from the previous chapter and drawing on both the analysis of Facebook conversations between group leaders and online supporters, and on interviews with a range of core organisers, Chapter 5 exposes the 'hidden' structure of emerging disability rights groups. In doing so, this chapter focuses particularly on the most innovative case study discussed in this book: The Broken of Britain. At a close examination, the tension between the participatory nature of this digital action network and its founders' preference for centralised 'brand management' contravened common wisdom in relation to 'horizontal' activist networks. While this can be explained at least in part as an attempt by the young bloggers-cum-activists at the centre of this group to address some of the traditional flaws of online grassroots networks (Bennett 2003), their emergence as disabled leaders and ability to use online media to relay the grievances of other disabled people can be seen as the cornerstone of a new type of 'peer-mediated citizenship'. This system lacks the type of internal accountability that would make it more representative. Yet, it undoubtedly constitutes an improvement on both the indirect representation provided by 'professionalised' charitable organisations and the marginalisation experienced by fringe protest groups that rely on disruptive tactics and contentious repertoires more generally.

Chapter 6 explores the influence of context on the digitalisation of British disability rights advocacy by comparing it to the use of new media technologies among American disability organisations. To do so, the traditional notion of context in Internet politics is expanded to account not only for predictable systemic factors, but also for time-sensitive circumstantial ones. The results of this comparison are surprisingly counter-intuitive. Despite America's reputation as a particularly fertile ground for innovative e-advocacy initiatives, British disability organisations were found to be the trendsetters in this case. Their U.S. counterparts emerged instead as a rather 'conservative' exception in a national context that is otherwise particularly inclined towards experimentation with online politics. Such unexpected results provided an important opportunity to reflect on the relationship between e-advocacy and the surrounding context, ultimately calling for a re-evaluation and better conceptualisation of the idea of crisis.

This last point is explored in detail in the book's conclusive chapter. In addition to the relationship between crisis and e-advocacy, Chapter 7 focuses on the new ecology of British disability activism uncovered in this book and discusses its effects on the citizenship levels of disabled Internet users. Furthermore, this chapter also advances reasonable hypotheses as to why such a vibrant campaigning environment ultimately failed to influence the U.K. government's agenda and achieve tangible policy goals. The book concludes by sketching an agenda for future work on disability, politics and new media. This builds directly on this study's findings and also proposes a range of other issues for researchers in disability and Internet studies to consider.

Overall, this book challenges established paradigms in both disability studies and Internet politics research, calling for a more nuanced approach to the relationship between disability and new media on one side, as well as a broader re-evaluation of the political significance of the Internet for disadvantaged groups on the other. Social science scholarship is at a crossroads. Not only are online media becoming increasingly integral to all aspects of social, economic and political life in democratic countries, but Internet use also leaves behind useful footprints that provide new ways of identifying and investigating emerging socio-political trends. This book seeks to make the most of these opportunities while at the same time avoiding losing sight of the broader context of advocacy, activism and policy-making. It is hoped that some of this project's findings will be relevant to grassroots advocates and campaign organisers wishing to harness the potential of new media in order to build more engaging, effective and empowering forms of citizen mobilisation.

References

Bennett, W.L., 2003. Communicating Global Activism: Strengths and Vulnerabilities of Networked Politics. *Information, Communication & Society*, 6(2), pp. 143–168.

Bimber, B., Flanagin, A.J., & Stohl, C., 2012. *Collective Action in Organizations: Interaction and Engagement in an Era of Technological Change*, Cambridge: Cambridge University Press.

Castells, M., 2012. *Networks of Outrage and Hope: Social Movements in the Internet Age*, Cambridge: Polity Press.

Dutton, W.H. & Blank, G., 2013. *Cultures of the Internet: The Internet in Britain*, Oxford: Oxford Internet Institute.

Ellcessor, E., 2016. *Restricted Access: Media, Disability, and the Politics of Participation*, New York: New York University Press.

Ellis, K. & Kent, M., 2011. *Disability and New Media*, London: Routledge.

Equality and Human Rights Commission, 2010. *How Fair is Britain? The First Triennial Review*. Available at: www.equalityhumanrights.com/about-us/our-work/key-projects/how-fair-britain/full-report-and-evidence-downloads (accessed 28 December 2015).

Fox, S., 2011. *Americans Living with Disability and Their Technology Profile*, Washington, DC: Pew Internet and American Life Project.

Gad, S., Ramakrishnan, N., Hampton, K. & Kavanaugh, A., 2012. Bridging the Divide in Democratic Engagement: Studying Conversation Patterns in Advantaged and Disadvantaged Communities. In 2012 International Conference on Social Informatics. Washington, DC: IEEE, pp. 165–176.

Gerbaudo, P., 2012. *Tweet and the Streets: Social Media and Contemporary Activism*, London: Pluto Press.

Goggin, G. & Newell, C., 2003. *Digital Disability: The Social Construction of Disability in New Media*, Lanham: Rowan & Littlefield.

Howard, P. & Chadwick, A., 2009. Conclusion: Political Omnivores and Wired States. In A. Chadwick & P. Howard, eds. *Routledge Handbook of Internet Politics*. London: Routledge, pp. 424–434.

International Telecommunication Union, 2012. *Measuring the Information Society 2012*. Available at: www.itu.int/en/ITU-D/Statistics/Documents/publications/mis2012/MIS2012_without_Annex_4.pdf (accessed 28 February 2016).

Lister, R., 2007. Inclusive Citizenship: Realizing the Potential. *Citizenship Studies*, 11(1), pp. 49–61.

Norris, P., 2001. *The Digital Divide: Civic Engagement, Information Poverty and the Internet Worldwide*, Cambridge: Cambridge University Press.

Roulstone, A., 1998. *Enabling Technology: Disabled People, Work, and New Technology*, Maidenhead: Open University Press.

Schur, L., Kruse, D. & Blanck, P., 2013. *People with Disabilities: Sidelined or Mainstreamed?*, New York: Cambridge University Press.

Warschauer, M., 2003. *Technology and Social Inclusion: Rethinking the Digital Divide*, Cambridge, MA: MIT Press.

Woliver, L., 1993. *From Outrage to Action: The Politics of Grassroot Dissent*, Urbana & Chigago: The University of Illinois Press.

1 Disabled People, Citizenship and New Media

Disability advocates around the world have fought some important battles in recent decades. As a result, disabled people's rights have advanced considerably on a global scale, becoming enshrined in the United Nations Convention on the Rights of Persons with Disabilities (CRPD) since 2006. Both the United States and the United Kingdom led the way in the development of disabled people's rights, pioneering the introduction of anti-discrimination legislation in 1990 and 1995, respectively. More broadly, these changes have occurred alongside a fundamental shift in debates on disability and society, which increasingly espouse the rhetoric and key principles of the independent living movement in the U.S., and the fundamental tenets of the social model of disability in the U.K. (Barnes 2007). However, more than 20 years after the passing of the Americans with Disabilities Act (ADA) and the U.K.'s Disability Discrimination Act (DDA), progress towards disabled people's full social, political and economic inclusion remains incomplete in these advanced countries. In particular, civic engagement and political participation continue to prove elusive for disabled citizens, who consequently have fewer opportunities than others to influence policy decisions likely to fundamentally affect their lives.

In order to understand what lies at the root of disabled people's exclusion from politics and policy-making, this chapter turns to both citizenship and disability scholarship. As disability scholars (Beckett 2005) and feminist writers (Lister 2007a, p. 49) noted, existing studies on democratic citizenship largely overlook disability, either because of its complex nature or due to a perceived lack of relevance to broader citizenship issues. To address this gap, it is useful to review the debates that underpinned the development of disability rights and relevant policy initiatives in the U.K. and the U.S. in recent decades. Empirical work is reviewed here that shows how so far disability policy has fallen short of promoting the development of full political rights for disabled people. The tendency for debates on disability policy to overlook instances of institutional discrimination within the formal and informal settings in which democratic politics is discussed has contributed in fundamental ways to the persisting entrapment of disabled people in a position of marginal citizenship on both sides of the Atlantic. As is discussed in detail below, formal participation channels such as elections and political parties remain off-limits to most disabled people. Disability rights activism has remedied this democratic gap in part. Yet, following the introduction of landmark legislation in the 1990s and until recently, these movements seemed to have lost much of their original thrust, while progress towards full citizenship for disabled people slowed down considerably. In particular, observers pointed out that U.K. disability groups switched their attention to a mere 'defensive engagement' of acquired rights, instead of fighting for their expansion (Beckett 2005, pp. 405–6). In addition, veteran disability scholars continue to this day to be outspoken critics of charitable organisations run by advocacy 'professionals' without disabled people in leadership positions, which in the last decade 'have experienced a resurgence, while the power and influence of the disabled people's movement has undoubtedly declined' (Oliver & Barnes 2012, p. 169).

Having traced the contours of the exclusion of disabled people from the civic arena, the second part of this chapter asks whether new media technologies could support the creation of a type of politics better suited to the needs of disabled citizens. In particular, the idea that online media could provide disabled Internet users with viable channels to meet, discuss and self-organise outside established advocacy groups is explored. 'Informal' opportunities to participate in politics online, it is argued, could help disabled people circumvent the institutionalised discrimination that plagues traditional channels of democratic participation and promote a more inclusive form of citizenship. With this in mind, this chapter reviews the existing literature on disability and new media, which, while still a niche field, has expanded considerably in recent years. A critical look at this literature reveals the dangers of approaching the relationship between disability and the Internet exclusively through the access and accessibility lens. Restricting scholarly investigation to the perspective of those among disabled people who cannot benefit from online media, or only benefit from it in limited measure compared to others, is bound to generate partial and potentially misleading conclusions. Instead, there is a need for a broader and more balanced approach to the issue of disability and new media technologies. This should overcome the dualism derived from digital divide theories and account for the experiences of the growing majority of disabled Britons and Americans who regularly use the Internet in spite of persisting access and accessibility difficulties.

Second Class Citizens: The Exclusion of Disabled People from the Civic Arena

A comprehensive debate on the relationship between citizenship and disability is yet to be had. This poses a problem for researchers wishing to investigate the reasons behind the confinement of disabled people to a condition of 'second-class' citizenship (Tisdall & Kay 2003, pp. 25–8) as it generates a lack of clear reference points, whether in the form of normative benchmarks or more flexible working criteria. However, reviewing the evolution of legislation, policy and activism concerned with disability issues can help to track developments in disabled people's position *vis-à-vis* the dynamic idea of citizenship (Faulks 2000, p. 3; Turner 1993, p. 2) and, more importantly, expose the roots of their political marginalisation. Article 29 of the CRPD, which was ratified by the U.K. in 2009 and has been signed but not yet ratified by the U.S., commits state parties to guaranteeing equal opportunities for disabled people to participate in political and public life, both through elections and referendums, as well as joining non-governmental organisations and other pressure groups. Nevertheless, both in Britain and America multiple competing conceptualisations of citizenship have shaped policy measures that so far have fallen short of promoting full political rights for disabled people.

Social Citizenship and State Welfare

For much of the post-war period until the 1990s, social policy in Western democracies found an important source of inspiration in the theory of 'social citizenship' championed by British sociologist Thomas Humphrey Marshall. At the centre of this paradigm was the assumption that, besides civil and political liberties, members of a democratic society also have a fundamental right to socio-economic equality and individual dignity. According to Marshall (1950), citizenship rights developed in an evolutionary fashion for which, after fundamental legal rights had been established in the seventeenth and eighteenth centuries and political rights secured in the nineteenth century, social rights were bound to follow in the second half of the twentieth century. This deterministic vision called for government action to ensure the realisation of socio-economic equality, with the development of the British Welfare State from the late 1940s onwards arguably providing the ultimate testimony of the liaison between theories of social citizenship and the intended outcomes of social policy innovations in the democratic West (Heater 2004, pp. 271–3).

Although social citizenship theory marked a substantial advancement in the debate on the range of individual and collective rights associated with democratic ideals, it was criticised also for its inability to promote 'full' citizenship for minorities and disadvantaged social groups. In particular, critics pointed out that this view overstated the importance of socio-economic rights to the detriment of political rights and related civic responsibilities (Roche 2002, p. 77). Policy measures inspired by social citizenship theories, it was argued, determined in fact a perverse watering down of citizenship for those who were already in a situation of disadvantage by exacerbating their dependency on state welfare while simultaneously overlooking the need for them to become involved in the relevant public decision-making processes (Heater 2004, p. 274). Marshall's view was tied too strongly to liberal ideals and excessively emphasised issues of socio-economic status over citizenship practices (Tisdall & Kay 2003, p. 21). The resulting policies took the acquisition of political rights for granted, supporting the development of an intrinsically incomplete type of citizenship (Faulks 2000, pp. 10–11). Furthermore, given the centrality of social class and the role of paid employment as a primary avenue for the achievement of socio-economic equality in this model, social citizenship has been criticised also for being primarily concerned with elevating the condition of white male workers (Turner 1986, pp. 86–7). As such, despite fostering important interventions for the reduction of poverty and deprivation (Lister 2007a, pp. 55–6), social citizenship was unable to cater for minority groups and guarantee sustainable dignity, fairness and empowerment for all in the long term (Fraser & Gordon 1994, p. 93).

In this framework, disabled people constitute a particularly problematic case due to their perceived inability to work and therefore benefit fully from socio-economic rights. Marshall tried to overcome this *impasse* by resolving to consider disabled people as entitled to state support without being required to contribute – at least economically – to society (Marshall 1950, pp. 45–6). This theoretical premise, strengthened by the framing of disability as an inescapable 'personal tragedy', fostered the establishment of a welfare system based on the idea of 'needy disabled people' that 'added to existing forms of discrimination and [...] created new forms of its own including the provision of stigmatised services' (Oliver 1996, pp. 75–6). In particular, means-tested state benefits, the role of medical 'experts' in welfare administration and the failure to involve disabled people in key decisions over their own lives, both at the individual and collective level, have been criticised repeatedly for their disempowering effects (C. Barnes & Mercer 2003). Put simply, these practices sanctioned disabled people's dependency on welfare systems that were not accountable to them and contributed to the consolidation of the stigma and negative stereotypes associated with disability, especially for people with learning difficulties and mental health problems (Drake 1999; Mercer et al. 1999, p. 154).

Dissociating socio-economic rights from participation in decision-making carries great risks for those that rely on charity-like welfare systems, who find themselves trapped between the bedrock of economic dependency on one side and the hard place of political marginalisation on the other. This issue assumes particular relevance in times of economic crisis and in conjunction with administrations that are committed to reducing welfare provision for economic, political or ideological reasons. Most notably, these issues became apparent in the 1980s during Margaret Thatcher and Ronald Reagan's 'New Right' politics in Britain and the United States respectively. In both countries, the hostility of government leaders towards some fundamental aspects of social citizenship, coupled with a period of economic instability and difficulties in influencing policy-making processes, put those dependent on state welfare in a highly vulnerable position (Dwyer 2004, pp. 61–6). Arguably, the erosion of social rights has continued in the U.K. in more recent years through the extensive austerity plans pursued since 2010 by the Conservative-led government, while in the U.S. social security has come under repeated attacks by Republican politicians during the Obama administration. Scholars such as Taylor-Gooby (2008) have pointed out that in Europe social citizenship is endangered by the growing emphasis that governments place on individual responsibilities over rights, as well as the rampant marketisation of public service provision. Therefore, contrary to Marshall's expectations, these trends revealed not only that citizenship does not always expand, but instead that it can contract also when the members of certain social groups are unable to exert effective political agency (Turner 1986, p. xii; 1993, pp. 6–8). An apparent symptom of this participation gap is the limited extent to which disabled citizens engage with formal political processes, most notably elections, which is rooted in a series of discriminatory barriers and fuels a vicious cycle of exclusion and disempowerment.

Disabled Voters and Elections

U.S. scholars in particular have paid great attention to opportunities for disabled citizens to exercise their basic political rights in elections. Overall, this work has shown that disabled Americans are substantially less likely to vote than non-disabled citizens in federal, state and local elections. For example, turnout among disabled people at the November 2012 elections was 5.7 per cent lower than among non-disabled people, which is equal to three million voters (Schur, Adya & Kruse 2013). While this represented a slight improvement on previous elections in 2008 and 2010 (Schur & Adya 2013, p. 832), and was consistent with the existence of a disability gap in voter turnout in many other democratic countries (Schur, Kruse & Blanck 2013, pp. 104–6), it confirmed that participation equality is yet to be achieved in the U.S. This contrasts sharply with the preference of most disabled Americans for 'big government' and their consequent desire to be able to influence politics through democratic channels such as elections (Schur & Adya 2013, p. 833).

Although some of the disability turnout gap can be explained as a consequence of other types of inequality – i.e. low levels of income, educational attainment and socialisation (Schur, Kruse & Blanck 2013, p. 107) – legislation and inadequate government measures have been widely blamed for this situation too. Both the ADA and the Help America Vote Act (HAVA), passed in 2002, contain a series of measures aimed at making voting more accessible for people with impairments. While this is not the place for a detailed discussion of the provisions made in this legislation, it is important to note that its patchy application and narrow interpretation by courts have led to improvements for some disabled Americans but not for others, depending on location and the types of impairments involved.

Various measures have been deployed in recent years to guarantee the accessibility of polling places for people with mobility problems. Nevertheless, as recently as 2008 nearly three-quarters of polling stations were found to have one or more significant impediments on the path between the parking and the voting areas (Government Accountability Office 2013). Furthermore, U.S. 'case law is silent on the modifications required to accommodate people with learning disabilities, mental retardation or other impairments that affect the ability to read or interpret written language' (Schriner & Batavia 2001, p. 671). This puts citizens with learning difficulties in an especially disadvantaged position when it comes to voting – a situation that also applies to the U.K. (Keeley et al. 2008; Redley 2008). More broadly, social policy too might foster low election turnout among disabled citizens because it tends to frame them as 'deserving' of and dependent on social security in ways that 'encourage withdrawal or passivity' (Shields et al. 2000, p. 197), which links back to the main critique of welfare systems modelled on the notion of social citizenship discussed earlier in this chapter.

While in Britain less research has been carried out about disabled people's involvement in elections and party politics than in the U.S., the available data paint an equally disappointing picture. This has led the U.K.'s Equality and Human Rights Commission to conclude that 'disabled people are generally less likely than non-disabled people to say that they can influence local decisions' (Equality and Human Rights Commission 2010, p. 602). Although disabled citizens have been as likely to turn out to vote as non-disabled people in recent U.K. elections (Equality and Human Rights Commission 2010, p. 591), access issues were found to be widespread at the 2010 General Election, when two-thirds of polling stations had one or more significant access barriers, showing no improvement on accessibility rates for the 2005 General Election (Gilbert et al. 2010, p. 25). Similar issues re-emerged at the time of the 2015 General Election, with Frances Ryan noting in *The Guardian* newspaper that not even the office of then disability minister Mark Harper was wheelchair accessible at that time, let alone many polling stations.[1]

Preliminary results for a survey of polling place accessibility at the 2015 U.K. General Election showed that over a quarter of disabled people who turned out to vote in person found it difficult to do so, while 17 per cent had problems with postal voting too (Mitchell-Pye 2015). In addition, disabled Britons continue to face significant barriers to being selected as election candidates (Equality and Human Rights Commission 2010, p. 592). In contrast with a growing tendency for parties to field candidates from under-represented groups – especially women – as a way of appealing to an increasingly diverse electorate, British political parties have been shown to be unlikely to select disabled candidates for fear that persisting misconceptions about the ability of disabled people to fulfil the duties of elected representatives may disadvantage them in the eyes of voters (C. Barnes & Mercer 2003, pp. 112–16).

Several types of intervention have been proposed to make 'formal' democratic processes more accessible to disabled citizens and ensure their enfranchisement. These range from fairly straightforward initiatives such as training polling station workers about the needs of disabled voters (Ward et al. 2009) to more wholesale changes such as the introduction of disability affirmative action in candidate lists (Guldvik & Lesjø 2014). Yet, the effectiveness of these and any other measures is dependent on a broader cultural shift in how disability and impairment are perceived and addressed, which will require considerable time to occur. In the meantime, it is essential to consider whether the disability gap in participation can be addressed through meaningful participation that occurs through other political processes.

While in fact the data discussed here provide a useful measure of disabled people's exclusion from formal political structures in the U.K. and the U.S., the relevance of other forms of democratic participation for their political inclusion should not be underestimated. In particular, the impact of disability rights activism and advocacy should be considered: to what extent have they empowered disabled people? To answer this question it is necessary to examine how governance systems try to involve disabled representatives in policy design and delivery, as well as to assess levels of democratisation within the disability movement. It is especially useful to focus on the U.K. context as the British government's continued commitment to radical austerity policies in the years since the global financial crisis has made it especially important for disabled citizens to find effective ways of voicing their opposition to such plans (Oliver & Barnes 2012, pp. 144–7).

The Limits of the U.K. Disability Discrimination Act

A useful place to start in assessing opportunities for disabled citizens to exercise their political rights is by exploring whether appropriate provisions are made in relevant legislation. The history of two landmark pieces of U.K. legislation – the DDA and the Community Care (Direct Payments) Act – is especially revelatory with regard to the ability of the U.K. governance system to engage disabled stakeholders and the resulting policy measures to promote sustained involvement in public decision-making.

From the late 1970s onwards, the tendency for public policy measures based on Marshall's idea of social citizenship to cast disabled people in a position of dependency was strongly criticised by disabled scholars and activists supporting a revolutionary conceptualisation of disability: the social model. Put simply, their main contention was that disablement does not originate from individual impairments. Instead, its causes are to be found in a range of exclusionary social barriers, including traditional approaches to welfare, that prevent people with impairments from participating fully and on a equal footing with others in all aspects of social life (see for instance, Abberley 1987; Finkelstein 1980; Oliver 1990; UPIAS 1976). Such a marked dichotomy between disability and impairment provided a fundamental catalyst for the growth of the British disabled people's movement throughout the 1980s. This was instrumental in pushing the issue of disability discrimination on the agenda (Campbell & Oliver 1996, pp. 146–158), leading to the introduction of innovative legislation in the mid-1990s in response to the petitioning from an unprecedented campaigning alliance that had been forged between disabled self-advocates and national disability charities (Barnes 2007, p. 208).

Building on the critique of policy measures based on the ideal of social citizenship discussed earlier in this chapter, social model scholars denounced the existing redistributive system as the source of a 'false' sense of citizenship for disabled people, who were trapped in a position of economic dependency and political exclusion. The only way to remedy this situation, they argued, was through an urgent 'participatory' transformation of the welfare system (Mercer et al. 1999, pp. 164–175). Fundamental to these claims and the political battle that ensued from them was the idea that citizenship can expand only through social struggle and political agency (Faulks 2000, p. 4), which previously had been instrumental to the achievements of the feminist and civil rights movements in the U.S. and elsewhere (Turner 1986, pp. 86–90). While some citizenship scholars remain sceptical with regard to the role of new social movements in the expansion of people's rights (Hadenius 2001, pp. 60–5), the ideas at the root of the social model of disability and their ability to inspire political action among disabled people undeniably contributed to re-shaping the U.K. approach to disability policy and re-framing the principles that support disability welfare provision in Britain (Campbell & Oliver 1996, pp. 86–91).

In 1995, the U.K. Parliament passed the DDA. This represented the culmination of over ten years of struggles by disabled campaigners and their allies, which involved 14 consecutive attempts to get similar legislation passed. The passing of the DDA was the result of a dramatic U-turn by the then Conservative government led by prime minister John Major, who was compelled to admit that disabled people indeed faced systematic discrimination in all aspects of social life, following the publication of quantitative and qualitative evidence collected by disabled researchers (C. Barnes 1991; Barton 1993). This constituted the first-ever organic attempt to tackle disability discrimination through specific legislation in the U.K. Thus, despite the DDA including a markedly medical definition of disability (Pearson & Watson 2007, pp. 105–7; Woodhams & Corby 2003, pp. 161–5) that was criticised by disability activists (C. Barnes & Mercer 2001, p. 18; Campbell & Oliver 1996, p. 16) and has remained unchanged in subsequent legislative revisions and updates (the DDA 2005 and the Equality Act 2010), it made for an important step towards disability equality. Twenty years on, however, this legislation continues to be criticised for being heavily and perhaps excessively oriented towards ensuring equality in the labour market and eliminating disability discrimination in the workplace compared to other aspects of social life (Floyd & Curtis 2001).

Indeed, such a focus on employment equality has not been exclusive to British disability discrimination law. For example, the ADA, passed in 1990, has also focused extensively on employment rights, introducing affirmative action measures to increase opportunities for disabled people to find jobs (Lunt & Thornton 1994). More recently, disability welfare provision was reviewed also in Australia as part of a welfare-to-work programme 'to produce *productive* citizens who are able to contribute to the national goal of maintaining competitiveness in the global economy' (Lantz & Marston 2012, p. 853). Moreover, the DDA has been expanded over the years to cover areas such as transport, education and the provision of public services (Pearson & Watson 2007). Nevertheless, the role that British legislation has bestowed upon employment, coupled with the shift to a work-oriented model of welfare as the basis for social rights (Dean 1999) and a more general emphasis on citizen obligations during the years of the New Labour (Dwyer 2004, pp. 71–4) and subsequent Conservative–Liberal governments (1997-onwards), bears an interesting relationship with both disability theory and the idea of social citizenship. The centrality attributed to paid work in anti-discrimination legislation echoed the influence of Marxist theory on original social model literature, which explained the oppression of disabled people as a by-product of capitalism (see, for instance, Oliver 1990). In turn, such a strong focus on employment rights was consistent also with Marshall's idea of work as a vehicle for the achievement of 'full' citizenship. Thus, one could argue that, in an attempt to facilitate the inclusion of disabled people, anti-discrimination legislation paradoxically embraced rather than challenged the notion of employment as a non-negotiable component of citizenship and overlooked instead the need to support other key aspects of social life, including political participation.

In recent years, the materialist conceptualisation of disability that inspired this type of policy intervention has been criticised by a new wave of disability scholars, who have suggested that the social model has in fact outlasted its original purpose and called for urgent changes to the way in which disability is conceptualised in social theory, legislation and other relevant policy measures (see, for instance, Armer 2004; Shakespeare & Watson 2001, 2010; Thomas & Corker 2002, p. 48; Tregaskis 2002, p. 461). Building on the work of feminist disability writers such as Morris (1992), French (1993) and Crow (1996), these authors have emphasised the need for theory to be re-aligned with the lived experiences of disabled people and for disability to be re-assessed as a multi-faceted combination of both environmental barriers and 'impairment effects' (Thomas 1999, 2010) in order to generate policy measures that adequately capture disablement and support disabled people's inclusion in the twenty-first century.

While a detailed review of this debate would reach beyond the scope of this book, arguments such as Shakespeare and Watson's (2001) claim that 'a mature society supports everyone on the basis, not of the work they have done, but of the needs they have' (p. 19) have highlighted the need to look beyond legislative and welfare systems that are primarily geared towards the utopian inclusion of all disabled people in the economic cycle of productivity. That is not to say that paid employment is not important for social participation, but rather to warn that over-emphasising its centrality to these processes might automatically exclude from citizenship those people, disabled and non-, who choose not to engage in paid employment or are prevented from doing so by environmental barriers. This concern has become especially relevant in an era 'when conditions of full employment can no longer be taken for granted and when welfare budgets have been under strain from the cost of supporting those without jobs' (Lister 2003, p. 20). These remarks are particularly relevant *vis-à-vis* the emphasis that the 2010–15 U.K. Conservative-led coalition government placed on work as a fundamental civic duty and entry to the labour market as the main aim of public welfare programmes (Roulstone 2011).

Prejudice and Exclusion in Policy-Making

In contrast with the DDA's strong focus on employment, another piece of landmark legislation aimed at ensuring that disabled people can be more involved in decision-making about the kind of support available to them was the Community Care (Direct Payments) Act 1996. This was based on the principles of independent living and on a person-centred approach to welfare, and offered disabled people cash payments in lieu of services. Despite some implementation issues, including some severe geographical disparities across the U.K. (Priestley et al. 2007, 2010), the Community Care (Direct Payments) Act sanctioned, at least on paper, the right of disabled people to choice in the personal sphere, thus laying the foundations for empowerment on a wider scale (Morris 1997).

Since the mid-1990s, direct payments have undoubtedly afforded many disabled Britons a greater share of control over their lives. However, scholars have since noted that the kind of 'empowerment' that this system supports is limited to the individual or local level, while a severe lack of meaningful involvement in system-wide decision-making processes continues to date. In other words, disabled people are in charge of spending their own support money, but continue to be excluded from decision-making processes that can fundamentally alter the welfare system as a whole. As Rummery (2006a) noted, this is consistent with a broader tendency for initiatives that sought to promote 'joined up' governance by bringing central government, local authorities and citizens closer together to fall short of their stated objectives. For example, the Disability Equality Duty (DED), which was enforced in late 2006, required public sector organisations to make provisions for the inclusion of disabled people in the design and delivery of policy and services. Yet, recent work has shown that the implementation of this measure has been affected by specific difficulties for public bodies to set up meaningful channels of engagement and collaboration with disabled people's organisations (Pearson et al. 2011). More broadly, evaluations of institutional forums designed to afford marginalised citizens opportunities to engage directly with policy-makers, including online consultations, have revealed also that these types of initiatives are largely unfit for purpose (Barnes et al. 2004).

As such, the predominant view within the literature is that policy-based interventions have failed to develop meaningful ways for disabled citizens to become involved in policy design and delivery, thus failing to boost their political agency (Rummery 2002, pp. 178–180). Designing paths for the involvement of people with complex needs is undoubtedly challenging, particularly in the case of those affected by learning difficulties (Beckman 2007; Stainton 2005). Yet, empirical research has shown also that there is a persisting attitude within institutions and society more broadly to regard impaired people as 'unable' or 'unwilling' to take on civic roles and the associated responsibilities, which precludes disabled people who would be eager to participate in public decision-making from doing so (Rummery 2006b, pp. 641–2). This prejudice mirrors the one encountered by disabled people in political parties as discussed above, entrenching exclusion at the local level. As Marion Barnes (2002) noted, the 'rules' of the democratic deliberation 'game' tend to privilege rationality over the emotional component of lived experiences, thus hindering the expression of disabled people's concerns and consequently casting them – together with other social groups such as children, young people and those living in poverty – as 'unqualified' for public decision-making. Crucially, Morris (2005) found this prejudice to be broadly reflected across policy 'initiatives to encourage "active citizenship" [that] tend not to treat disabled people as potential active citizens' and 'sometimes [. . .] have reaffirmed the assumption that disabled people are passive recipients of care' (p. 20). This final point echoes Marshall's out-dated view of the relationship between citizenship and disability, exposing the culture of exclusion that continues to hinder the involvement of disabled people in institutionalised politics, starting with participation in elections.

Having discussed the lack of a clear policy framework to support the development of disabled people's political rights, it is also useful to briefly review the evolution of disability activism in the U.K. in order to understand whether grassroots initiatives can effectively make up for the discrimination that characterises formal channels of participation in policy-making. Arguably, the simultaneous commitment of many disability scholars to both research and activism has inhibited the formulation of an in-depth critique of the disability movement. However, it is useful to reflect on the structure and ethos of the groups responsible for key disability rights battles in order to provide some clear points of reference for the investigation of their current successors.

Activists to the Rescue? The U.K. Disability Movement

The emergence of disabled people's self-advocacy groups from the 1970s was strictly connected to the growing popularity of social model ideas. Until then, the role of disabled Britons in the realm of organised disability interests was traditionally limited to that of passive recipients of 'charity' dispensed by voluntary organisations. Social model scholars argued that this type of arrangement was intrinsically disempowering and strongly criticised organisations such as the Cheshire Foundation (renamed Leonard Cheshire Disability in 2007) as well as the Spastics Society (renamed Scope in 1994) for perpetuating disabled people's oppression in the U.K. (Oliver 1990, p. 98). In particular, disability charities were accused of exclusionary practices and discriminatory attitudes that prevented service users from taking up positions of responsibility (Drake 1994) while at the same time undermining the confidence of the few disabled people who were involved in their governance structures. As Jenny Morris (1991) put it:

> [A] disabled person who holds a position within a conservative charitable organisation has been told all their lives [...] how inadequate and pitiable disabled people are. Small wonder then that such people, when asked to involve more disabled people in their organisation, commonly respond that there just isn't any capable person with the relevant expertise amongst the disabled community.
> (p. 177)

Inspired by the successes of the American independent living movement (Vaughn-Switzer 2003, pp. 70–6) and driven by a desire for direct representation, Britain's disability rights pioneers founded the Union of the Physically Impaired Against Segregation (UPIAS) in 1974. Simultaneously, a number of local self-advocacy groups were launched across the country, which eventually found coordination and a unitary voice at national level with the foundation of the British Council of Organisations of Disabled People (BCODP, later renamed the U.K. Disabled People's Council – UKDPC) in 1981. In particular, this umbrella organisation played an instrumental role in promoting the introduction of the landmark anti-discrimination legislation discussed earlier in this chapter (Barnes & Mercer 2001, pp. 14–16). Although the composite nature of the BCODP led to some internal disagreement among disability self-advocates (Campbell &

Oliver 1996, pp. 78–80), taken as a whole the original Disabled People's Organisations (DPOs) saw themselves as alternative to established disability charities, which '[did] not *want* us [disabled people] to control our own lives. These groups often separate[d] disabled people according to their impairment' (British Council of Disabled People 1997, p. 8), hampering the formation of a common identity and consequentially also the development of political agency for disabled people. This generated a rift between emergent, loosely structured and advocacy-oriented member-led groups on one side, and established, bureaucratic and service-focused charities on the other, which self-advocates accused of spreading disabling imagery through advertising material (Morris 1991, pp. 183–4) and actively campaigning against anti-discriminatory legislation to guarantee the preservation of the status quo (Oliver 1990, p. 105).

Unsurprisingly, such a bitterly divided disability community failed to promote significant advancements in disabled people's rights for some time. However, this changed with the foundation of the Voluntary Organisations for Anti-Discrimination Legislation (VOADL) Committee in 1985 (renamed Rights Now! in 1992), which 'heralded an uneasy alliance between organisations controlled by disabled people, such as the BCODP, and the more traditional organisations for disabled people like RADAR [the Royal Association for Disability Rights]' (Barnes & Mercer 2001, p. 16). Although the dynamics that underpinned the formation of this coalition remain contested, with some authors regarding Rights Now! as the result of the pressure exerted on 'household' charities by DPOs more than a spontaneous change of heart in the voluntary sector (Campbell & Oliver 1996, pp. 151–2), this experience is widely considered as a driving force behind the introduction of anti-discrimination legislation in the U.K., showing that substantial policy success is more likely to be achieved through targeted collaborative effort (Pearson 2012). That said, this coalition proved fragile and ephemeral as the introduction of the DDA in 1995 generated 'tensions between organisations willing to work with the government's own legislation (mostly organisations "for" disabled people) and those who were fundamentally opposed (overwhelmingly organisations "of" disabled people)' (Pointon 1999, p. 234), which led to a rapid dissolution of the campaigning alliance.

Although intuitively it could be tempting to consider these events as evidence of the impossibility of creating a unitary front in British disability activism, it is crucial instead to reflect on the way in which these organisations evolved after the dissolution of Rights Now!. While in fact a certain part of the literature continues to emphasise the exclusion of disabled people from strategic decision-making in charitable bodies (Drake 2002) and interpret statute changes in these organisations as opportunistic 'window dressing' (Oliver & Barnes 2012), others have pointed out that the lack of a sustainable merge between organisations 'for' and 'of' disabled people should not be mistaken for no change at all. Most notably, Tom

Shakespeare (2006) has warned against simplistic generalisations in this area, stressing how changes have occurred at both ends of the organisational spectrum so that 'the major disability charities have changed out of all recognition' (p. 159) and 'the traditional dichotomy between "organisations for" and "organisations of," which may have appeared useful in the 1980s, now fails to represent the complexity of organisations working with disabled people' (ibid., p. 161). In particular, national charities such as Scope have since reformed their governance structure, putting disabled people in control of strategic planning, at least in principle. Furthermore, these organisations have engaged also in an increasingly greater amount of advocacy work alongside their traditional focus on care and support services. At the same time, DPOs do not necessarily correspond any longer to those small membership groups that were once heralded as the backbone of the British disability movement (Oliver 1997). Rather, many of them have sought to attract public funding and donations, branching out into service provision. This has generated a context in which 'charities have become more like disability rights groups, and disability rights groups have become more like charities' (Shakespeare 2006, p. 161), for which 'a more rational approach would be more selective in its critique, and recognise the successes as well as the failures of the charitable sector' (ibid., p. 162).

Undoubtedly, these observations have introduced much needed nuance to the study of British disability activism. Yet, two key arguments have emerged also from recent literature that cast severe doubts on the ability of disability organisations in their current form to perform as effective channels for democratic participation and empowerment. On the one hand, veteran disability scholars like Colin Barnes (2007) claimed that 'while disability activism has had an important influence on disability policy in the U.K., this very success threatens to undermine its continuity and future' (p. 203). Such a pessimistic outlook rests primarily on the fact that disability organisations, including self-advocacy groups, have long been at risk of 'incorporation' or 'co-optation' by the government. Indeed, several factors contributed to this situation, including the 'joined up' governance approach championed by New Labour discussed above, as well as the desire of DPOs to attract public funding (Shakespeare 2006, p. 160) and gain credibility in the eyes of policy-makers in what is a very competitive advocacy environment. Nevertheless, these developments were criticised for putting additional distance between the leaders of these groups and those whom they seek to represent (Oliver & Barnes 2006).

On the other hand, much of the literature has noted also that the end of the campaigning alliance that brought about anti-discrimination legislation in the mid 1990s determined a crucial loss of momentum for British disability activism. Ultimately, this 'downsized' to what has been defined as 'defensive engagement' of acquired rights (Beckett 2005, pp. 405–6). Broadly speaking, this has been connected to two explanatory factors. As Beckett (2006a, 2006b) argued in her seminal work on citizenship and vulnerability, the continued exclusion of disabled people from institutional arenas has perpetuated a power imbalance that makes it especially difficult for disability activists to engage in pro-active efforts to strengthen and expand disabled people's rights. In addition, a second issue that has prevented unitary mass mobilisation from continuing in the long term has been the reluctance of many impaired people to identify as 'disabled', a label that they see as both negative and alien (Shakespeare & Watson 2001; Watson 2002). Although an in-depth examination of identity issues would go beyond the scope of this book, social movement theory has often highlighted the strong link that exists between shared identity and collective action (Benford & Snow 2000). Thus, while the battle for anti-discrimination legislation and independent living provided a common cause capable of bringing together a very diverse alliance of advocacy groups (Pearson 2012; Pearson & Riddell 2006, pp. 4–6), disability rights activists have since struggled to find unity and lacked the foundations to build new momentum.

Fragmentation Among U.S. Disability Advocates

A lot has been written about the history of the American disability rights movement and providing a comprehensive review of this literature would go beyond the scope of this book. However, it is useful to reflect on some of its key moments to better understand whether the limited extent to which British disability organisations have been able to support the meaningful engagement of disabled citizens in governance processes is an isolated case or part of a transnational trend in disability advocacy.

As was noted previously, Congress passed the ADA in 1990. This was then amended and updated in 2008 with the ADA Amendments Act, mainly to expand the definition of disability contained within the act and to ensure it covers a broader range of individuals. This legislative milestone was the result of a long-term advocacy effort that started with the establishment of the first Center for Independent Living by pioneering self-advocates such as Ed Roberts in Berkeley, California, in 1962. Although disability discrimination had been prohibited in federally-funded programmes and services since 1973 (American Rehabilitation Act), the ADA introduced comprehensive anti-discrimination provisions, making the U.S. the first country to do so. Key to this success was the ability of the American disability rights movement to frame the debate in terms of independence. In particular, the focus on independence for disabled Americans as a paramount goal simultaneously served a double purpose. First, it enabled advocates to campaign for an end to welfare dependency for disabled people, which resonated well with the 'small government' mantra of the Reagan administration and therefore proved popular with policy-makers. Second, it provided a more inclusive and attractive common cause around which the different components of the disability community could rally together compared to the civil rights frame that disability advocates had previously borrowed from African-American activists and towards which some of the more conservative elements of the disability community felt somewhat uncomfortable (Bagenstos 2009, pp. 27–32).

The issue of independent living generated an unprecedented and unsurpassed level of unity within the American disability rights movement. As veteran disability advocate Liz Savage remarked in Fred Pelka's (2012) fascinating oral history of the U.S. disability movement:

> No one group had the power to pull it [the ADA] off on their own. It was not people fighting over their own piece of the pie, to get federal money. [...] People stood up for each other based on their shared experience of discrimination.
>
> (p. 474)

However, similarly to the experience of the coalition of DDA campaigners in the U.K., the unity achieved by U.S. disability advocates in the late 1980s was short-lived. When the binding experience of pursuing a common tangible outcome faded away following the introduction of the ADA, deep-rooted tensions re-emerged in the American disability community, which grew increasingly fragmented and often organised along impairment-specific 'fault lines'. As Bagenstos (2009) noted:

> Though there is broad agreement within the [U.S. disability] movement on the social model of disability, that general consensus conceals a number of tensions that remain in the movement – tensions over whether disability is universal or demarcates a minority group, over the role of professionals, and over the notion of 'independence'.
>
> (p. 33)

In addition, the widespread use of litigation to achieve change in disability legislation has fostered an inherently un-cooperative climate among U.S. disability rights groups, despite acting as a very effective advocacy strategy. Inspired by the tactics of the civil rights movement and, at least until very recently, almost entirely alien to British disability organisations, litigation has been a cornerstone of disability rights advocacy in the U.S. for decades. Coupled with testimony, litigation has made a fundamental contribution to making the voices of disabled Americans heard in Congress and introducing the debate on the ADA in 1988. Over the years, some very important innovations have resulted from testimony on individual cases. The most recent of these is the introduction of legislation that provided for the replacement of the words 'mental retardation' with 'intellectual disability' in several instances of federal law in 2010, which has been dubbed 'Rosa's Law' from the name of the disabled child who inspired its introduction together with her family. This type of advocacy fits with a governance system that grants disability rights organisations, as well as other advocacy and interest groups, a specific place in the Washington policy-making apparatus. From a strategic point of view, this is arguably an effective model to 'get things done'. However, its focus on individual cases and the heavy involvement of formal disability organis-ations in this type of policy-making can put a break also on collective action and grassroots protest. Finally, the tendency for U.S. disability advocacy organisations to rely heavily on membership dues to self-fund, while strengthening the independence of these groups and their ability to negotiate, also constitutes a barrier for the many who would like to join and become involved but cannot afford it.

Overall, these advocacy patterns seem to have promoted the involvement of fewer people instead of many. At the same time, they also discourage collaboration across the range of groups that serve the disability com-munity, as was noted in many of the interviews with representatives from U.S. disability organisations carried out for this book that are discussed in Chapter 6. This is a system that can work very well when disability organisations are able to catalyse the support of key political allies in Congress and the White House. Indeed, it could be argued that disability rights have been protected and even expanded during the terms of the Obama administration. However, it is also a system that is not equipped to cope with crisis. In particular, limited collective participation and frag-mentation constitute inherent dangers for the future of effective disability advocacy in the U.S. First, competition between organisations that see political influence as a zero-sum game to the advantage of their respective, often impairment-specific, constituencies can be an obstacle to expanding disability rights 'at large'. Second, organisations that continue to rely on the traditional fee-paying membership model could find it difficult to quickly mobilise a very large mass of supporters if they were required to do so by emergency circumstances.

The picture that emerges from these considerations is one in which, although some positive steps towards ensuring 'fuller' citizenship for disabled people have indeed been taken both in the U.K. and the U.S., the finish line still lies a long way ahead. Changes in welfare administration, such as direct payments in Britain, have afforded some disabled people unprecedented control over their lives, leading to 'micro-empowerment' on an individual or, sometimes, local scale. However, as noted by feminist scholars, truly mean-ingful citizenship requires participation and the ability to influence public decision-making processes at a higher level (Siim 2000, p. 101). Several obstacles remain that make the current configuration of the political space in both countries unsuited to the needs of disabled people. These include:

- physical barriers (inaccessible building designs and transport issues);
- financial barriers (poverty and the impossibility to 'afford' civic participation);

- cultural barriers (disempowering attitudes reflected in practices of participation and representation);
- psychological barriers (largely a consequence of the above, these manifest themselves as a sense of 'powerlessness' and 'unsuitability' to civic and political participation among disabled people);
- institutional barriers (exclusionary practices embedded in representative and deliberative processes); and, finally,
- organisational barriers (a small number of disabled people in leadership positions within disability organisations, as well as a general fragmentation and lack of clear direction in the disability movement).

Indeed, most ordinary citizens, disabled and non-, are likely to encounter some of these obstacles on the path to civic engagement and political participation (Tonn & Petrich 1998). However, these barriers tend to affect disabled people in a disproportionate manner due to the discrimination they face in other domains of social life – especially work – and the lack of recognition and appropriate support for their needs. In particular, institutionalised barriers to political participation for disabled people have been inadequately addressed or *de facto* ignored by policy-makers (Morris 2005, pp. 24–5).

To evoke a classic governance metaphor, one could suggest that disabled people remain confined to the bottom tiers of the 'ladder of citizen participation' (Arnstein 1969), which corresponds to a position defined by Cohen (2009) as 'semi-citizenship'. To address this issue adequately, top-down policy interventions that aim to make the participation 'ladder' more accessible are not enough. Instead, this problem calls for a more general 're-articulation of the relationship between formal and informal politics, so that those who opt for the latter can nevertheless influence the former and those who choose the former are not cut off from the concerns and demands articulated in the latter' (Lister 2003, p. 165). The next section elaborates on this point, discussing how an expanded political space may promote the achievement of more meaningful levels of citizenship for disabled people.

Inclusive Citizenship Online: Eradicating Barriers and Expanding the Civic Arena

In recent years, the debate on citizenship has been reinvigorated by the work of scholars who argued that genuinely inclusive citizenship can only be achieved through a working compromise between liberal–social positions focused on rights and republican views emphasising civic obligations. Grounded in the work of Nancy Fraser (2003), the idea of inclusive citizenship was developed by other feminist scholars (Lister 2004) and development researchers (Kabeer 2005). This concept is centred on the assumption that 'full' citizenship for every member of society can be attained only on the condition that 'participatory parity amongst peers' is achieved first. As Fraser explained (2003, pp. 35–6), participatory parity is a 'two-dimensional' concept that rests upon two equally indispensable conditions, namely: a fair distribution of resources; and equal opportunities to participate in public life.

By avoiding the establishment of a hierarchy between rights and responsibilities, inclusive citizenship arguably resolves the tension between the social and civic republican conceptions of citizenship as it presents socio-economic redistribution and participation in public affairs as complementary – rather than oppositional and alternative – rights (Fraser & Gordon 1994). This highlights how previous understandings of citizenship have systematically excluded specific social groups because 'the status of human being was often selectively rather than universally applied' (Kabeer 2005, p. 10) depending on whether rights or responsibilities were emphasised. Thus, this view constitutes a pragmatic approach to citizenship in which both the misrecognition of rights and the obstacles to equal participation opportunities ought to be analysed on a case-by-case basis in order to be tackled adequately (Fraser 2003, pp. 45–8). This is less about emphasising legal rights and more about identifying and removing those socio-political, economical, institutional, cultural and psychological 'barriers that prevent the rights and responsibilities of citizenship from being fairly distributed' (Faulks 2000, p. 163).

Building upon the work of authors such as Longo (2001), Lister (2003, pp. 159–65) identified two ways in which politics needs to change to enable truly inclusive political citizenship for everyone. First, access to 'formal' politics – that of parties, election campaigns and representative institutions – ought to be improved through the removal of institutionalised barriers to participation. Second, the relationship between 'formal' and 'informal' politics too needs to be tightened. Ultimately, this calls for a bold expansion of the civic arena, implicitly recognising the limits of policy-based interventions – including affirmative action measures – in boosting participation among marginalised citizens. This argument rests upon the awareness that members of under-represented groups such as women, poor, young and disabled people are much more likely to engage in 'informal' political spaces concerned with 'everyday' issues at the local level than with the formal forums such as parties and elections (Siim 2000, p. 101). This goes beyond emphasising the centrality of political participation to the achievement of true equality (Levitas 2005) and questions the very essence of 'politics' as it is usually understood. Similarly, this is more than a mere revival of the debate between those who have invoked the primacy of traditional political institutions such as parties (Hadenius 2001, pp. 40–1) and those who championed more fluid social movement-like organisations as vehicles for change (Turner 1986, pp. 89–92). Instead, this proposal revolves around a re-evaluation of more elementary forms of 'micro-politics [...] embedded in the daily lives of individuals' (Mann, cited in Lister 2003, p. 27) as a way for 'marginal citizens' to access and develop fundamental political rights (Janoski & Gran 2002).

Although theoretical literature continues to outweigh empirical investigation in this area (Lister 2007a, p. 58), in the last decade qualitative work was carried out that illustrated the positive impact of programmes designed to involve people who experience social disadvantage in decision-making on issues that affect their lives directly (Lister 2004; Lister et al. 2005), with some scholars suggesting ways of building on these foundations (Lister 2007b). In addition, this research highlighted also how comprehensive engagement in public affairs and community life, and not participation geared towards particularistic group interests, most benefited marginalised citizens (Kabeer 2005, p. 12). With regard to disabled people, the ethos behind direct payments legislation in the U.K. went some way towards supporting this kind of expansion of the political space by promoting 'micro-empowerment'. However, the issues associated with the implementation of direct payments, as well as those characterising policy-based interventions more generally, highlighted the limits of policy interventions for re-shaping democratic governance into an overall more inclusive process to the advantage of disabled citizens.

In a review of social inequalities and human rights in the U.K., Riddell and Watson (2011) stressed that 'there is clearly a danger that Britain is locked in a high inequality equilibrium, which can only be disrupted by massive state-driven re-distribution, prompted by severe social unrest' (p. 202). This makes for an arguably persuasive, if concerning, scenario in the wake of mass anti-establishment mobilisations such as the transnational Occupy protests of 2011, anti-austerity networks such as the Spanish *Indignados* (Castells 2012; Gerbaudo 2012) and demonstrations against the G20 summits that took place following the 2008 global financial crisis (Bennett & Segerberg 2011). However, to gather a truly comprehensive picture of the shifting political landscape in this period of economic reform and emerging social tensions, it is useful to ask also whether there are other, less disruptive channels for marginalised citizens to express dissent and re-claim political agency. In the case of disabled people, it is necessary to look beyond both institutionally-sponsored paths to public engagement and traditional advocacy organisations to understand whether emerging alternative forces are in fact re-modelling the political space along Lister's inclusive vision. In particular, it is important to ask whether new media technologies are playing a role in helping disabled citizens overcome traditional barriers to participation by re-configuring the political arena into a more accessible space.

While some have argued that the Internet is 'a marginal resource for civic identity' for people on low incomes, who rely on state benefits, or are otherwise excluded from the societal mainstream (Mossberger et al. 2003, pp. 123–4; Olsson 2006, p. 85), participatory research carried out by scholars such as Hampton (2010) has shown instead that online technology can be an unexpected multiplier of social cohesion and a platform for the creation of 'communities of interest' for those who experience disadvantage. Using quasi-experimental methods, researchers found that, when provided with the necessary information technology (IT) infrastructure, people living in areas with high poverty rates were 'as motivated to participate and deliberate on local issues as people of other [more affluent] communities' (Gad et al. 2012, p. 10). At the root of these people's willingness to become engaged were common interests and latent affiliations that previously had been suppressed by physical and structural barriers to social interaction and community building. This research exposed the limitations of work that had looked at the Internet's significance for sociopolitical inclusion/exclusion by considering primarily quantitative survey data (Mossberger et al. 2008), and made a strong case for the qualitative contextualisation of online media use – and non-use – by members of marginalised and minority groups (Mehra et al. 2004). In light of these findings, it seems especially important to ask whether new media technologies can provide viable channels for disabled Internet users to meet, discuss, organise and be heard by public decision-makers.

New Media and Disability: The Story So Far

The idea that disabled people could benefit from new information and communication technologies (ICTs) is, strictly speaking, not new. In 1980, disabled scholar and activist Vic Finkelstein (1980) wrote that in a not too distant future 'impaired persons will [...] no longer be oppressed by disabling social conventions and disabling environments but will be absorbed in the mainstream of social interactions' (p. 37). At the centre of this vision was a strong belief in the transformative potential of technological development. Within this framework, ICTs were assumed to facilitate the empowerment of disabled people. Building upon this line of thought, other early cyber-enthusiasts went even further, claiming that although:

> the implications of such advanced technology as virtual reality will likely remain of concern for some time [...] the potential for aiding mankind – and in particular in improving the lives of those with disabilities – seems to make this quantum leap well worth the risk.
> (Nelson 1994, p. 208)

Such optimist positions echoed the deterministic scenarios depicted by political scientists like Barber (1984), who predicted that IT would herald an era of radical democratic renewal, direct participation and power redistribution in the not too distant future. Yet, since then no one has investigated the relationship between new media and disability politics in detail. Therefore, a meaningful debate on the effects of online communications on disabled people's political rights is long overdue.

Most of the empirical research on disability and new media to date has examined problems of Internet access and Web content accessibility. Theoretically, this work is rooted in the 'social shaping of technology' tradition and therefore postulates that the Internet, being socially constructed, tends to reproduce and possibly exacerbate the environmental barriers that typically exclude disabled people from central aspects of social and political life (Dobransky & Hargittai 2006; Goggin & Newell 2003). The most recent available data on online media usage in the U.K. appear to support this pessimistic view, indicating that, in 2013, 51 per cent of disabled Britons were using the Internet on a regular basis compared to 84 per cent of the general population (Dutton & Blank 2013). U.S. data paint a similar picture, with 54 per cent of disabled Americans using the Internet in 2012 versus 81 per cent of the general population (Fox 2011). Recent survey work with a range of impaired people in the U.K. has highlighted also that digital media can create new disabling barriers depending on a combination of access and lack thereof, technology features and impairments (Macdonald & Clayton 2013). Indeed, these findings should remind policy-makers and technology developers of the need to improve Internet access and accessibility by supporting the implementation of universal design principles. That said, it is encouraging also to note that a majority of disabled people in the U.K. and the U.S. are now regular Internet users.

Access and accessibility problems arguably resonate with fundamental theoretical arguments in both disability and Internet studies. On the one hand, the exclusionary design of some new technologies 'add[s] significant weight to a social barriers model of disability' (Roulstone 1998, p. 1). On the other hand, there has been a tendency among Internet scholars to conflate accessibility issues into the 'digital divide' paradigm (Vicente & López 2010; Warschauer 2003), which stresses the inequalities caused by disparity in Internet access, use and IT literacy (Norris 2001). Despite substantial progress in recent years, poverty, unemployment and low educational attainment remain crucial drivers in a lack of Internet use in countries such as the U.K. (Dutton & Blank 2013) and the U.S. (Zickuhr & Smith 2012). These problems continue to affect disabled people in a disproportionate manner (Aldridge et al. 2012) and therefore interact with accessibility issues to generate a heightened risk of digital exclusion for people with impairments. In light of these findings, the initial optimism for the 'liberating' potential of ICTs more recently turned into scepticism or even pessimism among disability scholars.

Over the years, the study of disability and new media has become increasingly less of a niche field and today includes a variety of publications across multiple fields. Constructionist concerns, however, have promoted a specific approach to disability and new media, which have been analysed almost exclusively through the lens of access and accessibility. For example, the journal *First Monday* devoted one of its most recent issues to evolving trends in digital accessibility (Ellis & Kent 2015). Much of this interest in disability and new media has been translated in the analysis of policy documents, accessibility standards and design protocols in search of 'virtual rights' for disabled people (Fitzpatrick 2000). Internet access and accessibility are also included in the CRPD (Article 9, par. g), which has led some scholars to refer to them as 'human rights' for disabled people given the growing centrality of Internet connectivity to the contemporary social fabric (Jaeger 2012, 2015). Sophisticated analyses of the legal battle for online equality for disabled people have emerged in recent years (Blanck 2014). Literature in this area has highlighted how accessibility generally continues to be an 'afterthought' for both content and technology developers, meaning that hardware, software and content are rarely designed to be universally accessible and need to be retrofitted for use by people with different impairments. This constitutes a global trend across democratic countries such as the U.K., the U.S. (Easton 2013), Australia (Ellis 2012) and Canada (Stienstra 2006). As Blanck (2014) noted:

> presently, to approach web content equality, many people with disabilities require modifications and accommodations in service design when reasonable and feasible to do so. These opportunities alone do not, and cannot, guarantee that, in all circumstances, people with disabilities will have the same outcomes from their activities on the web.
>
> (pp. 245–6)

While some of these scholars usefully hinted at the potential benefits of online media for disabled users, they did so mainly to underline arguments in support of universal design policies (Ellis 2010) and promote the inclusion of disabled representatives in Internet governance bodies such as the World Wide Web Consortium (Easton 2010). As part of this general trend, the same approach was applied also to the limited amount of research that has focused on disabled people's relationship with e-government and e-democracy initiatives to date, including current studies of local government accessibility online (McDonald et al. 2015). Universal access in particular has been interpreted either as a benchmark for success in evaluating e-government initiatives (Kuzma 2010; Stienstra & Troschuk 2005) and the provision of human services through the Internet (Watling & Crawford 2010), or as a key policy goal for disability rights advocates (Adam & Kreps 2009; Cheta 2004; D'Aubin 2007).

Undoubtedly, this research has had the merit of de-bunking the myth of the Internet as a 'panacea' for disabled people's social exclusion and establishing a principle for which 'control, and not technological innovation alone, will determine the potential benefits of communication technology for disabled people' (Thornton 1993, p. 348). As Warschauer (2003) noted, while 'some would suggest that ICT is a luxury for the poor,

[. . .] it is in effect becoming the electricity of the informational era' (p. 9) and 'the ability to access, adapt, and create new knowledge using new information and communication technology is critical to social inclusion' (ibid., p. 29). In light of these considerations, accessibility research speaks to some very real and fundamental concerns about disabled people's role in society. Disabled Internet users have only just started to gain visibility and a more nuanced research approach that considers the needs of people with communication difficulties (Parr et al. 2006) and learning impairments (Kennedy et al. 2011), alongside those of people with visual, auditory and motor impairments, is finally emerging. Internet access and accessibility therefore remain important problems and will constitute a crucial research area for the foreseeable future.

However, it seems reasonable to ask also whether the popularity of this approach inadvertently led researchers to overlook other aspects of the complex relationship between disabled people and new media that are worthy of investigation. The unrivalled predominance of accessibility studies signals a risky tendency to reduce a complex and multi-layered relationship to a single variable. Although this trend resonates with both social model and digital divide theories, such a stringent research focus fostered a lack of in-depth work on disabled people's own perspective with regard to new media technologies. This is particularly problematic because, as Pilling et al. (2004) pointed out in a seminal study on disability and the Internet in the U.K., a truly nuanced and exhaustive understanding of the relationship between disability and new media can only be achieved through a detailed exploration of the experiences of those disabled people who regularly engage in online communications in spite of persistent accessibility challenges.

Moreover, recent work on accessibility has registered substantial progress towards the development of more inclusive digital media and accessible online content. These changes have been ascribed to four main factors, including: more effective legislation introduced in countries that drive Internet development, chiefly the United States (Ellcessor 2010); the positive response of global technology companies such as Apple to universal design pleas coming from disabled users (Ellis & Kent 2011); legal challenges launched by disability rights advocates to show that reasonable accommodations must be made by online service providers and other vendors (Blanck 2014); and, finally, what Goggin and Newell (2007) termed 'the business of digital disability', i.e. the commercial value of accessible, universally-designed technology. This has prompted renewed calls for the investigation of the perspective of the growing majority of disabled people who 'increasingly, [. . .] rely on the [online] medium to provide more independence, work opportunities, and social interactions' (Ellis & Kent 2011, p. 59). As such, researchers are presented with a range of alternative options for analysing the relationship between disability and new media, exploring how different online technologies, in the hands of disabled Internet 'pioneers', may have different empowering effects in specific social life domains such as employment, personal relationships and civic engagement.

Looking Beyond Accessibility

In light of this, it is essential to re-align investigations of disability and new media with the lived experiences of disabled Internet 'pioneers'. This is not a case of underplaying the importance of accessibility issues, but rather one of pursuing a fuller understanding of the Internet's significance for disabled people. The fact that the online sphere undoubtedly reflects and possibly exacerbates some pre-existing disabling barriers need not overshadow the possibility that other obstacles, be those physical, cultural, psychological or organisational, may simultaneously be re-negotiated (Roulstone 1998, p. 129). In addition, gaining a better understanding of new media's significance for disabled users will augment pressure on both policy-makers and technology developers to tackle the issue of digital exclusion more effectively. In accordance with the principle of 'online groundedness' of social change, for which Internet research can anticipate new social trends at the same time as technology nurtures them (Rogers 2009, p. 8), focusing on disabled Internet users is poised to offer valuable insights into the future of political participation for disabled people.

Although at the time of writing too many disabled people remained locked out of online media, elements are emerging that could lead to positive developments in the coming years. In particular, universal design principles are becoming increasingly more widespread and the connection costs in advanced industrialised nations are falling at a staggeringly fast pace (International Telecommunication Union 2012, pp. 65–6). This is likely to reduce financial barriers and make access more ubiquitous for potential users on low incomes, especially through the expansion of mobile Internet services. In light of these considerations, the study of disability and new media should be expanded to assess the impact of digital technologies on the levels of citizenship of disabled users.

In the early 2000s, disabled Internet 'pioneers' were found to be enthusiastic about technology regardless of affordability and accessibility issues (Goggin & Newell 2004; Pilling et al. 2004; Sheldon 2004). In this period, authors like Johnson and Moxon (1998), Ritchie and Blanck (2003) and Polat (2005) emphasised the potential of the Internet for promoting political participation among people with impairments and strengthening the role of disability organisations in policy-making. Yet, following these speculative claims, just a handful of scholars ventured into empirical research with disabled Internet users. Virtually all of these studies used qualitative methods – primarily interviews – to investigate the perspective of disabled users on the impact of new media on daily life, focusing on aspects such as work, shopping and interpersonal relationships.

This work generated some useful preliminary insights into the significance of online media for disabled users. In particular, it highlighted the importance of discussion forums and blogs as platforms for the diffusion of alternative, unmediated representations of disability (Goggin & Noonan 2007; Thoreau 2006). In addition, it exposed the role of online communications as a booster and multiplier of interpersonal relationships for disabled users (Anderberg & Jönsson 2005) and revealed the benefits of online peer-support communities (Obst & Stafurik 2010), as well as mobile Internet connections (Goggin 2011) for disabled people. Following Roulstone's (1998) seminal study on the effects of technology on the relationship between disabled people and employment, others highlighted the advantages and disadvantages of both adaptive and mainstream IT for disabled workers. Overall, this research stressed the utopian character of full employment expectations for disabled people (Michailakis 2001) and confirmed that 'the fullest realisation of the benefits of enabling technology is highly dependant on a wider supportive and flexible environment' (Roulstone 1998, p. 129).

Throughout this pioneering work, close attention was paid to how disabled Internet users negotiated their identity, presented themselves and more generally built an online 'voice'. For example, Bowker and Tuffin (2002) noted that 'the idea that [online] identity can be constructed according to the demands of the situation is a powerful framework for disabled people' (p. 342), who greatly valued opportunities for not mentioning their impairments in online interactions with non-disabled people. Similarly, Moss et al. (2004) found that on the Internet people with aphasia had the freedom to build their own personal identity free from externally imposed 'roles'. Blogs and forums were particularly praised by participants in these studies for promoting 'alternative [disability] narrations that are not necessarily in accordance with the dominant paradigms, including those proposed by social model theorists' (Goggin & Noonan 2007, p. 165) and for expanding the geographical reach of peer-networks, enabling experience-sharing irrespective of distance and other physical barriers (Anderberg & Jönsson 2005, p. 729). Crucially, this meant that impairment and impairment-based discrimination were frequently discussed on these platforms (Thoreau 2006), which may contribute to building a group identity for disabled Internet users, mitigating some of the fragmentation issues outlined earlier in this chapter.

Indeed, the same studies also identified possible negative consequences stemming from the disappearance of impairment in the online sphere. In particular, the risk that the practice of routinely hiding impairment in online interactions may limit 'political action by rendering invisible the very phenomenon which invokes political debate, reaction, and a sense of solidarity amongst disabled people themselves' (Bowker & Tuffin 2002, p. 341) was noted, as well as the danger that this may increase the distance between disabled people and the rest of society. Nevertheless, empirical evidence ultimately led these scholars to conclude that the positive effects of online media on political participation for disabled Internet users would most likely outweigh the risks that came with it. As Anderberg and Jönsson (2005) pointed out in their detailed qualitative study with experienced disabled computer users, 'increased activity and knowledge, and the ability to form social networks will be an additional tool in the struggle for an equal and discrimination-free society' (p. 731).

Furthermore, survey research has revealed that Internet use among disabled people tends to be weighted heavily towards younger generations (Williams et al. 2008), who are also more civically engaged compared to their older counterparts (Schur et al. 2005). Crucially, these trends parallel those for the general population in democratic countries, where young users are far more often and more deeply engaged with online media, as well as especially inclined towards political uses of the Internet (Lupia & Philpot 2005; Owen 2006). While these patterns are certainly influenced by the socio-economic background of individual users (Livingstone et al. 2005) and their familiarity with technology (di Gennaro & Dutton 2006), the growing popularity of dedicated online spaces to promote civic engagement among young people has led some to question assumptions about youth's political apathy in countries such as the U.K. and Australia, inviting researchers to look instead beyond government-sponsored forums and focus more closely on youth-led platforms (Vromen 2008, 2011) as well as issue-focused online initiatives (Ward 2008). This adds a further dimension to the investigation of the relationship between disability and new media. As Mercer et al. (1999) noted, youth years are particularly crucial to the formation of disabled identities. Thus, it is important to ask whether online media – especially those promoting the expansion of peer-networks – can perform civic education and participation functions for young disabled people, boosting their sense of collective agency and possibly laying the foundations for generational renewal in disability advocacy.

Do the 'everyday' benefits experienced by disabled Internet users also translate into the political arena, or does the voice of disabled self-advocates continue to be silenced in online venues as it is in traditional representative processes? In other words, are new media technologies helping to re-configure politics along more 'informal' and thus inclusive lines to the benefit of disabled users? In order to tackle these questions, it is essential to assess whether online media are providing disabled users with opportunities to overcome the barriers that continue to prevent them from exercising their political rights fully. In addition to its relevance *vis-à-vis* physical access barriers and role in peer-community building outlined above, online communication has been credited also with the potential to reduce the 'distance' between citizens and political elites, enabling the former to organise themselves independently from formal institutions and pre-existing organisations (Shirky 2008). This is crucial for disabled users, who, as was discussed earlier, face both institutional and organisational hindrances to participation that continue to restrict their access to both 'formal' and 'informal' political spaces.

Even though disabled Internet users could come together and mobilise online, one could argue, barriers would continue to exist in the 'real' world, possibly reinforced by the shift of politically-minded disabled people to the 'virtual' sphere. Yet, interpreting online and offline politics as separate entities would erroneously mirror the fictional distinction between 'real' and 'virtual' that mired the study of the Internet in its infancy. More recently, a more mature understanding of online and offline interaction as complementary and deeply interconnected components of a single socio-political continuum has emerged (Rogers 2010, p. 242). As such, online media can do more than just provide a place to meet by serving also as tools to engage in new forms of 'digital' action, which can be equally if not more effective than traditional lobbying and street protest (Carty 2010). Thus, online organising may provide a genuine alternative to traditional advocacy formats for disabled Internet users as it has the potential to influence 'real' politics independent of the barriers that so far have determined their exclusion from the public arena.

Undoubtedly, a number of important questions remain unanswered at this stage. What elements of new media technologies are relevant and where exactly should one look for evidence of this transformation of the political space? Is this about acquiring information, the ability to form networks, the opportunity to change institutions from the ground up, or all of these things at once? Finally, what type of role, if any, should disabled Internet users be expected to perform in this hypothetical new political environment? Are they going to be leaders and drivers of change, or rather leave it to others, maybe existing organisations, to take the initiative? The next chapter turns to both theory and empirical evidence in Internet studies in order to discuss these issues in greater detail. In particular, the relationship between motivational factors and the formation of online networked 'communities' will be addressed, with a view to understanding what specific elements and circumstances may promote or hinder political discussion and online participation among disabled users.

Conclusions

In spite of substantial developments in anti-discrimination legislation and policy interventions inspired by the principles of independent living, disabled people in the U.K. and the U.S. continue to be confined to a position of 'semi-citizenship' (Cohen 2009). Within this context, the problem of disabled people's marginalisation in the political and civic arena is especially salient, resulting from the combined influence of a series of persistent exclusionary barriers. In particular, institutional barriers to participation have not been adequately challenged, while policy measures designed to encourage citizen participation in public decision-making have either failed to support the needs of disabled people or ignored them as legitimate political actors. At the same time, disability rights activists went their separate ways shortly after the introduction of landmark anti-discrimination legislation in the 1990s, limiting themselves to the defence of acquired rights rather than promoting their expansion. In this context, feminist citizenship theorists have put forward an unconventional perspective for which the realisation of a truly 'inclusive' model of citizenship will require a profound re-configuration of the relationship between 'formal' and 'informal' domains in politics. Alongside other traditionally disadvantaged groups, disabled people may have a lot to gain from this type of transformation. Yet, as policy intervention so far has fallen short on promoting this process and disability organisations have been either too weak or too close to politicians to fill the gap, change is poised to follow a different avenue.

As online media are becoming increasingly integral to political participation by affording new ways for citizens to mobilise and voice their views and concerns, it is therefore particularly important to investigate their role *vis-à-vis* the political exclusion of disabled people. While some pioneers in disability studies displayed great enthusiasm for the 'emancipatory' potential of ICTs, empirical research so far has concentrated overwhelmingly on access problems and accessibility standards. Although in opposite directions, both these approaches mirrored the determinism that riddled the study of the Internet in its infancy. Indeed, access and accessibility remain key issues that both researchers and policy-makers should address as a priority. However, at the same time their persistence does not provide a valid justification for underplaying the fact that a majority of disabled people in the U.K. and the U.S. now regularly use the Internet. This is likely to have consequences on both the political inclusion of disabled Internet users and disability advocacy practices more generally. Thus, choosing to ignore this phenomenon is not only patronising towards disabled users but it also means that so far researchers have missed out on understanding the significance of the digital transformation of the political arena for disabled people. In addition, from a broader Internet studies point of view, it is also of particular interest to establish how the Internet affects a social group that has traditionally been excluded from power.

These issues are to be approached with maximum cautiousness, avoiding any sort of premature assumption that may compromise the direction of the analysis. Formulating expectations of technology-enabled 'mass' empowerment as in Finkelstein's (1980) utopia would therefore be just as short-sighted as focusing solely on accessibility issues. Thus, the next chapter focuses on relevant literature in Internet studies in order to identify more nuanced expectations and lay the foundations for empirical analysis.

Note

1 See: www.theguardian.com/society/2015/mar/25/disabled-people-shut-out-lack-access-polling-stations (accessed 12 March 2016).

References

Abberley, P., 1987. The Concept of Oppression and the Development of a Social Theory of Disability. *Disability, Handicap & Society*, 2(1), pp. 5–19.

Adam, A. & Kreps, D., 2009. Disability and Discourses of Web Accessibility. *Information, Communication & Society*, 12(7), pp. 1041–1058.

Aldridge, H., Kenway, P., MacInnes, T. & Parekh, A., 2012. *Monitoring Poverty and Social Exclusion 2012*, York: Joseph Rowntree Foundation.

Anderberg, P. & Jönsson, B., 2005. Being There. *Disability & Society*, 20(7), pp. 719–733.

Armer, B., 2004. In Search of a Social Model of Disability: Marxism, Normality and Culture. In C. Barnes & G. Mercer, eds. *Implementing the Social Model of Disability: Theory and Practice*. Leeds: The Disability Press, pp. 48–64.

Arnstein, S.R., 1969. A Ladder of Citizen Participation. *Journal of the American Institute of Planners*, 35(4), pp. 216–224.

Bagenstos, S.R., 2009. *Law and the Contradictions of the Disability Rights Movement*, New Haven, CT: Yale University Press.

Barber, B.R., 1984. *Strong Democracy: Participatory Politics for a New Age*, Berkeley, CA: University of California Press.

Barnes, C., 1991. *Disabled People in Britain and Discrimination: A Case for Anti-Discrimination Legislation*, London: C. Hurst & Co.

——— 2007. Disability Activism and the Struggle for Change: Disability, Policy and Politics in the UK. *Education, Citizenship and Social Justice*, 2(3), pp. 203–221.

Barnes, C. & Mercer, G., 2001. The Politics of Disability and the Struggle for Change. In L. Barton, ed. *Disability Politics and the Struggle for Change*. London: David Fulton Publishers, pp. 11–23.

——— 2003. *Disability*, Cambridge: Polity Press.

Barnes, M., 2002. Bringing Difference into Deliberation? Disabled People, Survivors and Local Governance. *Policy & Politics*, 30(3), pp. 319–331.

Barnes, M., Knops, A., Newman, J. & Sullivan, H., 2004. The Micro-Politics of Deliberation: Case Studies in Public Participation. *Contemporary Politics*, 10(2), pp. 93–110.

Barton, L., 1993. The Struggle for Citizenship: The Case of Disabled People. *Disability, Handicap & Society*, 8(3), pp. 235–248.

Beckett, A.E., 2005. Reconsidering Citizenship in the Light of the Concerns of the UK Disability Movement. *Citizenship Studies*, 9(4), pp. 405–421.

———— 2006a. Understanding Social Movements: Theorising the Disability Movement in Conditions of Late Modernity. *The Sociological Review*, 54(4), pp. 734–752.

———— 2006b. *Citizenship and Vulnerability*, Basingstoke: Palgrave Macmillan.

Beckman, L., 2007. Political Equality and the Disenfranchisement of People with Intellectual Impairments. *Social Policy and Society*, 6(1), pp. 13–23.

Benford, R.D. & Snow, D.A., 2000. Framing Processes and Social Movements: An Overview and Assessment. *Annual Review of Sociology*, 26, pp. 611–639.

Bennett, W.L. & Segerberg, A., 2011. Digital Media and the Personalization of Collective Action. *Information, Communication & Society*, 14(6), pp. 770–799.

Blanck, P., 2014. *eQuality: The Struggle for Web Accessibility by Persons with Cognitive Disabilities*, Cambridge: Cambridge University Press.

Bowker, N. & Tuffin, K., 2002. Disability Discourses for Online Identities. *Disability & Society*, 17(3), pp. 327–344.

British Council of Disabled People, 1997. *The Disabled People's Movement: The Way Forward*, London: BCODP.

Campbell, J. & Oliver, M., 1996. *Disability Politics: Understanding Our Past, Changing Our Future*, London/New York: Routledge.

Carty, V., 2010. *Wired and Mobilizing: Social Movements, New Technology, and Electoral Politics*, London: Routledge.

Castells, M., 2012. *Networks of Outrage and Hope: Social Movements in the Internet Age*, Cambridge: Polity Press.

Cheta, R., 2004. Dis@bled People, ICTs and a New Age of Activism: A Portuguese Accessibility Special Interest Group Study. In W. van de Donk, B. Loader, & P.G. Nixon, eds. *Cyberprotest: New Media, Citizens and Social Movements*. London: Routledge, pp. 207–230.

Cohen, E.F., 2009. *Semi-Citizenship in Democratic Politics*, Cambridge: Cambridge University Press.

Crow, L., 1996. Including All of Our Lives: Renewing the Social Model of Disability. In C. Barnes & G. Mercer, eds. *Exploring the Divide: Illness and Disability*. Leeds: The Disability Press, pp. 55–72.

D'Aubin, A., 2007. Working for Barrier Removal in the ICT Area: Creating a More Accessible and Inclusive Canada. *The Information Society*, 23(3), pp. 193–201.

Dean, H., 1999. Citizenship. In M. Powell, ed. *New Labour, New Welfare State?* Bristol: The Policy Press, pp. 213–234.

di Gennaro, C. & Dutton, W., 2006. The Internet and the Public: Online and Offline Political Participation in the United Kingdom. *Parliamentary Affairs*, 59(2), pp. 299–313.

Dobransky, K. & Hargittai, E., 2006. The Disability Divide in Internet Access and Use. *Information, Communication & Society*, 9(3), pp. 313–334.

Drake, R.F., 1994. The Exclusion of Disabled People from Positions of Power in British Voluntary Organisations. *Disability & Society*, 9(4), pp. 461–480.

———— 1999. *Understanding Disability Policies*, Basingstoke: Palgrave Macmillan.

———— 2002. Disabled People, Voluntary Organisations and Participation in Policy Making. *Policy & Politics*, 30(3), pp. 373–385.

Dutton, W.H. & Blank, G., 2013. *Cultures of the Internet: The Internet in Britain*, Oxford: Oxford Internet Institute.

Dwyer, P., 2004. *Understanding Social Citizenship*, Bristol: The Policy Press.

Easton, C., 2010. The Web Content Accessibility Guidelines 2.0: An Analysis of Industry Self-Regulation. *International Journal of Law and Information Technology*, 19(1), pp. 74–93.

——— 2013. An Examination of the Internet's Development as a Disabling Environment in the Context of the Social Model of Disability and Anti-Discrimination Legislation in the UK and USA. *Universal Access in the Information Society*, 12(1), pp. 105–114.

Ellcessor, E., 2010. Bridging Disability Divides: A Critical History of Web Content Accessibility Through 2001. *Information, Communication & Society*, 13(3), pp. 289–308.

Ellis, K., 2010. A Purposeful Rebuilding: YouTube, Representation, Accessibility and the Socio-Political Space of Disability. *Telecommunications Journal of Australia*, 60(2), pp. 21.1–21.12.

——— 2012. It Means Inclusion: A Creative Approach to Disability and Telecommunications Policy in Australia. *Telecommunications Journal of Australia*, 62(2), pp. 27.1–27.3.

Ellis, K. & Kent, M., 2011. *Disability and New Media*, London: Routledge.

——— 2015. Disability and the Internet in 2015: Where to Now? *First Monday*, 20(9).

Equality and Human Rights Commission, 2010. *How Fair Is Britain? The First Triennial Review*. Available at: www.equalityhumanrights.com/about-us/our-work/key-projects/how-fair-britain/full-report-and-evidence-downloads (accessed 28 December 2015).

Faulks, K., 2000. *Citizenship*, London/New York: Routledge.

Finkelstein, V., 1980. *Attitudes and Disabled People*, New York: World Rehabilitation Fund.

Fitzpatrick, T., 2000. Critical Cyberpolicy: Network Technologies, Massless Citizens, Virtual Rights. *Critical Social Policy*, 20(3), pp. 375–407.

Floyd, M. & Curtis, J., 2001. An Examination of Changes in Disability and Employment Policy in the United Kingdom. In W. van Oorschot & B. Hvinden, eds. *Disability Policies in European Countries*. The Hague: Kluwer Law International, pp. 13–32.

Fox, S., 2011. *Americans Living with Disability and Their Technology Profile*, Washington, DC: Pew Internet and American Life Project.

Fraser, N., 2003. Social Justice in the Age of Identity Politics: Redistribution, Recognition and Participation. In N. Fraser & A. Honnoeth, eds. *Redistribution or Recognition? A Political-Philosophical Exchange*. London/New York: Verso, pp. 7–109.

Fraser, N. & Gordon, L., 1994. Civil Citizenship Against Social Citizenship? On the Ideology of Contract-Versus-Charity. In B. van Steenbergen, ed. *The Condition of Citizenship*. London: SAGE, pp. 90–107.

French, S., 1993. Disability, Impairment, or Something in Between. In C. Barnes, J. Swain, S. French & C. Thomas, eds. *Disabling Barriers, Enabling Environments*. London: SAGE, pp. 17–25.

Gad, S., Ramakrishnan, N., Hampton, K. & Kavanaugh, A., 2012. Bridging the Divide in Democratic Engagement: Studying Conversation Patterns in

Advantaged and Disadvantaged Communities. In 2012 International Conference on Social Informatics. Washington, DC: IEEE, pp. 165–176.

Gerbaudo, P., 2012. *Tweet and the Streets: Social Media and Contemporary Activism*, London: Pluto Press.

Gilbert, C., Sarb, C. & Bush, M., 2010. *Polls Apart 2010: Opening Elections to Disabled People*, London: SCOPE.

Goggin, G., 2011. Disability, Mobiles, and Social Policy: New Modes of Communication and Governance. In J. Katz, ed. *Mobile Communication: Dimensions of Social Policy*. New Brunswick: Transaction, pp. 259–272.

Goggin, G. & Newell, C., 2003. *Digital Disability: The Social Construction of Disability in New Media*, Lanham: Rowan & Littlefield.

——— 2004. Disabled E-Nation: Telecommunications, Disability, and National Policy. *Prometheus*, 22(4), pp. 411–422.

——— 2007. The Business of Digital Disability. *The Information Society*, 23(3), pp. 159–168.

Goggin, G. & Noonan, T., 2007. Blogging Disability: The Interface Between New Cultural Movements and Internet Technology. In A. Bruns & J. Jacobs, eds. *Uses of Blogs*. New York: Peter Lang Publishing, pp. 161–172.

Government Accountability Office, 2013. *Voters with Disabilities: Challenges to Voting Accessibility*, April 23, Washington, DC: Government Accountability Office.

Guldvik, I. & Lesjø, J.H., 2014. Disability, Social Groups, and Political Citizenship. *Disability & Society*, 29(4), pp. 516–529.

Hadenius, A., 2001. *Institutions and Democratic Citizenship*, Oxford: Oxford University Press.

Hampton, K.N., 2010. Internet Use and the Concentration of Disadvantage: Glocalization and the Urban Underclass. *American Behavioral Scientist*, 53(8), pp. 1111–1132.

Heater, D., 2004. *Citizenship: The Civic Ideal in World History, Politics and Education*, Manchester/New York: Manchester University Press.

International Telecommunication Union, 2012. *Measuring the Information Society 2012*. Available at: www.itu.int/en/ITU-D/Statistics/Documents/publications/mis2012/MIS2012_without_Annex_4.pdf (accessed 28 February 2016).

Jaeger, P.T., 2012. *Disability and the Internet: Confronting a Digital Divide*, Boulder, CO: Lynne Rienner.

——— 2015. Disability, Human Rights, and Social Justice: The Ongoing Struggle for Online Accessibility and Equality. *First Monday*, 20(9).

Janoski, T. & Gran, B., 2002. Political Citizenship: Foundations of Rights. In E.F. Isin & B.S. Turner, eds. *Handbook of Citizenship Studies*. London: SAGE, pp. 13–52.

Johnson, L. & Moxon, E., 1998. In Whose Service? Technology, Care and Disabled People: The Case for a Disability Politics Perspective. *Disability & Society*, 13(2), pp. 241–258.

Kabeer, N., 2005. The Search for Inclusive Citizenship. In N. Kabeer, ed. *Inclusive Citizenship: Meanings and Expressions*. London/New York: Zed Books, pp. 1–27.

Keeley, H., Redley, M., Holland, A.J., & Clare, I.C.H., 2008. Participation in the 2005 General Election by Adults with Intellectual Disabilities. *Journal of Intellectual Disability Research*, 52(3), pp. 175–181.

Kennedy, H., Evans, S. & Thomas, S., 2011. Can the Web Be Made Accessible for People with Intellectual Disabilities? *The Information Society*, 27(1), pp. 29–39.

Kuzma, J.M., 2010. Accessibility Design Issues with UK E-Government Sites. *Government Information Quarterly*, 27(2), pp. 141–146.

Lantz, S. & Marston, G., 2012. Policy, Citizenship and Governance: The Case of Disability and Employment Policy in Australia. *Disability & Society*, 27(6), pp. 853–867.

Levitas, R., 2005. *The Inclusive Society? Social Exclusion and New Labour*, Basingstoke: Palgrave Macmillan.

Lister, R., 2003. *Citizenship: Feminist Perspectives*, Basingstoke: Palgrave Macmillan.

—— 2004. A Politics of Recognition and Respect: Involving People with Experience of Poverty in Decision-Making that Affects their Lives. In J. Andersen & B. Siim, eds. *The Politics of Inclusion and Empowerment: Gender, Class and Citizenship*. Basingstoke: Macmillan, pp. 116–138.

—— 2007a. Inclusive Citizenship: Realizing the Potential. *Citizenship Studies*, 11(1), pp. 49–61.

—— 2007b. From Object to Subject: Including Marginalised Citizens in Policy-Making. *Policy & Politics*, 35(3), pp. 437–455.

Lister, R., Smith, N., Middleton, S. & Cox, L., 2005. Young People Talking about Citizenship in Britain. In N. Kabeer, ed. *Inclusive Citizenship: Meanings and Expressions*. London/New York: Zed Books, pp. 114–131.

Livingstone, S., Bober, M. & Helsper, E.J., 2005. Active Participation or Just More Information? Young People's Take-Up of Opportunities to Act and Interact on the Internet. *Information, Community and Society*, 8(3), pp. 287–314.

Longo, P., 2001. Revisiting the Equality/Difference Debate: Redefining Citizenship for the New Millennium. *Citizenship Studies*, 5(3), pp. 269–284.

Lunt, N. & Thornton, P., 1994. Disability and Employment: Towards an Understanding of Discourse and Policy. *Disability & Society*, 9(2), pp. 223–238.

Lupia, A. & Philpot, T.S., 2005. Views from Inside the Net: How Websites Affect Young Adults' Political Interest. *Journal of Politics*, 67(4), pp. 1122–1142.

McDonald, K.E., Williamson, P., Weiss, S., Adya, M. & Blanck, P., 2015. The March Goes On: Community Access for People with Disabilities. *Journal of Community Psychology*, 43(3), pp. 348–363.

Macdonald, S.J. & Clayton, J., 2013. Back to the Future, Disability and the Digital Divide. *Disability & Society*, 28(5), pp. 702–718.

Marshall, T.H., 1950. *Citizenship and Social Class*, Sterling, VA: Pluto.

Mehra, B., Merkel, C. & Bishop, A.P., 2004. The Internet for Empowerment of Minority and Marginalized Users. *New Media & Society*, 6(6), pp. 781–802.

Mercer, G., Shakespeare, T. & Barnes, C., 1999. *Exploring Disability: A Sociological Introduction*, Cambridge: Polity Press.

Michailakis, D., 2001. Information and Communication Technologies and the Opportunities of Disabled Persons in the Swedish Labour Market. *Disability & Society*, 16(4), pp. 477–500.

Mitchell-Pye, A., 2015. *Barriers to Voting – One in Four Disabled Voters Found Polling Stations Inaccessible*, London: Leonard Cheshire Disability. Available at: //www.leonardcheshire.org/what we-do/latest-news/news-and-blogs/barriers-voting-disabled-voters-polling-stations-inaccessible (accessed 15 June 2015).

Morris, J., 1991. *Pride Against Prejudice: Transforming Attitudes to Disability*, London: The Women's Press.

—— 1992. Personal and Political: A Feminist Perspective on Researching Physical Disability. *Disability, Handicap & Society*, 7(2), pp. 157–166.

—— 1997. Care of Empowerment? A Disability Rights Perspective. *Social Policy & Administration*, 31(1), pp. 54–60.

—— 2005. *Citizenship and Disabled People: A Scoping Paper Prepared for the Disability Rights Commission*. Available at: http://disability-studies.leeds.ac.uk/files/library/morris-Citizenship-and-disabled-people.pdf (accessed 28 February 2016).

Moss, B., Parr, S., Byng, S. & Petheram, B., 2004. 'Pick Me Up and Not a Down Down, Up Up': How Are the Identities of People with Aphasia Represented in Aphasia, Stroke and Disability Websites? *Disability & Society*, 19(7), pp. 753–768.

Mossberger, K., Tolbert, C.J. & McNeal, R., 2008. *Digital Citizenship: The Internet, Society, and Participation*, Cambridge, MA: The MIT Press.

Mossberger, K., Tolbert, C.J. & Stansbury, M., 2003. *Virtual Inequality: Beyond the Digital Divide*, Washington, DC: Georgetown University Press.

Nelson, J.A., 1994. Virtual Reality: The Promise of a Brave New World for Those with Disability. In J. A. Nelson, ed. *The Disabled, the Media, and the Information Age*. Westport, CT: Greenwood Press, pp. 197–209.

Norris, P., 2001. *The Digital Divide: Civic Engagement, Information Poverty and the Internet Worldwide*, Cambridge: Cambridge University Press.

Obst, P. & Stafurik, J., 2010. Online We Are All Able Bodied: Online Psychological Sense of Community and Social Support Found Through Membership of Disability-Specific Websites Promotes Well-Being for People Living with a Physical Disability. *Journal of Community & Applied Social Psychology*, 20(6), pp. 525–531.

Oliver, M., 1990. *The Politics of Disablement*, Basingstoke: Macmillan Education.

—— 1996. *Understanding Disability: From Theory to Practice*, Basingstoke: Macmillan.

—— 1997. The Disability Movement is a New Social Movement! *Community Development Journal*, 32(3), pp. 244–251.

Oliver, M. & Barnes, C., 2006. Disability Politics and the Disability Movement in Britain: Where Did It All Go Wrong? *Coalition*, June.

—— 2012. *The New Politics of Disablement*, Basingstoke: Palgrave Macmillan.

Olsson, T., 2006. A Marginal Resource for Civic Identity: The Internet in Swedish Working Class Households. *Javnost-The Public*, 13(1), pp. 73–88.

Owen, D., 2006. The Internet and Youth Civic Engagement in the United States. In S. Oates, D. Owen, & R. Gibson, eds. *The Internet and Politics: Citizens, Voters and Activists*. London: Routledge, pp. 20–38.

Parr, S., Watson, N. & Woods, B., 2006. Access, Agency, and Normality: The Wheelchair and the Internet as Mediators of Disability. In A. Webster, ed. *New Technologies in Healthcare: Challenge, Change, Innovation*. Basingstoke: Palgrave Macmillan, pp. 161–174.

Pearson, C., 2012. Independent Living. In N. Watson, A. Roulstone, & C. Thomas, eds. *Routledge Handbook of Disability Studies*. London: Routledge, pp. 240–252.

Pearson, C. & Riddell, S., 2006. Introduction – The Development of Direct Payments in Scotland. In C. Pearson, ed. *Direct Payments and the Personalisation of Care*. Edinburgh: Dunedin Academic Press, pp. 1–12.

Pearson, C. & Watson, N., 2007. Tackling Disability Discrimination in the United Kingdom: The British Disability Discrimination Act. *Washington University Journal of Law and Policy*, 23(95), pp. 95–120.

Pearson, C., Watson, N., Stalker, K., Lerpiniere, J., Paterson, K. & Ferrie, J., 2011. Don't Get Involved: An Examination of How Public Sector Organisations in England Are Involving Disabled People in the Disability Equality Duty. *Disability & Society*, 26(3), pp. 255–268.

Pelka, F., 2012. *What We Have Done: An Oral History of the Disability Rights Movement*, Amherst and Boston: University of Massachusetts Press.

Pilling, D., Barrett, P. & Floyd, M., 2004. *Disabled People and the Internet: Experiences, Barriers and Opportunities*, York: Joseph Rowntree Foundation.

Pointon, A., 1999. Out of the Closet: New Images of Disability in the Civil Rights Campaign. In B. Franklin, ed. *Social Policy, the Media and Misrepresentation*. London: Routledge, pp. 222–237.

Polat, R.K., 2005. The Internet and Political Participation Exploring the Explanatory Links. *European Journal of Communication*, 20(4), pp. 435–459.

Priestley, M., Jolly, D., Pearson, C., Riddell, S., Barnes, C. & Mercer, G., 2007. Direct Payments and Disabled People in the UK: Supply, Demand and Devolution. *British Journal of Social Work*, 37(7), pp. 1189–1204.

Priestley, M., Riddell, S., Jolly, D., Pearson, C., Williams, V., Barnes, C. & Mercer, G., 2010. Cultures of Welfare at the Front Line: Implementing Direct Payments for Disabled People in the UK. *Policy & Politics*, 38(2), pp. 307–324.

Redley, M., 2008. Citizens with Learning Disabilities and the Right to Vote. *Disability & Society*, 23(4), pp. 375–384.

Riddell, S. & Watson, N., 2011. Equality and Human Rights in Britain: Principles and Challenges. *Social Policy and Society*, 10(02), pp. 193–203.

Ritchie, H. & Blanck, P., 2003. The Promise of the Internet for Disability: A Study of On-Line Services and Web Site Accessibility at Centers for Independent Living. *Behavioral Sciences & The Law*, 21(1), pp. 5–26.

Roche, M., 2002. Social Citizenship: Grounds of Social Change. In E.F. Isin & B.S. Turner, eds. *Handbook of Citizenship Studies*. London: SAGE, pp. 69–86.

Rogers, R., 2009. *The End of the Virtual: Digital Methods*, Amsterdam: Vossiuspers UVA.

——— 2010. Internet Research: The Question of Method – A Keynote Address from the YouTube and the 2008 Election Cycle in the United States Conference. *Journal of Information Technology & Politics*, 7(2–3), pp. 241–260.

Roulstone, A., 1998. *Enabling Technology: Disabled People, Work, and New Technology*, Maidenhead: Open University Press.

——— 2011. Disabled People. In N. Yeates, T. Haux, R. Jawad, M. Kilkey & N. Timmins, eds. *In Defence of Welfare: The Impacts of the Comprehensive Spending Review*. Bristol: Social Policy Association, pp. 25–27.

Rummery, K., 2002. *Disability, Citizens and Community Care: A Case for Welfare Rights?* Burlington: Ashgate.

―――― 2006a. Introduction: Themed Section: Partnerships, Governance and Citizenship. *Social Policy and Society*, 5(2), pp. 223–225.

―――― 2006b. Disabled Citizens and Social Exclusion: The Role of Direct Payments. *Policy & Politics*, 34(4), pp. 633–650.

Schriner, K. & Batavia, A.I., 2001. The Americans With Disabilities Act: Does It Secure the Fundamental Right to Vote? *Policy Studies Journal*, 29(4), pp. 663–673.

Schur, L. & Adya, M., 2013. Sidelined or Mainstreamed? Political Participation and Attitudes of People with Disabilities in the United States. *Social Science Quarterly*, 94(3), pp. 811–839.

Schur, L., Adya, M. & Kruse, D., 2013. *Disability, Voter Turnout, and Voting Difficulties in the 2012 Elections*. Research Alliance for Accessible Voting.

Schur, L., Kruse, D. & Blanck, P., 2013. *People with Disabilities: Sidelined or Mainstreamed?* New York: Cambridge University Press.

Schur, L., Shields, T. & Schriner, K., 2005. Generational Cohorts, Group Membership, and Political Participation by People with Disabilities. *Political Research Quarterly*, 58(3), p. 487.

Shakespeare, T., 2006. *Disability Rights and Wrongs*, London: Routledge.

Shakespeare, T. & Watson, N., 2001. The Social Model of Disability: An Outdated Ideology? In S. Barnartt & B. Altman, eds. *Exploring Theories and Expanding Methodologies: Where We Are and Where We Need to Go*. Bingley: Emerald Group, pp. 9–28.

―――― 2010. Beyond Models: Understanding the Complexity of Disabled People's Lives. In G. Scambler & S. Scambler, eds. *New Directions in the Sociology of Chronic and Disabling Conditions*. London: Palgrave Macmillan, pp. 57–77.

Sheldon, A., 2004. Changing Technology. In J. Swain, S. French, C. Barnes & C. Thomas, eds. *Disabling Barriers – Enabling Environments*. London: SAGE, pp. 155–160.

Shields, T., Schriner, K., Schriner, K. & Ochs, L., 2000. Disenfranchised: People with Disabilities in American Electoral Politics. In B. Altman & S. Barnartt, eds. *Expanding the Scope of Social Science Research on Disability*. Stamford, CT: JAI Press, pp. 177–203.

Shirky, C., 2008. *Here Comes Everybody*, New York: Penguin.

Siim, B., 2000. *Gender and Citizenship: Politics and Agency in France, Britain and Denmark*, Oxford: Oxford University Press.

Stainton, T., 2005. Empowerment and the Architecture of Rights Based Social Policy. *Journal of Intellectual Disabilities: JOID*, 9(4), pp. 289–298.

Stienstra, D., 2006. The Critical Space Between: Access, Inclusion and Standards in Information Technologies. *Information, Communication & Society*, 9(3), pp. 335–354.

Stienstra, D. & Troschuk, L., 2005. Engaging Citizens with Disabilities in eDemocracy. *Disability Studies Quarterly*, 25(2).

Taylor-Gooby, P., 2008. *Reframing Social Citizenship*, Oxford: Oxford University Press.

Thomas, C., 1999. *Female Forms: Experiencing and Understanding Disability*, Buckingham: Open University Press.

———— 2010. Medical Sociology and Disability Theory. In G. Scambler & S. Scambler, eds. *New Directions in the Sociology of Chronic and Disabling Conditions*. London: Palgrave Macmillan, pp. 37–56.

Thomas, C. & Corker, M., 2002. A Journey Around the Social Model. In M. Corker & T. Shakespeare, eds. *Disability/Postmodernity: Embodying Disability Theory*. London/New York: Continuum, pp. 18–31.

Thoreau, E., 2006. Ouch!: An Examination of the Self-Representation of Disabled People on the Internet. *Journal of Computer-Mediated Communication*, 11(2), pp. 442–468.

Thornton, P., 1993. Communications Technology – Empowerment or Disempowerment? *Disability, Handicap & Society*, 8(4), pp. 339–349.

Tisdall, E. & Kay, M., 2003. A Culture of Participation? In S. Riddell & N. Watson, eds. *Disability, Culture and Identity*. Harlow: Pearson Education, pp. 19–33.

Tonn, B.E. & Petrich, C., 1998. Everyday Life's Constraints on Citizenship in the United States. *Futures*, 30(8), pp. 783–813.

Tregaskis, C., 2002. Social Model Theory: The Story So Far. *Disability & Society*, 17(4), pp. 457–470.

Turner, B.S., 1986. *Citizenship and Capitalism: The Debate over Reformism*, London: Allen & Unwin.

———— 1993. Contemporary Problems with the Theory of Citizenship. In B. S. Turner, ed. *Citizenship and Social Theory*. London: SAGE, pp. 1–18.

UPIAS, 1976. *Fundamental Principles of Disability*, London: Union of the Physically Impaired Against Segregation.

Vaughn-Switzer, J., 2003. *Disabled Rights: American Disability Policy and the Fight for Equality*, Washington, DC: Georgetown University Press.

Vicente, M.R. & López, A.J., 2010. A Multidimensional Analysis of the Disability Digital Divide: Some Evidence for Internet Use. *The Information Society*, 26(1), pp. 48–64.

Vromen, A., 2008. Building Virtual Spaces: Young People, Participation and the Internet. *Australian Political Studies Association*, 43(1), pp. 79–97.

———— 2011. Constructing Australian Youth Online. *Information, Communication & Society*, 14(7), pp. 959–980.

Ward, A., Baker, P.M.A. & Moon, N.W., 2009. Ensuring the Enfranchisement of People with Disabilities. *Journal of Disability Policy Studies*, 20(2), pp. 79–92.

Ward, J., 2008. The Online Citizen-Consumer: Addressing Young People's Political Consumption Through Technology. *Journal of Youth Studies*, 11(5), pp. 513–526.

Warschauer, M., 2003. *Technology and Social Inclusion: Rethinking the Digital Divide*, Cambridge, MA: MIT Press.

Watling, S. & Crawford, K., 2010. Digital Exclusion: Implications for Human Services Practitioners. *Journal of Technology in Human Services*, 28(4), pp. 205–216.

Watson, N., 2002. Well, I Know This is Going to Sound Very Strange to You, but I Don't See Myself as a Disabled Person: Identity and Disability. *Disability & Society*, 17(5), pp. 509–527.

Williams, B., Copestake, P., Eversley, J. & Stafford, B., 2008. *Experiences and Expectations of People with Disabilities*, London: Office for Disability Issues – Department for Work and Pensions.

Woodhams, C. & Corby, S., 2003. Defining Disability in Theory and Practice: A Critique of the British Disability Discrimination Act 1995. *Journal of Social Policy*, 32(02), pp. 159–178.

Zickuhr, K. & Smith, A., 2012. *Digital Differences*, Washington, DC: Pew Internet and American Life Project.

2 Online Mobilisation in Times of Crisis

Which online media platforms are more likely to help re-configure the civic arena in ways that support the inclusion of disabled Internet users? This is a complex question that connects to a broader debate about what exactly constitutes political participation online. In order to start addressing this issue, this chapter turns to previous work on the impact of new media technologies on the relationship between 'formal' and 'informal' politics, which at the centre of the idea of inclusive citizenship. The first part of this chapter reviews cyber-sceptical literature that looked at 'formal' online political activities. This is extremely valuable work, but its narrow focus on online initiatives such as election campaigns and public consultations has led it to over-emphasise the fact that online political forums are unlikely to foster participation among people who are disengaged from politics in the first place. In response to this, more recent work has pointed out the need for researchers to examine politically-relevant discussions in 'non-political' online spaces. These types of space may be especially relevant for users who are unfamiliar with or feel daunted by explicitly political forums because they help to re-configure the civic arena into a wider and more flexible environment where Internet users can become involved in politically-relevant debates by discussing their 'private' everyday interests.

In light of this, this chapter then considers what it takes for everyday political *talk* on online 'third spaces' to turn into collective *action*. Indeed, these platforms provide disabled Internet users with opportunities to meet, discuss shared interests and, possibly, organise around these in ways that do not presuppose a strong common identity. However, the leap between *talk* and *action* seems likely only in conjunction with specific events that catalyse the attention of disabled Internet users and trigger specific reactions. The role of disruptive events and emotions in this process – in particular anger – are discussed, presenting an issue-focused approach to investigate these mechanisms. Thereafter, this chapter considers several possible catalyst events that may have sparked a collective reaction among disabled Internet users in recent years. The radical reform of disability welfare introduced by the U.K. government between 2010–12 and the proposed cuts to Medicaid included in the Republican counter-budget of 2011 in the

U.S. are identified as potential mobilisation catalysts. The chapter then concludes by formulating a series of key questions about the use of online media in conjunction with these two events that drive the analysis in the remainder of this book.

'Formal' Politics Online: Forget About Egalitarian Utopias

It is useful to start by asking whether new media technologies have transformed 'formal' political processes in ways that could benefit disabled citizens. In a similarly optimistic fashion to the one that characterised early work on disability and information and communication technologies (ICTs), initial literature on Internet politics laid out somewhat utopian expectations that new media could facilitate 'forms of communication, interaction and organisation that undermine unequal status and power relations' (Spears & Lea 1994, p. 248) and foster participatory politics or even full-blown direct democracy (see, for instance, Rash 1995; Stromer-Galley 2000). Yet, these assumptions quickly made way for more sceptical and realist positions as research on e-democracy grew into the burgeoning field it is today. Many have argued that online political initiatives connected to 'formal' democratic processes simply replicated the inequality that traditionally separates ordinary citizens from elite groups, stressing that major political parties and resourceful interest groups are best placed for translating their offline primacy into the online sphere (Margolis & Moreno-Riaño 2009; Margolis & Resnick 2000). This, in turn, makes 'formal' online politics unsuited to the empowerment of minorities and disadvantaged groups such as disabled citizens.

Over the past 20 years, a large body of evidence has been collected that characterises online politics as 'business as usual'. Much of this work has highlighted that expecting powerful institutions such as political parties, central and local government to actively promote the development of revolutionary e-democracy initiatives was simply unrealistic (Bennett 2003; Wright 2006; Wright & Street 2007). In particular, two key democratic processes in which online media seem to have failed to inject equalising changes include elections and public policy consultations.

Although the literature on online election campaigns is too vast to discuss its many nuances in this book, it is useful to point out how most scholars in this area regard digital campaign efforts as the natural extension of what traditionally has been a carefully managed process of 'marketing' candidates to voters. As Howard (2006) put it, by 'redlining some constituents and communities and then narrowcasting political content, hypermedia campaigns diminish the amount of shared text in the public sphere' (p. 183). In other words, personalised messages and tailored interaction with voters are likely to create information cocoons that restrict pluralism instead of exposing users to a range of perspectives. Scholars such as Kreiss (2012) expanded on this by pointing out that it would be naïve to expect online election campaigns to support more participatory forms of democracy as, after all, their main objective is to win elections and therefore they 'simply are not designed to be the training grounds of radical democratic participation that many desire' (p. 183). Thus, it seems only logical that 'the decidedly undemocratic view of *controlled interactivity* is how most campaigns [continue to] operate' (Stromer-Galley 2014, p. 2). Indeed, some candidates in recent election cycles have introduced online initiatives that aimed to engage directly with disabled voters and these would be worthy of analysis (for example Barack Obama's 'People with Disabilities for Obama' online groups in the 2008 and 2012 U.S. presidential elections). Yet, digital election campaigns overall remain far from spurring the transformations required to support inclusive citizenship.

While the fact that online election campaigns have not generated opportunities for citizen empowerment may be unsurprising, e-consultations and digital rulemaking projects seem to hold greater potential for power re-distribution. However, work has shown that the 'managerial' approach taken by Western governments to online technology has restricted opportunities for e-deliberation, meaning that 'individuals may get better service as consumers from their governments, but as far as the possibilities of interactivity that are represented by the Internet are concerned, this is a bare minimum' (Chadwick & May 2003, p. 293). Also, early studies of citizen-input to rulemaking via electronic media went as far as suggesting that the use of new technologies by established and emerging interest groups had in fact led to a diminished quality of deliberation by promoting the use of template email messages for e-lobbying and consultation responses (Schlosberg et al. 2008). Crucially, this research has shown that 'e-democracy exercises [. . .] are ignored by elected politicians and are mistrusted by participating citizens who do not perceive there to be a credible link between their input and policy output' (Coleman & Blumler 2009, p. 115), while 'at its worst, pseudo-participation entails attempts by elites to domesticate and defuse participatory energies which [. . .] could become a threat to their power' (ibid.).

Paradoxically, much of this work confirmed the very same cyber-pessimist claims about the negative implications of the Internet for democratic participation that it had been set up to de-bunk, revealing that government-run online consultations and other deliberative platforms have tended to 'preach to the converted' instead of including those who generally have little or no opportunity to participate effectively to public decision-making (Norris 2003; Norris & Curtice 2006). Even online discussion platforms that had been designed with the genuine intention to engage disenfranchised users and extend citizen participation at the local level were found to be ultimately dominated by 'gladiators' who were already politically active and, whether consciously or not, pushed minority voices into a 'virtual' corner, perpetuating and potentially exacerbating their marginalisation (Albrecht 2006; Jensen 2006). In addition, the citizen experience with e-consultation spaces was found to be hampered also by exclusionary barriers that replicated some of the pitfalls of politics as we know it, both in terms of design and with regard to the overall impact of consultation processes on policy outputs (Tomkova 2009; Wright & Coleman 2012). Although citizens viewed the use of government-run e-democracy platforms such as the now defunct Number 10 petitions website as valuable democratic experiences, they were generally dissatisfied with official responses to grievances expressed electronically, which they 'perceived to be late, dismissive, impersonal and unengaged' (Wright 2016, p. 855).

These findings have contributed additional strength and further sophistication to the digital divide paradigm discussed in the previous chapter. Taken in isolation, these results have boosted the development of a broad theoretical strand for which online initiatives associated with formal politics, in spite of their potential for interaction, tend to reinforce existing elites and consequentially perpetuate the exclusion of disadvantaged groups (Weber et al. 2003). Thus, 'formal' online politics is far from promoting an inclusive transformation of the civic arena that would benefit disabled citizens. Instead, it appears more likely to expand and possibly exacerbate the discriminatory experiences described in Chapter 1.

Rebooting Internet Politics Research

At first impression, cyber-pessimist and cyber-sceptic research exposed a paradox. While the regime changes that followed the 2011 Arab Spring uprisings suggested that the Internet can precipitate – if not ignite – radical democratic transformations, online media would appear unable to support further democratisation in Western countries. That said, it is important to remember that 'formal' political processes such as elections and public consultations constitute only one aspect of democratic politics. Is it possible that so far researchers have looked for traces of democratic renewal in the wrong places, overlooking instead meaningful changes in other areas? As inclusive citizenship theory itself points at the difference between the 'formal' and 'informal' political sphere, and the latter is more relevant to disabled citizens, it seems appropriate to propose that changes at a more basic grassroots level than elections and formal e-consultations should be explored.

To this end, some prominent Internet politics scholars have questioned the very foundations of the cyber-sceptical and cyber-pessimist research mentioned above. Authors such as Wright (2012a) and Chadwick (2012) have argued that popular negative prophecies have *de facto* self-fulfilled because researchers have focused too much on government-run platforms and e-democracy initiatives explicitly branded as 'political'. Instead of asking 'what's really new about the new technology' (Newhagen 1998,

p. 112), researchers who concentrated on digital election campaigns, as well as government-sponsored discussion forums, and expected to find evidence of a radical democratic renewal, fell straight into the trap of applying out-dated frameworks to the study of an emerging media environment, mistaking a partial understanding of online politics for the whole picture. For example, even those studies that went against the pessimist 'tide' by highlighting a slight increase in the use of technology for political purposes did so by limiting themselves to measuring a small set of traditional indicators of political engagement such as 'searching for political information' and 'making contact with politicians' (see, for instance, di Gennaro & Dutton 2006). In other words, evidence of change has been sought in online spaces set up by the very same people who have a vested interest in the continuation of the status quo. Therefore, cyber-pessimist conclusions were strengthened by repeated attempts to test unrealistic expectations of a democratic 'revolution' on platforms that 'can [instead] be read as a strategy for disciplining civic energy within the constraining techno-political sphere of managed cyberspace' (Coleman & Blumler 2009, p. 115).

Following this critique of traditional e-democracy studies, a new body of research has started to emerge in very recent years that concentrates on 'everyday' online conversations in which politics and policy issues may also be discussed in conjunction with personal interests. In particular, scholars such as Wright have advocated a shift towards the study of 'third spaces' broadly defined as 'non-political online spaces where political talk emerges' (Wright 2012b, p. 5).

Everyday Concerns and Online 'Citizenship Training'

Most people learn how to be 'good' citizens outside formal institutional settings through ordinary conversations that take place in public venues. Ordinary places of daily interaction such as pubs, cafes and community centres have traditionally hosted politically-relevant talk, performing as citizenship 'training grounds' (Oldenburg 1989). As the frequency and scope of online social interactions continues to grow, it is reasonable to assume that seemingly 'mundane' online spaces that supplement in-person daily interactions – for example, price comparison websites or forums discussing entertainment – might play a role in the development of basic citizenship skills for many. In fact, online discussion venues might fulfil this function even more effectively than their offline precursors as they are free from some of the caveats that characterise physical spaces (Wright 2012b). In particular, while traditional public sphere theory, which values in-person interactions in public venues, emphasises the value of rational discussion over emotional talk (Habermas 1991), in online 'third spaces' the latter is seen as equally as relevant to 'citizenship training' as logical and evidence-based debate. Furthermore, discussions hosted on online 'third spaces' transcend the geographical boundaries associated with physical places, as well as the tendency for talk to focus primarily on local issues. Although a detailed examination of the nature of 'third spaces' would go beyond the scope of this book, it is important to note that this conceptualisation rejects theory-based objections to the ability of commercially-driven online platforms to support civic education, encourage political participation (Pajnik 2005) and boost citizenship (Coleman & Blumler 2009, p. 11). This widens the scope of online politics research to include a variety of non-obvious spaces that attract and engage a much greater number of users than the Internet's explicitly political corners discussed above.

Given that Internet-based media – in particular social networking sites – have blurred the distinction between private and public, much online conversation stems from individual interests and focuses on issues that would traditionally be associated with the 'private' sphere. This is particularly relevant for disabled Internet users, who may be more inclined to join platforms that focus on their everyday concerns and are not explicitly labelled as 'political', but on which they can nevertheless exercise basic citizenship skills. As Wojcieszak and Mutz (2009) explained, 'Internet users who are not sufficiently engaged in politics to self-select into explicitly political online chat rooms or message boards inadvertently encounter political views online in hobby and interest groups in particular' (p. 50). This is especially true for young people (Owen 2006; Vromen 2011), who are not nearly as disenfranchised as many assume but oriented instead towards alternative and more informal ways of participating in civic life focused on 'everyday' issues including lifestyle politics (Vromen & Collin 2010), and among whom social media use positively correlates with political engagement (Xenos et al. 2014). As was mentioned in Chapter 1, Internet usage among disabled people is skewed towards the younger generations even more dramatically than within the general population. Thus, these considerations assume particular relevance for the future of political engagement among disabled citizens.

Undoubtedly, analysing the interaction that takes place in 'everyday' online venues presents great challenges due to the difficulties involved in distinguishing politically-relevant content from what is just 'chatter' (Graham 2008). This explains, at least in part, why this type of research only started to emerge at a time in which Internet scholarship has entered a new age of maturity (Chadwick & Howard 2009). One way in which some have sought to circumvent methodological challenges was by carrying out surveys with users of non-political interactive spaces. This work revealed that users are widely aware of the fact that much 'participation in non-political chats or message boards regularly involves some discussion of political topics and controversial public issues' (Wojcieszak & Mutz 2009, p. 45). Yet, a real breakthrough in this field has come from more recent developments in the area of deliberative analysis, which have strengthened the idea of online 'third spaces' both theoretically (Lupia 2009) and methodologically (Dahlberg 2004), providing researchers with increasingly refined tools for the investigation of naturally occurring online conversations. Pioneering empirical work has highlighted how seemingly frivolous online talk about, for example, reality TV shows in fact provides an indirect channel to discussions about political issues (Graham 2010, 2012; Graham & Harju 2011). In contrast with the exclusionary role played by Internet 'gladiators' in government-sponsored forums as discussed above, this research also exposed the positive influence of 'super-users' in non-political platforms as facilitators of discussion and debate (Graham & Wright 2013). While so far much of this work has focused on U.K. case studies, pioneering research in countries of relatively recent democratisation has stressed the importance of 'mundane' discussion forums for the growth of civil society groups in those contexts too (Bakardjieva 2012).

This alternative interpretation of online participation strongly resonates with the ideal of inclusive citizenship. In particular, the unconventional and flexible conceptualisation of where in the online sphere one should expect to find 'politics', and the expanded definition of 'political' contribute to a substantial extension of the civic arena, promoting the re-evaluation of informal politics that feminist scholars indicated as a fundamental condition for the realisation of 'participatory parity'. If, then, political talk is mixed with, or disguised as, 'everyday' conversation, users who otherwise are disenfranchised and excluded from public debates stand a better chance to be able to participate in politically-relevant online interaction, whether consciously or not. This could activate a virtuous mechanism that enhances their civic culture, making them fuller citizens (Dahlgren 2002). This is in stark opposition to the effects of government-run e-democracy platforms, which have frequently been designed with 'fully informed' and 'hyperactive' users in mind (Vedel 2006, p. 232). In the case of disabled users, this is particularly relevant as it signals the existence of alternative channels where psychological barriers to participation such as feelings of inadequacy and powerlessness may be circumvented by discussing public issues and articulating political opinions through the lens of one's personal interests and daily experiences.

Overall, this expanded approach to online politics highlights one of the Internet's main affordances for disabled users. Flexible or possibly even inadvertent access to politically-relevant conversations constitutes a decisive step towards civic education and an opportunity to familiarise with the 'building blocks' of public discourse (Mansbridge 1999). That said, effective political participation, online as well as offline, requires more than mere *talk*. As Vedel (2006) pointed out, 'exchanging ideas and opinions is only one step in the democratic process' (p. 233). Rather, 'power continues to reside in government agencies, elected legislatures and transnational, intergovernmental bodies' (Coleman & Blumler 2009, p. 135), for which 'there need to be channels of common discourse between the official and informal political spheres' (ibid., p. 136). Thus, a fundamental pre-requisite for meaningful participation is the ability of a given group to exhibit some form of coordinated collective *action* capable of targeting and influencing public decision-makers (Scott 1985, pp. 299–301).

A recent analysis of online platforms focused on 'everyday' concerns such as the British parenthood portal Netmums and financial advice website MoneySavingExpert showed that collective action can indeed emerge in online 'third spaces', and does so most often in conversation threads that start off as non-political (Graham et al. 2015a). In addition, health and social welfare issues have been extremely popular conversation topics on these and other similar platforms, which have performed as 'incubators' of a diffused anti-austerity sentiment and helped to spur mobilisation against government cuts to public spending following the 2008 global financial crisis (Graham et al. 2015b). To better understand the relevance of these emerging trends for disabled citizens, it is crucial to understand the mechanisms by which *talk* can generate agency and collective *action*, either in traditional forms such as street protest and petitions, or as new, innovative and unpredictable online repertoires. A useful place to start is by reviewing the relationship between new media technologies and the way in which people come together in groups. The key concept here is that of 'network society'.

À *La Carte* Participation? Disabled People in the Network Society

The idea that online media can promote coordinated collective action has long been associated with that of 'network society'. Although social network theory emerged long before the Internet became commercially available in the mid-1990s, it has become increasingly sophisticated and extremely popular in recent decades following the expansion of digital media. Network society theorists have credited the Internet with the proliferation of 'communities of choice', which people join on the basis of their own interests and are more horizontal and fluid than geographically-bound 'communities of place'. Some have argued against the use of the term 'community' to describe the social structures that emerge from connections based on personal interests (Baym 2010, pp. 72–3). However, others have pointed out that these types of 'weak' ties are in fact likely to enable better informed deliberation and support mutual understanding among more diverse and distant groups (Granovetter 1973), making communities more agile and inclusive. Because people join on the basis of personal interest instead of location, individuals can take part in multiple groups at the same time, regardless of distance (Castells 2002, pp. 125–9). This shows that citizen engagement is not disappearing due to a decline in social capital, as some claimed (Putnam 2000). Instead, it is being re-configured (Wellman 1979; Wellman et al. 1988, p. 133; Wellman et al. 2001) through new social structures that have the potential to support unconventional forms of political agency in the twenty-first century (Norris 2002, p. 24). Just as it would be a mistake to assume that online relationships are of inferior quality compared to in-person interaction, as some have done (Matzat 2010), it would be wrong to measure new activist communities against traditional understandings of participation and citizenship (Papacharissi 2010, pp. 12–13).

The Internet's growth and increasingly ubiquitous connectivity have been credited with augmenting the speed and magnitude of this social transformation (Castells 2000, 2004, pp. 9–13). Thanks to its networked structure, the Internet is arguably suited, at least in theory, to promoting less hierarchical forms of organisation free from the influence of gate-keepers and in which power tends to be distributed across a plurality of actors rather than centralised in the hands of the few (Wellman et al. 1988, p. 137). A substantial amount of empirical evidence has been collected that supports these assumptions (Chadwick 2006, pp. 103–7), indicating that direct control over mass communication – described by Castells (2004) as 'self-directed mass communication' (p. 13) – can ultimately empower individual network actors. In this model, online discussion in 'everyday' third spaces represents the first step towards the formation of 'communities' that can mobilise users around shared but also deeply personal interests while leaving them free to withdraw at any time (Olsson 2008, p. 665, p. 671). This is especially relevant for groups that, like disabled people, are concerned with issues of social justice and feel un-represented by existing advocacy bodies (Castells 2007, pp. 248–9). Online networks made up of ordinary citizens with shared interests have been able to take on established organisations that did not adequately represent their needs and challenge state institutions that denied them basic rights. For example, online patient networks in the United States successfully took on main-stream non-profit organisations that did not advocate effectively (Brainard & Siplon 2002, pp. 166–70).

This process has experienced an even greater acceleration in the past ten years with the expansion of Web 2.0 technology (O'Reilly 2012), which has blurred the distinction between users and producers of content, and through the proliferation of 'always-on' lifestyles brought on by mobile Internet growth (boyd 2012). In particular, it has been argued that the ambivalent nature of social networking platforms such as Facebook and Twitter, which are both 'public' and 'private' media at the same time (Baym & boyd 2012; boyd 2007; boyd & Ellison 2008), can facilitate user mobilisation on 'public' issues from within a user's own 'private' sphere (Häyhtiö & Rinne 2008, p. 14; Papacharissi 2009, p. 244). In this context, 'neither the personal nor the political are prevalent, but rather a peculiar mixture of both, which simultaneously renders citizenship less political than it was in the past, but also more autonomously defined' (Papacharissi 2010, p. 162). Although the lack of clear boundaries between 'public' and 'private' makes things potentially confusing, the creation of a fluid continuum echoes the arguments put forward by inclusive citizenship theorists with regard to the transformation of the civic arena. This is because:

> [C]ollective actions of all kinds entail individuals' transition from a private domain of interest and action to a public one. [. . .] When boundaries between private and public domains are porous and easily crossed [. . .] people's negotiation of the boundary typically involves less intentionality and calculation [and] the transition may even be unintentional.
>
> (Bimber et al. 2005, pp. 377–8)

Thus, the growing focus on private aspects of the political debate, as well as the identification of online platforms as 'personal' spaces, may reasonably facilitate participation for users who, like disabled people, are traditionally excluded from government-sponsored forums by accessibility issues, as well as feelings of powerlessness and inadequacy (Wellman et al. 2003).

The individual sits at the centre of networked participation (Wellman et al. 2002, p. 160), which is 'shaped around an agenda that is personal' (Papacharissi 2010, p. 162). Yet, the political efficacy of 'communities of choice' continues to depend on their ability to deploy coordinated action to reach the domain of 'formal' politics where policy decisions are taken (Wellman et al. 2003). Some have criticised the centrality of the individual in this model, pointing out that in fact this may determine a loss of efficacy for citizen-initiated politics and, ultimately, foster disempowerment. Scholars such as Bimber (1998) argued that the dependence of online networks on 'private' interests characterises them as 'thin' communities, giving members an easy way out and possibly leading to an excessive personalisation of political action and dangerous fragmentation of participation. More broadly, the possibility to set up highly personalised news-feeds and choose to communicate only with other like-minded people has been interpreted as a source of growing polarisation (Sunstein 2007). In light of these considerations, some have argued that 'network openness does not lead us directly to democracy' (Fenton 2012, p. 142) and therefore 'new media *may* be liberating for users, but not necessarily democratising for society' (ibid.). While this is a legitimate interpretation of the overall trajectory of contemporary democratic participation, in the case of disabled Internet users these arguments ought to be weighed against the specific benefits associated with this emerging structure of engagement.

Most notably, online networks that revolve around shared interests are poised to re-align interaction and participation with the lived experiences of disabled users. This is because, compared to traditional organisations, they lower the entry threshold by eliminating the need to subscribe to either an ideologically-charged explanation of exclusion or a controversial 'disabled' identity. More broadly, this has been conceptualised as a potential solution to the problem of 'free-riding' (Bennett & Segerberg 2012; Bimber et al. 2005), for which in traditional offline contexts many of those who have a stake in collective action prefer 'piggybacking' on the efforts of others as they consider direct participation to be too costly in terms of time and resources (Olson 1965). Thus, whereas in recent years organisations 'for' and 'of' disabled people have struggled to successfully aggregate and empower their primary constituents, as discussed in the previous chapter, online networks may offer disabled Internet 'pioneers' a more straight-forward, less onerous and inclusive alternative to reach out to others in a similar situation, talk and possibly organise on the basis of specific interests. This, however, does not mean that identity, which has traditionally been at the root of collective action in social movements (Chesters & Welsh 2006, pp. 130–4; Tarrow 2011), simply does not matter anymore. Rather, in this context, common identity constitutes less of a pre-requisite for mobilisation and more of an element that is negotiated throughout the process of mobilisation, ultimately pertaining to the long-term sustainability of networks more than their immediate viability (Cavanagh 2007, p. 75; Häyhtiö & Rinne 2008, p. 18).

Personal interests, beliefs and connections have traditionally been at the root of aggregation in social movements, which individuals generally join after carrying out, consciously or unconsciously, a cost-benefit analysis oriented towards specific gains that are perceived either rationally or emotionally (della Porta & Diani 1999, pp. 112–8). If, then, the Internet is promoting a more individualistic culture, at the same time this can be a vehicle for discovering and activating 'latent' ties among users who otherwise would have little chance to get in touch with one another, kick-starting a process that can generate new forms of coordinated collective action (Haythornthwaite 2005). Online media can arguably defy 'informational' obstacles to human interaction by enabling users to find out about 'shared interests, shared desires, or common experiences and acquaintances' (Bimber et al. 2005, p. 382) more readily than in physical settings. This is especially relevant to disabled users penalised by physical access barriers or who generally lack opportunities to meet with others who share a similar life experience on a regular basis.

In a recent essay, Bennett and Segerberg (2012) coined the term 'connective action' to describe digitally-enabled protest that revolves around highly personalised action frames. This personalisation of protest presents opportunities for the creation of a 'better organised pluralism' that reflects specific grievances more effectively and can remedy the shortcomings of existing advocacy organisations by putting their constituents directly in charge (Coleman 2005, p. 211). That said, this also carries a significant risk for further fragmentation if too many users decide to go their own way and fail to coordinate with others to form a critical mass of protesters. Empirical research is essential to verify whether online networks concerned with specific issues are veering towards effective new forms of collective action or, instead, amplify pre-existing rifts and divisions. To understand the effect of these new community dynamics on disabled Internet users, there are at least two avenues that could be pursued. The first option is to start by looking at existing organisations, while the second one takes a step back and focuses on issues before organisations.

Looking for Evidence: The Limits of Organisation-Based Approaches

Intuitively, the Web presence of existing disability organisations may look like a useful place from which to start to investigate the implications of new media for disabled users' citizenship. In recent years, a number of established advocacy organisations in both the U.K. and the U.S. have assimilated participatory elements typical of social movement groups into their repertoires, offering flexible opportunities for user-engagement and shifting power to their grassroots. This ultimately generated 'hybrid' structures that mix both hierarchical and participatory features (Chadwick 2007). Although for some organisations these changes seemed the result of a calculated strategy in an era when citizens have the opportunity to self-organise online and established organisations risk losing relevance, this trend nevertheless influenced many traditionally bureaucratic and centralised organisations. For example, the proliferation of member-driven blogs within British political parties has injected additional pluralism and raised the influence of the so-called 'virtual grassroots', especially in the periods between elections (Gibson et al. 2013). Thus, it would be interesting to ask whether groups 'for' and 'of' disabled people too have embraced participatory online media in response to a growing demand for 'entrepreneurial engagement' from disabled users who had opportunities to familiarise with digital technology in 'third spaces' and demanded a more active role in organisational agenda setting (Bimber et al. 2009, 2012; Flanagin et al. 2006).

However, previous work that explored the use of new media technologies among a range of Scottish disability organisations has shown that, as recently as 2012, many of them continued to lag substantially behind comparable organisations active in other advocacy areas in terms of digital media adoption (Trevisan 2012, 2014a). Indeed, it is inevitable that some groups perform better than others as e-democratic actors depending on their pre-existing structure, underpinning ideology and overall mission (Burt & Taylor 2008). Yet, the results of this work were strikingly negative across the entire organisational spectrum. Scottish disability organisations effectively operated as alternative 'filters' of user-participation, revealing a resistance to participatory technology and user-generated content that was confirmed in interviews with their officers. In particular, there was a real dearth of opportunities for users to share their concerns in an un-mediated fashion. For example, any personal disability story that appeared on the blogs of these organisations had been carefully selected and edited, or even written, by staff members instead of self-advocates. Paradoxically, this use of online media put more distance between disabled people and those who advocate on their behalf instead of promoting self-representation and user control. Moreover, when these organisations had engaged in social networking sites, this was invariably as part of an effort to mobilise users around a pre-determined agenda (Trevisan 2012, p. 397).

With hindsight, this is perhaps not so surprising considering that the main reasons given by the representatives of Scottish disability organisations interviewed for this study to explain their limited use of participatory media were limited budgets and accessibility difficulties, which made these platforms a bad choice for connecting with people with complex needs (Trevisan 2014a). The delay in embracing digital technologies derived, at least in part, from an attempt to invest the limited resources available in other, more effective ways of communicating with disabled people and not from a deliberate choice to limit discussion. In this, Scottish disability organisations were similar to other non-profits that serve disadvantaged people, which for a long time preferred not to engage with interactive media due to their perceived lack of relevance to their constituents (Siapera 2005). More broadly, however, established and institutionalised campaigning organisations operating in a number of other areas have often demonstrated an ambivalent attitude towards online media by virtue of the tension existing between the open nature of participatory platforms and a natural preference for centralised control in organisations (Brainard & Siplon 2002, 2004; Wright & Coleman 2012).

Given the fluid nature of e-advocacy repertoires and technological innovation more generally, it is important to keep an eye on possible future digital transformations in the disability non-profit sector. That said, the results of this preliminary investigation suggest that focusing directly on advocacy organisations is not the most useful way to start exploring the interaction among disability, new media technologies and citizenship. There are two main reasons for this. First, investigating a single-handedly picked set of established organisations restricts the scope of this research in the same way as early work on e-democracy focused excessively on government-run platforms, which led to the skewed cyber-pessimistic conclusions outlined earlier in this chapter. A broader approach is required in order to capture any new initiative and more spontaneous forms of action that may have grown out of everyday online spaces in which disabled Internet users can connect with one another outside of formal organisations. Second, it seems unrealistic to expect participatory change to originate from established disability rights organisations under ordinary circumstances, given that in recent years these groups have concentrated mainly on defending acquired rights, as the previous chapter illustrated. Instead, a more promising path starts with looking for a 'trigger' of spontaneous mobilisation and catalyst of organisational change in the form of an issue or event that radically challenges the status quo and pushes both new and experienced advocates to act.

In Search of a Catalyst: Issue-Focused Participation

Social movement theorists have long postulated that sudden disruptions of the status quo can lead otherwise disengaged and disenfranchised citizenries towards direct participation in politics (Woliver 1993). In particular, 'threats to interests, values, and, at times, survival that different groups and individuals experience' (Tarrow 2011, p. 86) foster mobilisation. In contrast with other types of civic action, which privilege individuals and groups that are rich in both time and resources, reactions to threats tend to involve poor groups because it is 'those with the most to lose who are most likely to engage in contention, since they face the greatest threat from inaction' (ibid.). While disability advocates, especially in Britain, have struggled to organise disabled people around a proactive agenda since the introduction of comprehensive anti-discrimination legislation in the 1990s, the need to respond to external threats may be a more successful catalyst of mobilisation in the disability community. In addition, reactive mobilisation is consistent also with the 'headline chasing' strategy pursued by many new advocacy groups (Karpf 2010). Instead of trying to shape the political agenda by proactively 'sponsoring' certain topics, emergent organisations prefer to use online media to campaign on the issues that are already at the forefront of the public debate at any given moment. Strategically, this seems a logical move as trying to steer a debate that is already on-going is likely to require fewer resources than trying to push new issues on the agenda. This practice tends to be associated with generalist groups. However, 'niche' and issue-focused ones have started to take a similar approach too, using online media to reach and mobilise new supporters when their issue of choice climbs to the top of the political agenda (Karpf 2010, p. 34; 2012, p. 50). For these reasons, it is important to define exactly what kinds of issues are capable of performing this role.

In general, networked participation tends to be centred on 'personal' interests and 'private' issues (Baym 2010, p. 90). This tendency has been widely criticised for furthering individualism and contributing to an alleged decline of engagement in community matters and common causes (Curran 2012). However, such critical perspective fails to recognise that, 'as boundaries are more easily crossed between private and public, the mechanisms of collective entrepreneurship become available to a larger array of actors, especially those with fewer resources' (Flanagin et al. 2006, p. 41). More broadly, work on resistance and collective action among socially-oppressed people in the pre-Internet era also showed that 'bread-and-butter issues are the essence of lower-class politics' (Scott 1985, p. 296). Therefore, 'to require lower-class resistance that is somehow "principled" or "self-less" is not only utopian [but], more fundamentally, a misconstruction of the basis of class struggle' (ibid.).

These arguments resonate with 'pragmatist' voices within the disabled people's movement. As Germon (1998) remarked, 'none of us is motivated by altruism. We are in this struggle because ultimately we benefit. It is both naïve and unreasonable to expect that we will not be concerned with our own liberation' (p. 248). Turbine (2007) usefully elaborated on this point in her work on human rights, which has shown that conversations about 'everyday problems' among groups experiencing oppression, disillusioned with state bureaucracy and confined to a condition of partial citizenship constitute a proxy for discussing collective rights issues. As she noted, 'everyday problems' fosters participation in informal networks that have 'the potential [. . .] to act as a springboard for respondents to pursue formal approaches [to policy-making]' (Turbine 2007, p. 178). A similar connection exists between personal aspects of disabled people's daily routines and social policy – especially state welfare provisions – given that the latter impacts the livelihoods of most disabled people in a direct way. In this context, online discussion platforms provide disabled users with a channel to discuss personal yet at the same time politically-relevant issues without becoming associated with any formal organisation or committing to a particular ideology.

That said, not every discussion of personal issues is the same, as not every one of them leads to mobilisation. As Bennett and Segerberg pointed out (2012):

> The transmission of personal expression across networks may or may not become scaled up, stable, or capable of various kinds of targeted action depending on the kinds of social technology [. . .] and the kinds of opportunities that motivate anger or compassion across large numbers of individuals.
>
> (p. 754)

Instead, mobilisation is more likely to occur as a reaction to external events, 'crises' or controversial policy agendas that touch upon the personal domain and at the same time are perceived as violations of fundamental rights, which are therefore capable of rapidly uniting otherwise fragmented communities against a common target (Coleman & Blumler 2009). For this reason, a useful strategy for studying online political participation among disabled Internet users involves the identification of a key catalyst issue followed by a broad overview of the organisations, groups and campaigns that revolve around it from which particularly significant case studies can be selected from in-depth analysis (Figure 2.1). A key question then is whether in recent years there have been any specific events that may have sparked this type of reaction among disabled Internet users.

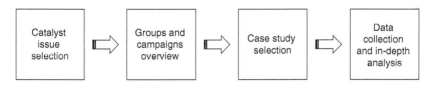

Figure 2.1 Issue-focused research process.

The Catalysing Power of the U.K. Welfare Reform

Several events have occurred in the U.K. in recent years that fit the 'catalyst' profile outlined earlier (i.e. a disruptive or controversial event, issue or agenda that negatively affects disabled people directly and calls for a rapid, strong and possibly exceptional collective response). The most prominent of these include:

a   A radical reform of state welfare provision and drastic public expenditure cuts proposed by the then Conservative–Liberal Democrat coalition government in the second half of 2010 and finalised with the Welfare Reform Act 2012;

b   The Equality Act 2010, which controversially merged several pieces of anti-discrimination legislation (the Equal Pay Act, the Sex Discrimination Act, the Race Relations Act and the Disability Discrimination Act) into one single document;

c   The United Nations (UN) Convention on the Rights of Persons with Disabilities (CRPD), given that the British government was due to report on progress towards its implementation in 2011.

Among these, the event that stood out as having the greatest potential for mobilisation was without doubt the debate on the Welfare Reform Act.

Following the global financial crisis of 2008, a new agenda promoting fiscal responsibility and austerity measures emerged in several European countries. Plans for public expenditure reduction and welfare cuts in particular generated strong reactions in countries such as Spain – with the *Indignados* movement – and debt-ridden Greece, where austerity continues to be a contentious issue to this day. As was mentioned above, anti-austerity sentiments in the U.K. erupted on 'everyday' Internet discussion forums among people worried about how they would cope with cuts to public services, changes to state welfare and budget reductions in the National Health Service (NHS). While established organisations such as the Trades Union Congress (TUC) promoted anti-austerity campaigns, including public demonstrations, part of this anger was also channelled towards the formation of grassroots groups such as UK Uncut, which organised protest rallies across the country. Arguably, the election of left-wing MP Jeremy

Corbyn to leader of the British Labour Party in 2015 could be interpreted as a result of a shift in the political mood of young people, who make up many of the new members that joined that party after it lost the May 2015 general election. As Sloam (2014) noted:

> [T]hese [economic] crises have been so effective in mobilizing young people, because they operate both on a personal (micro-) and societal (macro-) level, connecting young people's individual experiences of youth unemployment, university tuition fees, etc. to broader economic and political issues such as economic inequality.
>
> (p. 227)

In other words, a new wave of political engagement originated from experiences that were deeply personal but at the same time also shared by millions. Indeed, concerns have been raised about the ephemeral nature of issue-focused participation (Lin & Dutton 2003) and its ability to foster long-term engagement (Lusoli & Ward 2006, p. 68), which are addressed later in this book. However, these movements have introduced a generation disillusioned with 'politics as usual' to emerging forms of direct participation that involve both online and offline actions.

Within this broader context of contention, the welfare reform had a special significance for disabled Britons. While in fact the U.K. government sought to bundle changes to disability welfare into its comprehensive austerity plan, both in draft legislation and in the ways in which this was communicated to the news media, social policy scholars have strongly contested the idea that disability welfare changes would be primarily efficiency-driven. Looking at the evolution of Conservative Party policy in recent decades, authors such as Bochel (2011) concluded that plans to reform the welfare system by the then coalition government in 2010 were rooted in a neo-liberal ideology that characterised them as 'largely a continuation of Thatcherite approaches' (p. 20) and therefore 'more than an immediate response to a large account deficit [. . .] that takes the country in a new direction, rolling back the state to a level of intervention below that of the United States – something which is unprecedented' (Taylor-Gooby & Stoker 2011, p. 14). It is useful to briefly summarise the proposed changes in order to understand why this was the case.

Shortly after the May 2010 general election, the then Conservative–Liberal Democrat coalition government announced a drastic reduction in welfare spending as part of an emergency budget presented in June 2010. More detailed plans for a comprehensive reform of the benefits system were presented at the Conservative Party conference in October 2010 and relevant draft legislation was eventually introduced to the House of Commons in February 2011. It was immediately apparent that the benefits offered specifically to disabled people were a key target for reform. Government plans included proposals for replacing the Disability

Living Allowance (DLA),[1] a non-means tested and tax-free benefit available to all disabled people, with a new Personal Independence Payment (PIP) for all working age claimants (16–64-year-olds). New legislation that included these measures was eventually passed in March 2012 and PIPs started to be rolled out progressively from April 2013 (Table 2.1). PIP was part of a larger package of reforms that the Department for Work and Pensions (DWP) argued would tackle the problem of benefit fraud, which was estimated to be worth as much as £5.2 billion per year.[2]

This plan was strongly criticised by academics and prominent figures in the disability community because it radically reformed the process of benefit eligibility for disabled claimants by introducing a new points-based assessment system modelled on the controversial Working Capability Assessment (WCA) medical test that was already in use to determine eligibility for another benefit (Employment and Support Allowance). Under the new rules, existing DLA recipients were not moved automatically to the new system. Instead, everyone was asked to re-apply for PIPs and go through the new points-based medical assessment. Both disability scholars and advocates denounced this as a way to eradicate social model principles from welfare provision and return to a purely medicalised concept of disability (Grant & Wood 2011). Many also criticised the outsourcing company selected for carrying out PIP assessments, Atos Origin, which at the time was already responsible for the controversial WCAs mentioned above. Much of the government's own rhetoric surrounding welfare reform cast a great proportion of DLA recipients as 'undeserving poor' claiming benefits to which they were in fact not entitled (Patrick 2011). In addition, public opinion on these issues was stirred by the tendency of a large part of the British press – particularly tabloid newspapers – to portray disabled benefit claimants as 'welfare cheats' and 'fraudsters' (Briant et al. 2013). Interestingly, these negative frames used to describe disability benefits recipients clashed with the DWP's own data, which at the time estimated that only 0.5 per cent of all the DLA applications made each year were in fact fraudulent (Department for Work and Pensions 2012, p. 13).

As Roulstone (2011a) noted, changes to disability benefits were particularly regressive towards a social group with little political capital and for which it would be difficult to respond effectively to this challenge. According to Oliver and Barnes (2012), such measures generated a paradox. Although they were ostensibly designed to reduce state dependency among disability welfare recipients, their most immediate effect would be to plunge a large proportion of disabled people into poverty instead. For these reasons, it could be argued that these reforms threatened core benefits for many disabled people, thereby challenging their right to live independently. Given the centrality of welfare policy to the public discourse on disability in Britain (Rummery 2002), such radical modifications to the benefits system could be interpreted as not only a mere

Table 2.1 Timeline of the U.K. disability welfare reform (2010–12)

Date	Event
6 May 2010	U.K. General Election
12 May 2010	Conservative–Liberal Democrat coalition government formed
22 June 2010	Emergency budget presented to parliament
30 July 2010	Government consultation on welfare reform opens
1 October 2010	Government consultation on welfare reform closes
3 October 2010	March against the Conservative Party conference in Birmingham
20 October 2010	Government Spending Review presented to parliament
11 November 2010	DWP releases '21st Century Welfare' report on results of welfare reform consultation and 'Universal Credit: Welfare That Works' white paper
6 December 2010	Consultation on changes to the Disability Living Allowance (DLA) opens
13 December 2010	Closure of the Independent Living Fund (ILF) by 2015 is announced
6–12 December 2010	'Mobilise for DLA' week sponsored by several disability charities
16 February 2011	Welfare Reform Bill (WRB) introduced to the House of Commons
18 February 2011	Consultation on DLA changes closes
9 March 2011	Second WRB reading in the Commons
23 March 2011	Government budget presented to parliament; Trafalgar Square demonstration against cuts in London
26 March 2011	Trades Union Congress (TUC) march against the cuts in London
4 April 2011	Results of the DLA consultation and government response are released
11 May 2011	The Hardest Hit (coalition of disability organisations) march in London
15 June 2011	3rd WRB reading in the Commons
16 June 2011	WRB introduced to the House of Lords
13 September 2011	2nd WRB reading in the Lords
22 October 2011	Local Hardest Hit marches across the U.K.
14 November 2011	Lords committee discusses proposed changes to DLA
28 November 2011	Lords committee returns WRB to the Commons
30 November 2011	Government U-turn on plans to scrap DLA mobility component for recipients in residential care
1 December 2011	'Fulfilling Potential' discussion document on the future of disability policy in the U.K. launched by Office for Disability Issues
31 January 2012	3rd WRB reading in the Lords
8 March 2012	Welfare Reform Act 2012 gains Royal Assent

redistribution issue but also as a re-definition of equality rights that foreshadowed the withdrawal of other types of support as 'proposed cuts in health and social care risk reversing hard won debates around personalised and enabling packages in the form of direct payments and personal budgets' (Roulstone 2011b, p. 27). In a similar fashion to the sentiments that supported the fight for anti-discrimination legislation and the introduction of direct payments in the early to mid-1990s (Pearson 2012; Pearson & Riddell 2006), this generated a strong motivation for political action, prompting those with previous campaigning and self-advocacy experience in particular to speak out against the dangers of 'rolling back' the welfare state (Morris 2011).

Thus, the welfare reform was poised to affect the very livelihoods of disabled Britons in the long term, threatening some of their fundamental rights. This made it a 'political' issue with 'personal' implications relevant to all disabled people, including those not versed in political debates and too young to remember about the battles for anti-discrimination and direct payment legislation in the 1980s and 1990s. Given the crucial role that 'expressions of sentiment' play in expanding and activating online networks (Papacharissi 2015), the widespread anger that welfare reform proposals caused among the British disability community increased the chances for mobilisation. In addition, as a pan-disability issue, the welfare reform had the potential to activate latent ties and trigger unity among disabled Internet users with a range of different experiences and without the need for a pre-existing group identity (Haythornthwaite 2005). This made it an ideal issue to patch together – at least temporarily – a community that in recent years had become increasingly fragmented. Furthermore, the Labour Party's arguably reluctant approach to opposing these measures, particularly during their first reading in the House of Commons, emphasised the need for those who were against them to organise independently outside the parliamentary system. This combination of factors created a particularly favourable environment for the development of citizen-led initiatives and the growth of disability protest groups.

In addition, focusing on the U.K. welfare reform was advantageous for comparative reasons too. Roughly at the same time when the U.K. welfare reform was going through parliament, U.S. disability rights advocates were busy fighting a series of proposals for radical cuts to Medicaid – the public healthcare plan that meets the medical needs of most disabled Americans – that were included in the federal budget plan proposed by Representative Paul Ryan in April 2011. Although there were some substantial differences between the scope and implications of the U.K. welfare reform on one side and the plans for Medicaid cuts on the other, the co-occurrence, controversial nature and similar remit of these policy plans invited a useful international comparison. This is discussed in detail in Chapter 6, which puts the experience of British disability advocates with new media technologies in perspective by contrasting it with that of their American counterparts and uses comparative findings to reflect on the influence of the local context on the shape and efficacy of disability rights e-advocacy.

A final step that corroborated the relevance of the U.K. welfare reform as a potential catalyst for online grassroots advocacy among disabled Internet users was to verify the level of interest that it sparked online. Indeed, the vast amount of coverage that British news media dedicated to the then coalition government's welfare plans and their controversial nature suggested that people with an interest in disability issues, if not the general public, would be very aware of controversial benefit changes, may use the Web to find more information about them and, possibly, discuss them with other interested parties. A useful way to test this assumption and start exploring how anger and concerns could have translated into online activity was to look at Google Trends data for the period in which the welfare reform debate was most intense.

Tracking User-Interest with Google Trends

The very act of searching for keywords connected to a given topic implies a specific interest in an issue, person or event. Despite the rise of social media as information providers, search engines remain the primary channel through which Internet users access online information in democratic countries such as the U.K. (Dutton & Blank 2013) and the United States (Purcell et al. 2012). Internet users continue to show great levels of trust in the ability of search engines – especially Google – to provide them with the information they need (Sanz & Stančík 2014), to the point that they question their own ability to search properly before doubting the effectiveness of Google's algorithms (Hillis et al. 2013). This is especially the case among young people who have no experience of the Internet prior to Google (Gunter et al. 2009; Purcell et al. 2012). Thus, search engine usage patterns can be extremely revelatory with regard to user-interests, offering useful opportunities to capture emerging social trends as expressed by online information flows.

Google Trends is a freely available online tool that elaborates archived Google search records to show fluctuations in the popularity of any given keyword or set of keywords, provided that a minimum number of relevant searches were carried out during the period under investigation. In recent years, this tool has become popular with journalists, who have included Google Trends data in their coverage of a wide range of topics from Christmas shopping to election campaigns. Besides journalistic reporting, a growing number of scientific publications have started to include Google Trends data in recent years, especially in the areas of public health and epidemiology (Nuti et al. 2014). Also, Google recently launched a Google Trends Twitter account on which it shares insights about important search trends, often in near real time.

Individual Google Trends scores are derived from actual search records that are normalised on a scale ranging between 0 to 100, where 100 is assigned to the day, week or month – depending on the length of the period under examination – in which the given keywords were searched most frequently. All the other values are then calculated in function of their distance from the top score. Google Trends scores are plotted on a line chart and can be downloaded in CSV format for further examination. It ought to be noted that Google Trends does not grant access to raw search data and in some ways operates as a 'black box' where the output is clear but input not so. This calls for caution when social scientists bring Google Trends data into their work, limiting opportunities for further statistical elaboration. Also, while most Internet users in countries such as the U.K. and the U.S. habitually use Google to find information online, not all of them do, which suggests that it would be inappropriate to use Google Trends data as a substitute for key social trends indicators collected in more traditional ways such as through surveys (Trevisan 2014b). Nevertheless, Google Trends can provide extremely useful insights into the perceived salience of specific issues among Google users (Scharkow & Vogelgesang 2011; Scheitle 2011). In particular, it is especially useful to compare Google Trends charts with the timeline of related events, as well as relevant news coverage, in order to better understand which events, if any, catalyse the attention of users.

In light of this, it was interesting to consider search trends for common terms connected to disability issues, as well as more specific ones linked to disability welfare[3] for the period between the 2010 general election and November 2011, during which the debate on changes to disability welfare was most intense. In particular, Google Trends data showed that many of the greatest peaks in disability-related keyword searches on Google.co.uk occurred on key dates in the welfare reform's timeline (see Table 2.1 for a detailed timeline of the U.K. welfare reform debate). As is highlighted in Figure 2.2, substantial interest surges for both 'disability' and 'disability welfare' searches were registered during the week in which the then newly formed Conservative–Liberal Democrat coalition presented an emergency budget to parliament (22 June 2010) and the one in which a Comprehensive Spending Review was announced (20 October 2010), which outlined long-term plans to replace all existing disability welfare payments with a single benefit (PIPs). While these weeks stood out in particular due to sharp increases and relatively rapid decreases in disability-related searches, a closer cross-examination of the Google Trends and policy-making time-lines also showed that many other smaller interest surges occurred around key welfare reform dates.

Most notably, additional peaks occurred in conjunction with very important moments in the policy process, including: the opening (6 December 2010) and closing (18 February 2011) of the consultation on DLA changes; the introduction of the Welfare Reform Bill (WRB) to the House of Commons (16 February 2011); the presentation of the government's budget to parliament (23 March 2011); the release of the DLA consultation results (4 April 2011); and the introduction of the WRB to the House of Lords (16 June 2011). In addition, other search peaks occurred in conjunction with major protest events such as the Trades Union

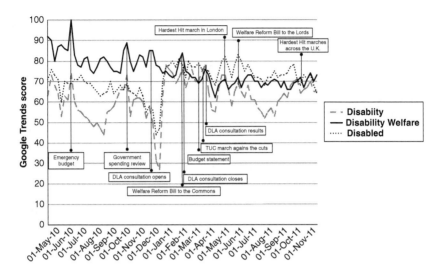

Figure 2.2 Interest in disability issues on Google.co.uk (May 2010–November 2011).

Congress (TUC) march against public expenditure cuts (26 March 2011) and the demonstrations organised by a coalition of disability organisations against welfare cuts in London (11 May 2011), as well as eight other cities across the country (22 October 2011).

Indeed, not every single surge in Google searches for information about disability and disability welfare occurred on an important date in the welfare reform calendar and vice-versa. This suggests that some types of events may be more prone to stimulating online activity than others, possibly depending on their nature, magnitude and visibility on the news media. This would be an interesting hypothesis to test, but one that goes beyond the scope of this book. That said, these results show that the co-occurrence between the two most prominent 'spikes' in user interest for disability-related topics and key moments in the welfare reform's timeline (22 June and 20 October 2010) was not exceptional and isolated, but rather part of a broader and more nuanced search trend revolving around the policy process. This is somewhat counter-intuitive as complex policy-making procedures tend to be of interest to a select group of people who are civically and politically active, as was discussed earlier in this chapter, while Google Trends captures data across a much broader section of Internet users. This appears to corroborate the assumption that disability welfare changes catalysed the attention of a large mass of users that included many who typically would not be involved in, or even pay attention to, policy-making.

Conclusions

Since the mid-1990s, much social science scholarship branded e-democracy and online mobilisation as 'niche' phenomena for geeks and political junkies that are likely to discourage ordinary citizens from participating, strengthen the power of existing elites and foster the creation of new ones. Undoubtedly, these conclusions were based on an impressive body of empirical evidence – one based primarily on quintessentially 'political' online spaces designed and governed by the same institutional actors that have traditionally dominated offline politics. Yet:

> [T]oday technology is different, [...] in the contemporary environment people are now more able than ever to act however they see fit, readily acting beyond the constraints imposed by a context for collective action once largely dominated and controlled by organizations.
>
> (Bimber et al. 2012, pp. 178–9)

This calls for the Internet's potential for political participation and civic engagement among traditionally disadvantaged social groups, for whom the online medium has generally been considered irrelevant, to be re-assessed. In particular, online media may have a lot to offer to that majority of disabled people who today identify themselves as regular Internet users. Online 'third spaces', and especially social media platforms, may facilitate their involvement in politically-relevant discussions as part of 'everyday' talk with other users, both disabled and non-. Online relationships and discussion may foster the growth of flexible forms of participation focused on shared interests and capable of circumventing traditional organisations and their exclusionary practices, as well as institutionalised barriers to participation, creating new channels for disabled people to exert influence on the 'formal' domain of politics where decisions are taken.

At the same time, digitally-enabled participatory transformation is most likely to occur in conjunction with disruptive events that provide a strong incentive for otherwise inactive citizens to aggregate and mobilise while bypassing established advocacy organisations or even the need for a pre-constituted common identity. This is especially relevant in the case of disabled users, as the lack of a strong group identity traditionally has been a hindrance to the expansion of disability activism. This strategy has the additional benefit of capturing online initiatives without relying on a priori categorisations, thus avoiding the mistake of applying prescriptive and outdated frameworks to emerging online phenomena that has affected many studies of Internet politics.

Between the second half of 2010 and 2012, the U.K. government enacted a radical reform of disability welfare provisions that catalysed the attention of scholars, campaigners and 'ordinary' disabled people for whom opportunities to live independently were dramatically and unexpectedly threatened by government cuts. The 'personal' consequences of proposed legislation and its relevance for disabled people's 'everyday' lives made this an issue likely to come up in conversations on online 'third spaces' that involved disabled Internet users, lowering the threshold for participation in political discussion. Google Trends data showed a link between key moments in the welfare reform timeline and major surges in interest for information on disability-related issues in the U.K. This corroborated the impression of benefit changes as important catalysts of disability-related online activity. At the same time, American disability advocates were focusing on fighting proposed cuts to Medicaid, the public social care programme on which most disabled Americans rely to cover their medical costs. This provided a useful opportunity for comparing the British case internationally.

Given the level of interest that British Google users showed towards disability welfare changes, the controversial nature of these proposals, and their potential for mobilisation, it is important to ask whether this flurry of online activity was being channelled into any forms of coordinated collective action capable of challenging the government's agenda effectively. If so, what did these group efforts look like? Which online platforms did they use and how? How did they compare with previous campaigns by the U.K. disability rights movement and interact with the wider socio-political context? Who led these efforts? And, ultimately, did these groups promote the development of a more inclusive model of citizenship for disabled Internet users? Chapters 3, 4 and 5 address these questions by discussing data collected both on- (Facebook content analysis, Web link analysis) and off-screen (in-depth interviews with activists and advocates). Chapter 6 takes this discussion one step further by comparing disability rights e-advocacy in Britain to its American counterpart in order to better understand the influence of a range of contextual factors on the technological choices of disability advocates and the ways in which emergent digital tactics are integrated with more established practices to influence policy-makers.

Notes

1 DLA was first introduced in 1992 to cover some of the additional living costs associated with disability. It was a non-means-tested and tax-free benefit that included both a care and a mobility component. The U.K. government initially announced it would scrap the mobility component for disabled people living in residential care with the introduction of PIPs from 2013, but eventually removed this element from the Welfare Reform Bill in November 2011. However, the replacement of DLA with PIP went ahead as planned including the controversial points-based eligibility tests performed by Atos, which started to be implemented in April 2013.
2 For details see: www.gov.uk/government/news/welfare-reform-bill-restoring-the-welfare-system-to-make-work-pay (accessed 10 June 2016).

3 Terms investigated with Google Trends included: 'disability'; 'disabled'; and a composite index of specific terms connected to disability welfare: 'disability benefit(s), disability welfare, disability (living) allowance, employment and support allowance (ESA)'. The first two were deliberately chosen in order to capture interest trends touching upon any area of disability. The keyword combination focusing on disability welfare was included to generate a more specific overview of online interest in the main issue at stake for disabled people.

References

Albrecht, S., 2006. Whose Voice is Heard in Online Deliberation?: A Study of Participation and Representation in Political Debates on the Internet. *Information, Community and Society*, 9(1), pp. 62–82.

Bakardjieva, M., 2012. Mundane Citizenship: New Media and Civil Society in Bulgaria. *Europe-Asia Studies*, 64(8), pp. 1356–1374.

Baym, N.K., 2010. *Personal Connections in the Digital Age*, Cambridge: Polity Press.

Baym, N.K. & boyd, D., 2012. Socially Mediated Publicness: An Introduction. *Journal of Broadcasting & Electronic Media*, 56(3), pp. 320–329.

Bennett, W.L., 2003. New Media Power: The Internet and Global Activism. In N. Couldry & J. Curran, eds. *Contesting Media Power: Alternative Media in a Networked World*. New York: Rowman & Littlefield, pp. 17–37.

Bennett, W.L. & Segerberg, A., 2012. The Logic of Connective Action: Digital Media and the Personalization of Contentious Politics. *Information, Communication & Society*, 15(5), pp. 739–768.

Bimber, B., 1998. The Internet and Political Transformation: Populism, Community, and Accelerated Pluralism. *Polity*, 31(1), p. 133.

Bimber, B., Flanagin, A.J. & Stohl, C., 2005. Reconceptualizing Collective Action in the Contemporary Media Environment. *Communication Theory*, 15(4), pp. 365–388.

——— 2012. *Collective Action in Organizations: Interaction and Engagement in an Era of Technological Change*, Cambridge: Cambridge University Press.

Bimber, B., Stohl, C. & Flanagin, A.J., 2009. Technological Change and the Shifting Nature of Political Organisation. In A. Chadwick & P.N. Howard, eds. *Routledge Handbook of Internet Politics*. London: Routledge, pp. 72–85.

Bochel, H., 2011. Conservative Social Policy: From Conviction to Coalition. In C. Holden, M. Kilkey, & G. Ramia, eds. *Social Policy Review 23*. Bristol: Policy Press, pp. 7–24.

boyd, D., 2007. Social Network Sites: Public, Private, or What? *Knowledge Tree* 13, May.

——— 2012. Participating in the Always-On Lifestyle. In M. Mandiberg, ed. *The Social Media Reader*. New York: New York University Press, pp. 71–76.

boyd, D. & Ellison, N.B., 2008. Social Network Sites: Definition, History, and Scholarship. *Journal of Computer-Mediated Communication*, 13(1), pp. 210–230.

Brainard, L.A. & Siplon, P.D., 2002. Cyberspace Challenges to Mainstream Non-profit Health Organizations. *Administration & Society*, 34(2), pp. 141–175.

———— 2004. Toward Nonprofit Organization Reform in the Voluntary Spirit: Lessons from the Internet. *Nonprofit and Voluntary Sector Quarterly*, 33(3), pp. 435–457.

Briant, E., Watson, N. & Philo, G., 2013. Reporting Disability in the Age of Austerity: The Changing Face of Media Representation of Disability and Disabled People in the United Kingdom and the Creation of New 'Folk Devils'. *Disability & Society*, 28(6), pp. 874–889.

Burt, E. & Taylor, J., 2008. How Well Do Voluntary Organizations Perform on the Web as Democratic Actors? Towards an Evaluative Framework. *Information, Communication & Society*, 11(8), pp. 1047–1067.

Castells, M., 2000. *The Rise of the Network Society*, Oxford: Blackwell Publishing.

———— 2002. *The Internet Galaxy: Reflections on the Internet, Business, and Society*, Oxford: Oxford University Press.

———— 2004. Informationalism, Networks, and the Network Society: A Theoretical Blueprint. In M. Castells, ed. *The Network Society: A Cross-Cultural Perspective*. Cheltenham: Edward Elgar, pp. 3–48.

———— 2007. Communication, Power and Counter-Power in the Network Society. *International Journal of Communication*, 1(1), pp. 238–266.

Cavanagh, A., 2007. *Sociology in the Age of the Internet*, Maidenhead: Open University Press.

Chadwick, A., 2006. *Internet Politics: States, Citizens and New Communication Technologies*, Oxford: Oxford University Press.

———— 2007. Digital Network Repertoires and Organizational Hybridity. *Political Communication*, 24(3), pp. 283–301.

———— 2012. Web 2.0: New Challenges for the Study of E-Democracy in an Era of Informational Exuberance. In S. Coleman & P. Shane, eds. *Citizenship and Vulnerability*. Cambridge, MA: The MIT Press, pp. 45–73.

Chadwick, A. & Howard, P., 2009. Introduction: New Directions in Internet Politics Research. In A. Chadwick & P. Howard, eds. *Routledge Handbook of Internet Politics*. London: Routledge, pp. 1–10.

Chadwick, A. & May, C., 2003. Interaction between States and Citizens in the Age of the Internet: 'e-Government' in the United States, Britain, and the European Union. *Governance*, 16(2), pp. 271–300.

Chesters, G. & Welsh, I., 2006. *Complexity and Social Movements: Multitudes at the Edge of Chaos*, London: Routledge.

Coleman, S., 2005. The Lonely Citizen: Indirect Representation in an Age of Networks. *Political Communication*, 22(2), pp. 197–214.

Coleman, S. & Blumler, J.G., 2009. *The Internet and Democratic Citizenship: Theory, Practice and Policy*, Cambridge: Cambridge University Press.

Curran, J., 2012. Reinterpreting the Internet. In J. Curran, N. Fenton, & D. Freedman, eds. *Misunderstanding the Internet*. London: Routledge, pp. 34–66.

Dahlberg, L., 2004. Net-Public Sphere Research: Beyond The 'First Phase'. *Javnost-The Public*, 11(1), pp. 27–43.

Dahlgren, P., 2002. In Search of the Talkative Public: Media, Deliberative Democracy and Civic Culture. *Javnost-The Public*, 9(3), pp. 5–25.

della Porta, D. & Diani, M., 1999. *Social Movements: An Introduction*, Oxford: Blackwell Publishing.

Department for Work and Pensions, 2012. *Fraud and Error in the Benefit System: 2011/12 Estimates (Great Britain)*. Available at: www.gov.uk/government/uploads/system/uploads/attachment_data/file/244844/fem_1112.pdf (accessed 28 February 2016).

di Gennaro, C. & Dutton, W., 2006. The Internet and the Public: Online and Offline Political Participation in the United Kingdom. *Parliamentary Affairs*, 59(2), pp. 299–313.

Dutton, W.H. & Blank, G., 2013. *Cultures of the Internet: The Internet in Britain*, Oxford: Oxford Internet Institute.

Fenton, N., 2012. The Internet and Social Networking. In J. Curran, N. Fenton, & D. Freedman, eds. *Misunderstanding the Internet*. London: Routledge, pp. 123–148.

Flanagin, A.J., Stohl, C. & Bimber, B., 2006. Modeling the Structure of Collective Action. *Communication Monographs*, 73(1), pp. 29–54.

Germon, P., 1998. Activists and Academics: Part of the Same or a World Apart? In T. Shakespeare, ed. *The Disability Reader*. London: Continuum, pp. 244–255.

Gibson, R.K., Gillan, K., Greffet, F., Lee, B.J. & Ward, S., 2013. Party Organizational Change and ICTs: The Growth of a Virtual Grassroots? *New Media & Society*, 15(1), pp. 31–51.

Graham, T., 2008. Needles in a Haystack: A New Approach for Identifying and Assessing Political Talk in Nonpolitical Discussion Forums. *Javnost-The Public*, 15(2), pp. 17–36.

——— 2010. Talking Politics Online within Spaces of Popular Culture. *Javnost-The Public*, 17(4), pp. 25–42.

——— 2012. Beyond 'Political' Communicative Spaces: Talking Politics on the Wife Swap Discussion Forum. *Journal of Information Technology & Politics*, 9(1), pp. 31–45.

Graham, T. & Harju, A., 2011. Reality TV as a Trigger of Everyday Political Talk in the Net-Based Public Sphere. *European Journal of Communication*, 26(1), pp. 18–32.

Graham, T. & Wright, S., 2013. Discursive Equality and Everyday Talk Online: The Impact of 'Superparticipants'. *Journal of Computer-Mediated Communication*, 19(3), pp. 625–642.

Graham, T., Jackson, D. & Wright, S., 2015a. From Everyday Conversation to Political Action: Talking Austerity in Online 'Third Spaces'. *European Journal of Communication*, 30(6), pp. 648–665.

——— 2015b. 'We Need to Get Together and Make Ourselves Heard': Everyday Online Spaces as Incubators of Political Action. *Information, Communication & Society*, 19(10), pp. 1373–1389.

Granovetter, M.S., 1973. The Strength of Weak Ties. *American Journal of Sociology*, 78(6), pp. 1360–1380.

Grant, E. & Wood, C., 2011. Disability Benefits. In N. Yeates, T. Haux, R. Jawad, M. Kilkey & N. Timmins, eds. *In Defence of Welfare: The Impacts of the Comprehensive Spending Review*. Bristol: Social Policy Association, pp. 28–29.

Gunter, B., Rowlands, I. & Nicholas, D., 2009. *The Google Generation: Are ICT Innovations Changing Information-Seeking Behaviour?* Oxford: Chandos Publishing.

Habermas, J., 1991. *The Structural Transformation of the Public Sphere: An Inquiry into a Category of Bourgeois Society*, Cambridge: Polity Press.

Häyhtiö, T. & Rinne, J., 2008. Introduction: Seeking the Citizenry on the Internet – Emerging Virtual Creativity. In T. Häyhtiö & J. Rinne, eds. *Net Working/ Networking: Citizen Initiated Internet Politics*. Tampere: Tampere University Press, pp. 11–38.

Haythornthwaite, C., 2005. Social Networks and Internet Connectivity Effects. *Information, Community and Society*, 8(2), pp. 125–147.

Hillis, K., Petit, M. & Jarrett, K., 2013. *Google and the Culture of Search*, New York: Routledge.

Howard, P., 2006. *New Media Campaigns and the Managed Citizen*, Cambridge: Cambridge University Press.

Jensen, J.L., 2006. The Minnesota E-Democracy Project: Mobilising the Mobilised? In S. Oates, D. Owen, & R. Gibson, eds. *The Internet and Politics: Citizens, Voters and Activists*. London: Routledge, pp. 39–58.

Karpf, D., 2010. Advocacy Group Communications in the New Media Environment. In *8th APSA Political Communication Pre-conference meeting*. Washingon, DC 1 September.

——— 2012. *The MoveOn Effect: The Unexpected Transformation of American Political Advocacy*, New York: Oxford University Press.

Kreiss, D., 2012. *Taking Our Country Back: The Crafting of Networked Politics from Howard Dean to Barack Obama*, Oxford: Oxford University Press.

Lin, W.-Y. & Dutton, W.H., 2003. The 'Net' Effect in Politics The 'Stop the Overlay' Campaign in Los Angeles. *Party Politics*, 9(1), pp. 124–136.

Lupia, A., 2009. Can Online Deliberation Improve Politics? Scientific Foundations for Success. In D. Todd & S. Peña, eds. *Online Deliberation: Design, Research, and Practice*. Stanford, CA: CSLI Publications, pp. 59–70.

Lusoli, W. & Ward, S., 2006. Hunting Protestors: Mobilisation, Participation and Protest Online in the Countryside Alliance. In S. Oates, D. Owen, & R. Gibson, eds. *The Internet and Politics: Citizens, Voters and Activists*. London: Routledge, pp. 52–71.

Mansbridge, J., 1999. Everyday Talk in the Deliberative System. In S. Macedo, ed. *Deliberative Politics: Essays on Democracy and the Internet*. Oxford: Oxford University Press, pp. 211–239.

Margolis, M. & Moreno-Riaño, G., 2009. *The Prospect of Internet Democracy*, Farnham: Ashgate.

Margolis, M. & Resnick, D., 2000. *Politics as Usual: The Cyberspace 'Revolution'*, London: SAGE.

Matzat, U., 2010. Reducing Problems of Sociability in Online Communities: Integrating Online Communication With Offline Interaction. *American Behavioral Scientist*, 53(8), pp. 1170–1193.

Morris, J., 2011. *Rethinking Disability Policy*. Available at: www.jrf.org.uk/report/rethinking-disability-policy (accessed 28 February 2016).

Newhagen, J.E., 1998. Hitting the Agenda Reset Button: Matching Internet Research with Development. *Convergence: The International Journal of Research into New Media Technologies*, 4(4), pp. 112–119.

Norris, P., 2002. *Democratic Phoenix: Reinventing Political Activism*, Cambridge: Cambridge University Press.

——— 2003. Preaching to the Converted? Pluralism, Participation and Party Websites. *Party Politics*, 9(1), pp. 21–45.

Norris, P. & Curtice, J., 2006. If You Build a Political Web Site, Will They Come?: The Internet and Political Activism in Britain. *International Journal of Electronic Government Research*, 2(2), pp. 1–21.

Nuti, S.V., Wayda, B., Ranasinghe, I., Wang, S., Dreyer, R.P., Chen, S.I. & Murugiah, K., 2014. The Use of Google Trends in Health Care Research: A Systematic Review. *PLoS ONE*, 9(10), p. e109583.

Oldenburg, R., 1989. *The Great Good Place: Cafés, Coffee Shops, Community Centers, Beauty Parlors, General Stores, Bars, Hangouts and How They Get You Through the Day*, New York: Paragon House.

Oliver, M. & Barnes, C., 2012. *The New Politics of Disablement*, Basingstoke: Palgrave Macmillan.

Olson, M., 1965. *The Logic of Collective Action: Public Goods and the Theory of Groups*, Cambridge, MA: Harvard University Press.

Olsson, T., 2008. The Practises of Internet Networking – A Resource for Alternative Political Movements. *Information, Communication & Society*, 11(5), pp. 659–674.

O'Reilly, T., 2012. What is Web 2.0? Design Patterns and Business Models for the Next Generation of Software. In M. Mandiberg, ed. *The Social Media Reader*. New York: New York University Press, pp. 33–52.

Owen, D., 2006. The Internet and Youth Civic Engagement in the United States. In S. Oates, D. Owen, & R. Gibson, eds. *The Internet and Politics: Citizens, Voters and Activists*. London: Routledge, pp. 20–38.

Pajnik, M., 2005. Citizenship and Mediated Society. *Citizenship Studies*, 9(4), pp. 349–367.

Papacharissi, Z., 2009. The Virtual Sphere 2.0: The Internet, the Public Sphere, and Beyond. In A. Chadwick & P. Howard, eds. *Routledge Handbook of Internet Politics*. London: Routledge, pp. 230–245.

——— 2010. *A Private Sphere: Democracy in a Digital Age*, Cambridge: Polity.

——— 2015. Affective Publics and Structures of Storytelling: Sentiment, Events and Mediality. *Information, Communication & Society*, 19(3), pp. 307–324.

Patrick, R., 2011. Deserving or Undeserving? The Coalition, Welfare Reform and Disabled People. In *Social Policy Association Conference*. University of Lincoln, 4–6 July.

Pearson, C., 2012. Independent Living. In N. Watson, A. Roulstone, & C. Thomas, eds. *Routledge Handbook of Disability Studies*. London: Routledge, pp. 240–252.

Pearson, C. & Riddell, S., 2006. Introduction – The Development of Direct Payments in Scotland. In C. Pearson, ed. *Direct Payments and the Personalisation of Care*. Edinburgh: Dunedin Academic Press, pp. 1–12.

Purcell, K., Brenner, J. & Rainie, L., 2012. *Search Engine Use 2012*, Washington, DC: Pew Internet and American Life Project.

Putnam, R.D., 2000. *Bowling Alone: The Collapse and Revival of American Community*, New York: Simon & Schuster.

Rash, W., 1995. *Politics on the Net: Wiring the Political Process*, New York: Freeman.

Roulstone, A., 2011a. Coalition Disability Policy: A Consolidation of Neo-Liberalism or Benign Pragmatism? In *Social Policy Association Conference*, University of Lincoln, 4–6 July.

———— 2011b. Disabled People. In N. Yeates, T. Haux, R. Jawad, M. Kilkey & N. Timmins, eds. *In Defence of Welfare: The Impacts of the Comprehensive Spending Review.* Bristol: Social Policy Association, pp. 25–27.

Rummery, K., 2002. *Disability, Citizens and Community Care: A Case for Welfare Rights?* Burlington: Ashgate.

Sanz, E. & Stančík, J., 2014. Your Search – 'Ontological Security' – matched 111,000 Documents: An Empirical Substantiation of the Cultural Dimension of Online Search. *New Media & Society*, 16(2), pp. 252–270.

Scharkow, M. & Vogelgesang, J., 2011. Measuring the Public Agenda using Search Engine Queries. *International Journal of Public Opinion Research*, 23(1), pp. 104–113.

Scheitle, C.P., 2011. Google's Insights for Search: A Note Evaluating the Use of Search Engine Data in Social Research*. *Social Science Quarterly*, 92(1), pp. 285–295.

Schlosberg, D., Zavestoski, S. & Shulman, D.S.W., 2008. Democracy and E-Rulemaking: Web-Based Technologies, Participation, and the Potential for Deliberation. *Journal of Information Technology & Politics*, 4(1), pp. 37–55.

Scott, J.C., 1985. *Weapons of the Weak: Everyday Forms of Peasant Resistance*, New Heaven, CT: Yale University Press.

Siapera, E., 2005. Minority Activism on the Web: Between Deliberative Democracy and Multiculturalism. *Journal of Ethnic and Migration Studies*, 31(3), pp. 499–519.

Sloam, J., 2014. 'The Outraged Young': Young Europeans, Civic Engagement and the New Media in a Time of Crisis. *Information, Communication & Society*, 17(2), pp. 217–231.

Spears, R. & Lea, M., 1994. Panacea or Panopticon? The Hidden Power in Computer-Mediated Communication. *Communication Research*, 21(4), pp. 427–459.

Stromer-Galley, J., 2000. Democratizing Democracy: Strong Democracy, US Political Campaigns and the Internet. In P. Ferdinand, ed. *The Internet, Democracy and Democratization.* London: Frank Cass, pp. 36–58.

———— 2014. *Presidential Campaigning in the Internet Age*, New York: Oxford University Press.

Sunstein, C.R., 2007. *Republic.com 2.0*, Princeton, NJ: Princeton University Press.

Tarrow, S.G., 2011. *Power in Movement: Social Movements and Contentious Politics*, Cambridge: Cambridge University Press.

Taylor-Gooby, P. & Stoker, G., 2011. The Coalition Programme: A New Vision for Britain or Politics as Usual? *The Political Quarterly*, 82(1), pp. 4–15.

Tomkova, J., 2009. E-Consultations: New Tools for Political Engagement of Facades for Political Correctness? *European Journal of ePractice*, 7(March), pp. 45–54.

Trevisan, F., 2012. ICTs for Empowerment? Disability Organizations and the Democratizing Potential of Web 2.0 in Scotland. In A. Manoharan & M. Holzer, eds. *E-Governance and Civic Engagement: Factors and Determinants of E-Democracy.* Hershey: IGI Globa, pp. 381–404.

———— 2014a. Scottish Disability Organizations and Online Media: A Path to Empowerment or 'Business as Usual?' *Disability Studies Quarterly*, 34(3).

———— 2014b. Search Engines: From Social Science Objects to Academic Inquiry Tools. *First Monday*, 19(11).

Turbine, V., 2007. Russian Women's Perceptions of Human Rights and Rights-Based Approaches in Everyday Life. In R. Kay, ed. *Gender, Equality, and Difference During and After Socialism*. Basingstoke: Palgrave Macmillan, pp. 167–186.

Vedel, T., 2006. The Idea of Electronic Democracy: Origins, Visions and Questions. *Parliamentary Affairs*, 59(2), pp. 226–235.

Vromen, A., 2011. Constructing Australian Youth Online. *Information, Communication & Society*, 14(7), pp. 959–980.

Vromen, A. & Collin, P., 2010. Everyday Youth Participation? Contrasting Views From Australian Policymakers and Young People. *Young*, 18(1), pp. 97–112.

Weber, L.M., Loumakis, A. & Bergman, J., 2003. Who Participates and Why? An Analysis of Citizens on the Internet and the Mass Public. *Social Science Computer Review*, 21(1), pp. 26–42.

Wellman, B., 1979. The Community Question: The Intimate Networks of East Yorkers on JSTOR. *American Journal of Sociology*, 84(5), pp. 1201–1231.

Wellman, B., Boase, J. & Chen, W., 2002. The Networked Nature of Community: Online and Offline. *It & Society*, 1(1), pp. 151–165.

Wellman, B., Carrington, P. & Hall, A., 1988. Networks as Personal Communities. In B. Wellman & S. D. Berkowitz, eds. *Social Structures: A Network Approach*. Cambridge: Cambridge University Press, pp. 130–184.

Wellman, B., Quan-Haase, A., Witte, J. & Hampton, K., 2001. Does the Internet Increase, Decrease, or Supplement Social Capital?: Social Networks, Participation, and Community Commitment. *American Behavioral Scientist*, 45(3), pp. 436–455.

Wellman, B., Quan-Haase, A., Boase, J., Chen, W., Hampton, K., Díaz, I. & Miyata, K., 2003. The Social Affordances of the Internet for Networked Individualism. *Journal of Computer-Mediated Communication*, 8(3).

Wojcieszak, M.E. & Mutz, D.C., 2009. Online Groups and Political Discourse: Do Online Discussion Spaces Facilitate Exposure to Political Disagreement? *Journal of Communication*, 59(1), pp. 40–56.

Woliver, L., 1993. *From Outrage to Action: The Politics of Grassroot Dissent*, Urbana & Chigago: The University of Illinois Press.

Wright, S., 2006. Design Matters: The Politics Efficacy of Government-Run Discussion Boards. In S. Oates, D. Owen, & R. Gibson, eds. *The Internet and Politics: Citizens, Voters and Activists*. London: Routledge, pp. 72–89.

———— 2012a. Politics as Usual? Revolution, Normalization and a New Agenda for Online Deliberation. *New Media & Society*, 14(2), pp. 244–261.

———— 2012b. From 'Third Place' to 'Third Space': Everyday Political Talk in Non-Political Online Spaces. *Javnost-The Public*, 19(3), pp. 5–20.

———— 2016. 'Success' and Online Political Participation: The Case of Downing Street E-Petitions. *Information, Communication & Society*, 19(6), pp. 843–857.

Wright, S. & Coleman, S., 2012. The Third Sector as E-Democratic Actors. In S. Coleman & P. Shane, eds. *Connecting Democracy: Online Consultations and the Flow of Political Communication*. Cambridge, MA: The MIT Press, pp. 209–227.

Wright, S. & Street, J., 2007. Democracy, Deliberation and Design: The Case of Online Discussion Forums. *New Media & Society*, 9(5), pp. 849–869.

Xenos, M., Vromen, A. & Loader, B.D., 2014. The Great Equalizer? Patterns of Social Media Use and Youth Political Engagement in Three Advanced Democracies. *Information, Communication & Society*, 17(2), pp. 151–167.

3 Keep Calm and Tweet On
British Disability Advocacy Goes Digital

Moving from the idea that mobilisation and grassroots advocacy often flourish in response to events that disrupt the status quo, this chapter provides an overview of the groups that used new media technologies to oppose a radical reform of disability welfare in the U.K. between 2010 and 2012. What kinds of groups turned to new media to voice dissent against these policy proposals? To what extent did the Web presence of these groups facilitate interactive and participatory advocacy? Were disabled self-advocates and ordinary users involved in these efforts and, if so, in what roles? And, finally, what other actors did these groups connect to and interact with in the online sphere? This chapter addresses these questions by identifying the British disability advocacy groups – both established and emergent – that were most visible on the Internet at the peak of the welfare reform debate and therefore had the greatest chance to attract supporters, both disabled and non-. Their e-advocacy strategies are explored through a detailed inventory of their technological preferences, interviews with key figures within a range of these groups and Web link analysis with IssueCrawler.

Three main types of groups emerged that relied on online media to oppose the then Conservative-led coalition's government plan to reform disability welfare. These included: formal disability organisations (both 'professionalised' charities and self-advocacy groups); experienced disabled activists who had been part of the disabled people's movement in the 1980s and 1990s, and joined forces again to protest against the welfare reform; and, finally, a new generation of technology-savvy disabled bloggers who came together as an advocacy group for the first time in the wake of the welfare reform controversy. In particular, disabled bloggers were able to take advantage of their familiarity with technology to launch a new 'genre' in British disability advocacy. They provided potential supporters with a flexible range of opportunities for becoming involved in the activities they launched, which arguably occupied an intermediate position between those promoted by formal organisations and the ones sponsored by more 'militant' protest groups.

After discussing this new typology of British disability advocacy, this chapter focuses in detail on three emblematic case studies, including:

The Hardest Hit; Disabled People Against Cuts (DPAC); and The Broken of Britain. In particular, the nature of each of these groups and their relationship with technology is explored in detail, laying the foundations for further investigation on their potential for user-empowerment in the remainder of this book. While the findings discussed in this chapter show that each group had adopted a different online advocacy repertoire depending on its ethos, history and ambitions, results also revealed that the use of social media platforms had become ubiquitous across the entire organisational spectrum. This marked an important departure from the reluctance of both disability non-profits and self-advocacy groups to embrace participatory technology until recently (Trevisan 2012, 2014) and injected new vitality into British disability advocacy at a time of crisis. However, the three approaches to e-advocacy outlined here also prompted fundamental questions about their potential to empower disabled Internet users and raise their stakes in citizenship. Chapters 4 and 5 address these questions by discussing in detail the use of Facebook in each of the three groups that are introduced here.

One Issue, a Plurality of Online Players and Spaces

The first step in exploring the potential implications of the online activities connected to U.K. disability welfare reform for the empowerment of disabled Internet users was to understand whether anger and user-interest were being channelled into any forms of coordinated collective action. This was not simply a case of putting together a general overview of the groups that used the Internet to campaign against disability welfare changes. Instead, it was important to determine which initiatives were most visible and readily accessible to disabled Internet users who were worried about this issue.

In order to do so, it was useful to begin by considering the options that Internet users had to find information about how to participate in opposing disability welfare changes. Indeed, some people may have learnt about advocacy groups or grassroots campaigns in 'everyday' online discussions with other users. However, as was discussed in the previous chapter, Internet search continues to be the most popular and common way of finding online information about a specific topic, issue or event. For this reason, keyword searches helped to identify the online initiatives that users had the greatest opportunity to encounter, be they supported by 'usual suspects' such as professionally run non-profits and established self-advocacy groups, or more spontaneous grassroots networks. While it should be noted that search algorithms privilege certain sites over others, tending to favour traditionally dominant online actors (Hindman 2009; Mager 2012), what matters here is that looking at popular search results essentially replicates the choice available to most Internet users interested in finding out what groups and campaigns were opposing government policy. In doing so, this points the analysis in the direction of those online initiatives that were most likely to attract substantial online traffic.

Searching Google.co.uk for a series of keyword combinations linked to disability benefits and activism[1] when the welfare reform debate had intensified (October 2010–January 2011) uncovered a number of groups that made extensive use of digital tools to oppose changes to the disability benefits system at the national level. The same keyword searches were carried out also on Facebook.com in order to capture groups that did not rank high on Google results (i.e. they were not on the first page) and therefore were less likely to be seen by users (Jansen & Spink 2005, p. 371; 2006, p. 257) but at the same time were popular on social media (for example, the successful 'Toy Like Me' campaign mentioned at the very beginning of this book, which did not have a website and operated primarily on Facebook). This strategy made it possible to detect some important grassroots initiatives before they gained visibility in major news media outlets such as *The Guardian* and *The Independent*. In addition to established organisations such as the Disability Alliance, the UK Disabled People's Council, Scope and Mencap, several new groups that used the Internet to advocate against changes to disability welfare were uncovered. Searches continued until theoretical saturation was reached and no more new types of online initiatives were found.

These groups could be categorised inductively (George & Bennett 2004, pp. 240–4) on the basis of three criteria, namely:

- their structure (How formalised was their membership? Did they have centralised headquarters?);
- their relationship with established disability organisations (Were they entirely new groups or did they branch out of existing ones? Did they collaborate with existing organisations or see them as competitors?);
- their relationship with technology (Did they run their operations entirely online, or did they blend both online and offline repertoires?).

Overall, there were three distinct types of advocacy groups active in this area (Table 3.1). These included:

a   **Formal organisations:** established organisations (including professionalised charities, self-advocacy groups and 'hybrid' bodies) that often formed temporary *ad hoc* coalitions to campaign against changes to disability welfare;
b   **'Digitised' activists:** groups of experienced disabled self-advocates rooted strongly in the social model of disability and independent living principles who in the 1980s and 1990s had been involved in the fight for anti-discrimination legislation, either in a personal capacity or as part of self-advocacy groups; after meeting at protest rallies, several of

Table 3.1 Top organisations, groups and coalitions that opposed the U.K. disability welfare reform on Google.co.uk and Facebook.com

Campaigns by formal organisations	'Digitised' activists	Digital action networks
	Campaign for a Fair Society	The Broken of Britain
The Hardest Hit	Disabled People Against Cuts (DPAC)*	Where's the Benefit?*
Mobilise for DLA	Benefit Claimants' Fightback	Spartacus Network*
Make ESA Fit for Work (Citizens Advice Bureau)		

Note: *indicates on-going effort as of early 2016.

these activists set up a Web presence in an attempt to campaign separately from established disability organisations;

c **Digital action networks:** online-only initiatives created by young disabled bloggers-cum-activists – digital media were integral not only to the tactics of these groups, but also to their very existence as their founders were geographically dispersed across the U.K. and, in all likelihood, would not have met each other if they had not been able to do so online.

This initial overview suggests that both the British disability advocacy landscape and its relationship with new media technologies underwent some substantial changes between 2010 and 2011. First, established organisations that had parted ways following the introduction of anti-discrimination legislation as discussed in Chapter 1 used the Internet to launch new joint initiatives against the radical reform of disability welfare. Second, self-advocates that had previously tended to shun online platforms, such as in the case of Scottish disabled people's organisations discussed in Chapter 2, were now engaged with these new forms of media. Third, disabled Millennials were leveraging their familiarity with social media platforms to set up new and possibly innovative forms of advocacy and protest. Each of these group types and their relationship with technology is discussed in detail in the reminder of this chapter and the next two chapters through the analysis of three emblematic case studies.

It is interesting to note that keyword searches identified two more types of online spaces that hosted a substantial amount of conversation about disability welfare changes, namely: Web portals for carers and disabled children's parents; and discussion forums hosted on commercial sites such as Moneysavingexpert.co.uk ('Disability & Dosh' board) and Benefitsandwork.co.uk. While the involvement of carers and parents' organisations constitutes no surprise given their stakes in welfare reform, the presence of commercial discussion forums in this mix reiterates the importance of 'everyday' online spaces as incubators of politically-relevant discussion (Chadwick 2012; Wright 2012a, 2012b). Investigating the conversations that occur on these kinds of forums promises to reveal the dynamics for which talk on disability policy may emerge from 'everyday' topics. As this book concentrates on initiatives that promoted action rather than just talk and were directed at disabled Internet users rather than carers or parents, these two additional platforms are not examined in detail here. That said, future research should focus on these online discussion venues too as more reliable methods for analysing user-generated content automatically are developed.

Great Expectations or Business as Usual?

At a first look, the presence of disabled bloggers among those using the Internet to oppose disability welfare changes could seem to corroborate the popular assertion that digital communications foster the 'mass amateurisation' of activism (Shirky 2008). However, a closer examination of the composition of these groups showed that to be a premature conclusion. Not only were the digital action networks run by disabled Millennials flanked by groups of experienced self-advocates on one side and established disability organisations on the other, but groups from all three categories revolved also around sets of key organisers who provided content, guidance and direction. Although this raises the issue of internal democracy in these groups, it also resonates with the social movement principle for which grassroots initiatives, much like special interest groups, tend to 'naturally' organise around experienced leaders (Burstein 1999; Campbell 2005), which in turn boosts their chances of achieving concrete, tangible change (Woliver 1993, p. 4). Whether they sought to implement a hierarchical control structure or merely steer collective deliberation processes, the centrality of lead campaigners emerged repeatedly throughout the research carried out for this book. Leadership and participatory practices within both established and emerging groups are addressed in detail later in this book.

Despite this basic commonality, however, groups in each of the categories listed above had a distinct relationship with technology and used new media platforms in different ways. In order to better understand what set the three group types apart from one another, it is useful to discuss in detail three emblematic groups selected among those that operated at the national level, ranked among the top results on Google.co.uk and Facebook.com, and therefore had the greatest potential to attract a large number of Internet users interested in this issue. These included:

1　**The Hardest Hit,** a joint campaign endorsed by more than 50 established British disability organisations;

2   **Disabled People Against Cuts (DPAC)**, a group set up by experienced disability activists who met during a protest at the 2010 Conservative Party annual conference in Birmingham; and
3   **The Broken of Britain**, an online-only campaign run by a network of young disabled bloggers such as Kaliya Franklin and other self-advocates such as the late Rhydian Fon James.

All these groups started to campaign online against changes to disability welfare between the second half of 2010 and early 2011. They used new media platforms to raise their profile and quickly gained considerable visibility on British news media. Each of them was selected as it epitomised the most distinctive traits of one of the group types illustrated above. The remainder of this chapter illustrates how each of these groups used new media platforms and employs Web link analysis to map their relationships with the broader online context. The next two chapters provide a detailed account of how these groups used Facebook, focusing in particular on what this revealed about the relationship between core organisers and rank-and-file supporters in each group. The results of 12 semi-structured interviews with leading figures from these groups (Table 3.2) are discussed alongside the data gathered on-screen (Dahlberg 2004; Witschge 2008). The interviews took place between May and October 2011, and queried participants about four main issues, including: changes in advocacy practices in the Internet age; online tactics and strategy; how the groups understood their online target audiences; and the role played by catalyst events in mobilising and organising disabled people (for a copy of the interview guide, see Appendix A). As in previous work on political blogs (Fossato et al. 2008) and online activism (Gillan 2009; Olsson 2008), interviews were instrumental in acquiring a sense of the specific campaign strategies pursued by these groups and clarify some of the reasons at the root of their choices.

Given the importance of opportunities for genuine two-way communication and enhanced levels of user-control over advocacy initiatives for user empowerment (McMillan 2002, p. 276), the inventory matrix used to map the Web presence of these groups focused particularly on interactive features. Several scholars have developed sophisticated online media inventories for political actors such as parties (Gibson & Ward 2000; Gibson et al. 2003; Lilleker & Jackson 2011), candidates (Stromer-Galley 2007), activist networks (Bennett & Segerberg 2011; Gillan 2009) and even terrorist groups (Qin et al. 2007). This work crucially informed the scheme devised for this study. However, unlike much previous work, this project looked beyond websites and blogs to also include several aspects of social media and map the Web presence of disability rights groups more comprehensively. The matrix covered four main areas of interaction and communication, including: personalisation and user-input; broadcast information features; social media and community

Table 3.2 Overview of British disability groups

U.K. organisations	Interviews	HQ location	Website
Disabled People Against Cuts (DPAC)^	2	U.K.-wide network (offline & online)	www.dpac.uk.net
The Broken of Britain	2	U.K.-wide network (online-only)	www.thebrokenofbritain.blogspot.com
Scope*^	1	London	www.scope.org.uk
The MS Society*^	2	London	www.mssociety.org.uk
Inclusion London*^	1	London	www.inclusionlondon.org.uk
United Kingdom Disabled People's Council (UKDPC)*	1	London	www.ukdpc.net
Leonard Cheshire Disability (LCD)*^	1	London	www.lcdisability.org.uk
Royal National Institute of Blind People (RNIB)*^	1	London	www.rnib.org.uk
National Autistic Society (NAS)*^	1	London	www.autism.org.uk
Mencap*	—	London	www.mencap.org.uk
Disability Alliance*^	—	London	www.disabilityalliance.org (from 2012: www.disabilityrightsuk.org)
National Centre for Independent Living (NCIL)*	—	London	www.ncil.org.uk (from January 2012: www.disabilityrightsuk.org)
Royal Association for Disability Rights (RADAR)*^	—	London	www.radar.org.uk (from January 2012: www.disabilityrightsuk.org)
Mind*^	—	London	www.mind.org.uk
Ambitious About Autism*^	—	London	www.ambitiousaboutautism.org.uk
Action for ME*^	—	Bristol	www.afme.org.uk

Notes: *indicates members of 'The Hardest Hit' coalition; ^indicates members of the Disability Benefits Consortium.

applications; and collective action resources (see Appendix B for details). A 'clicktivism plus' variable was added to track the practice of encouraging supporters to personalise advocacy messages (e.g. template emails, etc.) to be sent directly to policy-makers, which was popular among British disability groups, as well as among their American counterparts, as is discussed in Chapter 6. The online media inventory was completed at the apex of the disability welfare reform debate between 2011 and 2012. Results are summarised in Table 3.3 and discussed for each case study in the remainder of this chapter.

Web link network analysis was used also to explore the context in which these groups operated: What was their relationship with other disability activists and the broader 'galaxy' of anti-austerity initiatives that flourished in the U.K. between 2010 and 2012? Did they pursue connections with institutional actors such as government departments, political parties or the news media? Hyperlinks helped answer these questions because they are both the enablers and the most explicit manifestation of the relationships that exist between the people behind Web pages (Baulieu 2005, pp. 190–1; Rogers 2010a). Thus, Web link analysis can expose otherwise less visible social connections (Rogers 2010b). This task was completed using Issue-Crawler,[2] which is a free online-based tool. A number of recent Internet politics studies have used IssueCrawler data, including work on political parties (Gibson et al. 2013; Oates 2012, 2013), peace activists (Gillan 2009; Gillan et al. 2008) and anti-G20 protesters (Bennett & Segerberg 2011). In keeping with the trend established in this work, entire networks are adopted as units of analysis here and IssueCrawler visualisations are discussed with specific reference to the types of websites involved, the types of organisations behind them, the nature of central nodes (i.e. those receiving the greatest number of in-links), the presence of any identifiable sub-networks and whether The Hardest Hit, DPAC and The Broken of Britain acted as central, peripheral or broker nodes in their respective networks.

Formal Disability Organisations: The Hardest Hit Campaign

The Hardest Hit campaign was the largest and arguably most visible of the digital initiatives launched by disability rights groups in the wake of the U.K. welfare reform. It mobilised thousands of disabled people, online as well as in person, particularly in conjunction with the street demonstrations it organised in London on 11 May 2011 (Figure 3.1) and eight other cities across the U.K. on 22 October that same year. Crucially, these events went beyond the traditional lobbying repertoire of disability non-profits, which typically shun confrontation in favour of softer tactics. This provides a first indication of how the groups behind The Hardest Hit believed that the coalition government's welfare agenda required an 'extraordinary' response from disability advocates.

Table 3.3 Online media repertoires at the height of the welfare reform debate (March 2012)

		The Hardest Hit (Coalition of formal organisations)	DPAC ('Digitised' activists)	The Broken of Britain (Digital action network)
Personalisation & user-input	Audience segmentation	No	No	No
	Share personal stories	Yes	No	Yes
	Polls/surveys	No	No	No
	Clicktivism plus	Yes	No	Yes
Broadcast info (top-down comms)	Email action network	No	No	No
	Other email list or discussion groups	No	Yes	No
	RSS feed	No	No	Yes
	E-newsletter	No	No	No
	Events calendar	No	No	No
	Personal contact details for officers	No	No	No
	Generic contact details	Yes	Yes	Yes
Community (horizontal comms)	Discussion forum	No	No	Yes (only members)
	Official blog(s)	No	Yes (comments)	Yes (comments)
	Members-only area	No	No	No
	Twitter	No	Yes	Yes
	Facebook 'fan' page	Yes	No	Yes
	Facebook 'group' page	No	Yes	No
	YouTube	No	No	Yes (only individual videos)

(Continued)

Table 3.3. (continued)

		The Hardest Hit (Coalition of formal organisations)	DPAC ('Digitised' activists)	The Broken of Britain (Digital action network)
Community (horizontal comms) – continued	Flickr	Yes	Yes	No
	Join button	No	Yes	No
	Donate button	No	Yes	No
	Share button	No	Yes	Yes
Action resources	E-petitions link	No	No	Yes
	E-postcard or template letter	Yes	No	No
	Campaign or advocacy section on website	Yes	Yes	Yes
	Maps/events listings	No	Yes	No
	Virtual protest page(s)	No	Yes	No

Figure 3.1 The Hardest Hit's first demonstration in London, 11 May 2011.
Source: Courtesy of Matthew Winyard, RNIB.

The driver behind The Hardest Hit was the decision by more than 50 disability organisations, many of which were members of the Disability Benefits Consortium (DBC),[3] to join forces against what was considered an unprecedented 'threat' to disabled people's future. Given the involvement of virtually all the most prominent British disability non-profits, it may seem tempting to class The Hardest Hit as a 'mainstream' campaign. Yet, on closer inspection, this broad coalition appears more innovative than expected.

First, The Hardest Hit successfully combined the idea of an issue-based advocacy campaign with a specific focus on disabled people's rights. This was in contrast to the approach taken by other anti-cuts networks such as UK Uncut, which involved a very broad range of constituencies affected by the government's austerity agenda, from unemployed people to those struggling to find affordable housing and more. Although The Hardest Hit's lack of connection with the other components of the anti-cuts movement – which was confirmed also by the results of Web link analysis that are discussed below – could be interpreted as a potential weakness, it reflected the preoccupation of disability organisations with ensuring that the disability community's voice should not be overshadowed by other, better-organised or simply more vocal opponents of austerity. Arguably, The Hardest Hit's specific focus on disability welfare avoided such dispersion.

Second, The Hardest Hit brought together a wide range of disability organisations, including both professionally-run charities such as Scope, Mencap and Leonard Cheshire Disability, and member-led self-advocacy groups such as the United Kingdom's Disabled People's Council (UKDPC), Inclusion London and the National Centre for Independent Living (NCIL).

This marked a historic occurrence in British disability activism. Such a convergence of organisations had only ever happened once before, in the 'golden age' of anti-discrimination campaigns in the early 1990s, when a coalition called Rights Now! was launched (Barnes & Mercer 2001). The Hardest Hit included an even greater number of organisations than Rights Now!. In light of this, it is reasonable to assume that online technology fundamentally facilitated the development of a composite advocacy coalition. As Bimber (2003) noted with reference to Internet-enabled advocacy coalitions in the U.S., online media enable the creation of common campaign 'hubs' in which multiple organisations can collaborate free from burdensome commitments of an ideological or financial nature and without the risk of losing their individual 'brands' and identities. The Hardest Hit took advantage of this opportunity to form a common anti-austerity front while allowing its member organisations to continue with the rest of their business as usual. Online communications also eliminated the need for 'physical' campaign headquarters based at one of the participating organisations as in the case of Rights Now! (Pointon 1999, p. 227), emphasising the collaborative nature of this initiative.

In interviews, representatives of the organisations involved in The Hardest Hit repeatedly mentioned the advantages of using the Internet as a common campaign 'shop front'. As one of the communication specialists in charge of The Hardest Hit's Facebook page explained in an interview:

> It was challenging to keep everyone together but technology really helped, [...] I think we reached a fine balance between sending out joint messages and updates specific to each organisation.
> (Communications officer, U.K. charity, July 2011)

This shows that online media played a crucial role in enabling a joint and coordinated response to the then coalition government's welfare plans among established disability organisations. Strategically, this was very important as it facilitated the mobilisation of a critical mass of supporters much larger than if individual organisations had campaigned separately as they had done in previous years, as was discussed in Chapter 1. Although it was unclear whether the temporary unity that British formal disability organisations built around their anti-austerity efforts would translate into other joint initiatives and closer integration in the longer run, those interviewed seemed open to this possibility following their positive experience with The Hardest Hit. As a policy specialist from one of the member-led groups involved put it:

> I don't think there is such a thing as a 'disability movement' just now but maybe The Hardest Hit is the start of a new one.
> (Policy coordinator, U.K. self-advocacy group, July 2011)

These words effectively encapsulated the cautious optimism towards this collaborative 'experiment' that was shared by all those involved with The Hardest Hit who were interviewed for this research.

At the same time, participants also emphasised the role of the 'emergency' climate created by welfare reform proposals in promoting the use of online media for campaign purposes more generally. As a communications officer from one of The Hardest Hit's sponsor organisations explained:

> Although we would probably have set up one [social media presence] anyway, the welfare cuts undoubtedly precipitated that decision.
> (Communications officer, U.K. charity,
> September 2011)

These considerations suggest that at least two key factors contributed to the emergence of a joint campaign such as The Hardest Hit. On the one hand, Internet-based media reduced the 'cost' of collaborative advocacy for disability organisations. On the other hand, the unique nature of the U.K. welfare reform as a participation catalyst accelerated the adoption of digital technology among groups that until recently had been very reluctant to engage with social media. This is interesting also in comparison to the U.S. case, where a similar *ad hoc* coalition failed to materialise around the fight against Medicaid cuts. This seems to suggest that the nature of the issues at stake is particularly relevant in this context. These issues are explored in detail in Chapter 6. Meanwhile, at this stage it is useful to discuss The Hardest Hit's choice of online media, which revealed some fundamental traits of the relationship between formal disability organisations and digital communications.

User-Participation in the Hardest Hit's Online Repertoire

The Hardest Hit's website (Figure 3.2) clearly highlighted the issue-driven character of this joint campaign. In addition, it identified all the organisations involved in the coalition and provided links to their respective websites, which in some cases were reciprocated while in others not. For the most part, site content included key information about the welfare reform, the legislative process associated with it and details of specific campaign initiatives such as the demonstrations in March and October 2011 mentioned earlier. Users were given the opportunity to add their comments at the bottom of each piece of content posted by the organisers. Although the total number of user comments on the website was relatively low, with the majority of posts counting at most a handful of user replies, this signalled a positive attitude towards inter-creativity among the organisations involved (Meikle 2010). In particular, the website actively encouraged supporters to contribute their own content by sharing their experiences and expectations in a section titled

Figure 3.2 The Hardest Hit's homepage.

'Your Stories'. This section featured several personal narratives that chronicled the experiences of disabled people with the benefits system and illustrated the dramatic impact that welfare reform was likely to have on their lives.

The practice of soliciting personal content and posting it on a campaign website is potentially controversial, as it could be readily linked to the traditional tendency among disability non-profits to elicit 'real-life' disability stories from supporters, which can then be filtered, edited and arguably distorted in order to fit a specific campaign narrative (Barnett & Hammond 1999). Although in recent years these organisations have replaced pitiful 'personal tragedy' stories (Barnes 1992) with more positive representations of disability in their publicity material (Pointon 1999), the narratives featured on The Hardest Hit's website had been posted by those in charge of the page and not directly by users. Therefore, it was unclear to what extent disabled people had been involved in crafting the final version of their own stories, as disability scholars have advocated for the past two decades (Doddington et al. 1994, pp. 219–20).

Overall, the inclusion of personal stories of disability in The Hardest Hit's campaign tactics may seem a step backwards in terms of interactivity as it possibly gave users the impression of being co-creators of campaign messages while in fact their contributions were mediated at the central level. Nevertheless, this was not just 'business as usual'. This is because The Hardest Hit also pleaded with supporters to post their personal stories directly on its Facebook page and send personalised messages to MPs. In these cases, users had full control over their personal narratives, which appeared unedited on Facebook as well as in messages to policy-makers. These 'DIY' lobbying channels clash with the initial impression of a managed campaign. In particular, their presence in The Hardest Hit's action repertoire raises the issue of whether conflating *personal* and *political* issues in fact empowered ordinary users by enabling them to articulate their views on complex policy matters through the lens of 'everyday' rights (Turbine 2007). At the same time, the inclusion of personal stories of disability in online advocacy was not exclusive to The Hardest Hit. Instead, both the DPAC and The Broken of Britain embraced personal issues as a discussion topic on social media, a form of attack against government plans and a way to challenge widespread media stereotypes of disabled people as 'benefit cheats' (Briant et al. 2013). This made personal disability stories central to the strategies of the new wave of British disability dissent discussed in this book, as is explained in detail further on in this chapter and in Chapter 4.

With regard to social and interactive media more generally, it is interesting to note that at the height of the disability welfare reform debate The Hardest Hit had engaged in comparatively fewer of these platforms than either of the other British groups analysed in this book (see Table 3.2 for details). As of March 2012, when the welfare reform was signed into law, The Hardest Hit maintained Facebook and Flickr accounts. These allowed any user to post original contributions and start conversations, irrespective of whether they had even 'liked' these pages. This represented a leap forward for disability non-profits, which previously had considered social media almost exclusively as marketing and fundraising tools, as opposed to places for initiating a conversation with potential supporters (Trevisan 2012, 2014). That said, this campaign had no discussion forum or YouTube channel. Perhaps most strikingly for a campaign that sought to reach public decision-makers, The Hardest Hit only joined Twitter in August 2012 – months after the conclusion of the welfare reform legislative process and when the implementation of the new benefit rules was already underway – and did not run any type of email list, including e-action alerts.

One reasonable explanation for this 'minimalistic' approach to online communications would be that it was a result of the challenges involved in coordinating the very diverse range of disability organisations in this coalition and the consequent need to compromise between specific strategic requirements and individual perspectives on participatory media. Indeed, keeping the use of participatory media at a minimum was likely to have persuaded more organisations to join the coalition and lend their support. Additional reasons for The Hardest Hit's limited online media repertoire, including tactical effectiveness and resource-optimisation, were revealed in interviews with those in charge of its online operations. As a communication specialist from one of the non-profits involved explained:

> [T]here was a group of about ten charities who had a person who looked after the [Hardest Hit] website [. . .] so it was a way of sharing out the workload and we concentrated on certain channels, especially Facebook, but also used our existing accounts.
>
> (Communications officer, U.K. charity, July 2011)

Thus, although only The Hardest Hit's website and Facebook page projected a truly collaborative image, this campaign was promoted also through the existing Web outlets of its sponsor organisations including websites, Twitter and YouTube accounts, as well as specialised forums. This made up, at least in part, for the lack of a dedicated email alert list by enabling campaigners to reach users who had shown a positive inclination towards advocacy initiatives on previous occasions. In other words, The Hardest Hit's member organisations made a strategic choice to capitalise on their existing networks in order to speed the mobilisation process instead of trying to attract and activate a new 'audience' from scratch. More cynically, this approach preserved the exclusive relationship between each organisation and its existing network of supporters, ensuring that they would not shift to potential competitors. Most notably, this was demonstrated by the lack of a common action alert email list, which was meant to prevent any disputes in relation to the ownership of shared supporter information once the campaign would terminate. This signalled the intention of The Hardest Hit's sponsor organisations to curb its electronic 'legacy' in an effort to ensure the *ad hoc* and time-limited character of this collaborative initiative.

From a user's perspective, The Hardest Hit provided a limited amount of choice and flexibility with regard to online advocacy opportunities. Undoubtedly, the inclusion of customisable template messages (i.e. e-postcards/letters) to distribute to policy-makers and the decision not to offer fixed 'clicktivism' features (e.g. e-petitions, online polls) were consistent with a general tendency to move away from 'push-a-button' tactics towards more sophisticated solutions by both British and American formal disability organisations as is discussed in detail in Chapter 6. Yet, in contrast with the other British advocacy groups analysed in this book, The Hardest Hit did not experiment with readily available online media such as Twitter and other platforms to create innovative ways for disabled Internet users to participate in the campaign. For example, this coalition did not offer virtual protest pages for those unable to attend its street demonstrations. Thus, the limited range of participatory options displayed by this collaborative campaign was problematic as it fundamentally restricted the ability of its online operations to cater for the wide range of support and accessibility needs experienced by disabled users.

The Hardest Hit in Context

Although The Hardest Hit's own website blocked IssueCrawler from operating on it, it was possible to map the online environment that surrounded this collaborative campaign by using as starting points the URLs of the home pages of its most prominent member organisations. Starting from the websites of the 14 disability non-profits and member-led groups whose logos were featured on The Hardest Hit's homepage in early 2011, a co-link crawl was carried out. In addition to mapping the network surrounding some of the most high-profile British disability organisations, this generated a useful visualisation of the links leading into The Hardest Hit's website from other websites. Three key observations can be advanced on the basis of the map generated by IssueCrawler (Figure 3.3).

First, the websites of the disability organisations involved in The Hardest Hit were connected to each other by a widely distributed set of links. These connections, if not all very strong, joined together groups concerned with different impairments, as well as pan-disability organisations. Although not all the seed URLs were retained in the resulting network (UKDPC and

Figure 3.3 Online network immediately surrounding The Hardest Hit's sponsor organisations.

Inclusion London were notable exclusions), the absence of clearly defined sub-networks organised around different types of impairment clashes with the traditional image of a fragmented disability sector, which was discussed in Chapter 1. IssueCrawler cannot clarify whether these links pre-dated the establishment of The Hardest Hit coalition and therefore may have contributed to its formation, or instead were a secondary output of that very joint effort. That said, this 'snapshot' still highlighted how contact and cooperation among The Hardest Hit's member organisations had reached beyond the shared website and Facebook page discussed above.

Second, it is also interesting to note that none of these organisations served as a network 'hub'. While the Disability Alliance's website in fact received links from a number of other disability groups, this did not make it an 'intermediary' between nodes. Instead, most websites were connected to each other directly. The absence of a node in a clear central position increased the flexibility of this network and, potentially, granted it additional resilience. These are important, if somewhat unexpected, results that provide some interesting contrast with the U.S. situation, in which an online coalition of disability organisations failed to materialise, as is confirmed by hyperlink analysis discussed in Chapter 6. That said, it ought to be noted that not all the websites belonging to The Hardest Hit's member organisations included a link to the joint campaign's Web portal. This echoes the tension that some of these groups felt between the need to promote a collaborative initiative on one side and their determination to preserve their own online 'audience', which resulted in the establishment of a basic Web presence for The Hardest Hit, as discussed previously in this chapter. Similarly, an additional explanation for this is the residual fear among member-led groups to possibly become too close to professionally-run non-profits, which has affected trust between these two components of the British disability community for a long time, as is discussed in Chapter 1.

Third, government websites and those of other state agencies occupied prominent positions in this network, with www.direct.gov.uk receiving the most in-links out of all the nodes that were retrieved. Other nodes in this category included both the portals of government branches directly concerned with disability issues, such as the Department for Work and Pensions, as well as third party bodies such as the National Health Service (NHS) and the Equality and Human Rights Commission. The in-links that these institutional websites received from The Hardest Hit's member organisations resonate with the desire of the latter to be seen as legitimate representatives of disabled people and official parties in policy formulation. However, it is interesting to note also the absence from this network of institutional websites such as www.Number10.gov.uk, which at the time used to enable users to petition the government directly, or platforms such as www.theyworkforyou.com, which help users monitor parliamentary activity.

Overall, The Hardest Hit's choice of online media spoke of both the opportunities and challenges associated with seeking to conciliate the strategic priorities and tactical perspectives of a variety of disability organisations. Nevertheless, the composite nature of this coalition constituted a strategic advantage, as, historically, initiatives that bring a range of different stakeholders together around a common cause have tended to be more successful than individual efforts carried out separately by different groups (Woliver 1993, pp. 153–4). As an issue-driven alliance, The Hardest Hit followed in the footsteps of Rights Now!, its 1990s predecessor. Yet, as a technology-enabled coalition, it also constituted a more immediate and less cumbersome, if potentially very fragile, inter-organisational operation. Web link analysis also uncovered unexpected connections among many of The Hardest Hit's member organisations, somewhat mitigating the perception of the British disability advocacy sector as deeply fragmented. Furthermore, this coalition's determination to keep its Web outlets open to comments from any user denoted a positive step towards more participatory forms of e-advocacy, which break the traditional tension between the open nature of social media and the preference for controlled interaction and managed campaigns that is typical of organisations.

Arguably, The Hardest Hit's online infrastructure was designed to be effective in the short term. In spite of the optimism demonstrated by some of those interviewed for this project, this raised doubts about its suitability for long-term cooperation. In early 2016, the website and Twitter accounts of The Hardest Hit were still accessible, but appeared to have been inactive for more than a year. In addition, its Facebook page had not been updated in over six months. It would seem that, as the debate on welfare reform lost intensity after the relevant legislation received final approval in March 2012, online collaborative advocacy lost its appeal for established disability organisations in Britain. Since 2012, the U.K. government has brought forward a series of additional disability welfare changes, such as the closure of the Independent Living Fund (ILF). Although none of these measures has affected nearly as many disabled people as the switch between the Disability Living Allowance (DLA) and Personal Independence Payments (PIPs), they are nevertheless relevant to a number of disability organisations. Yet, in these cases, British formal disability organisations have chosen to campaign individually or in very small groups of two or three instead of arranging a collaborative effort comparable to The Hardest Hit.

Digitised Activists: Disabled People Against Cuts (DPAC)

DPAC (Figure 3.4) was established in October 2010 by a group of experienced disabled activists independent of formal disability organisations. Following a protest rally at the Conservative Party conference in Birmingham, these self-advocates set up a Web presence as a way to continue their work in the longer term. Many of this group's founders had been involved in the 1980s and 1990s campaigns that led to the

Figure 3.4 DPAC's homepage.

introduction of the Disability Discrimination Act (DDA) and direct payments legislation. This strongly anchored DPAC in the social model of disability and independent living tradition. Although this group's name mentions public expenditure cuts explicitly, DPAC used its online outlets to present itself as 'something more' than just an anti-austerity movement. Having turned down an invitation to join The Hardest Hit in March 2011, DPAC activists considered themselves as a more genuine grassroots alternative to that coalition.

These positions echoed the scepticism that some disability writers continue to express with regard to the effectiveness of the participatory practices that many disability non-profits adopted in recent years, as discussed in Chapter 1. In an interview carried out for this book, one of DPAC's founders explained that:

> DPAC is focused on human rights for disabled people, we started because of the austerity programme but things are much broader than that. This government has an ideological stance and we hope to bring disabled people together to fight that.
>
> (DPAC founder, June 2011)

DPAC's ambition to go beyond benefit cuts was apparent at its first national conference, which took place in London on 29 October 2011 and covered a broad range of disability-related issues in addition to the welfare system, from disability hate crime to transport policy. On this occasion, conference participants also voted to elect a steering group tasked with overseeing the coordination of further campaigns in these other areas. This activist spirit was reflected in DPAC's choice of online media, which also appeared to be geared towards fostering maximum inclusivity.

Inclusivity and Action in DPAC's Online Repertoire

In addition to a website complete with a blog section, DPAC's Web presence at the height of the U.K. welfare reform debate included a Facebook group page and both Twitter and Flickr accounts (see Table 3.2 for details). In early 2016, this had expanded to include a YouTube account and a Facebook 'fan' page.[4] A close look revealed that this online media repertoire was in line with the ethos and *modus operandi* typical of new social movements (della Porta 2005), for which small, less resourceful and loose activist groups tend to approach new media in a more participatory way than established governmental and non-profit organisations (Mosca & della Porta 2009; Pickerill 2004). This had the potential to be especially conducive to meaningful interaction between ordinary users and the steering group mentioned above. In particular, DPAC's Facebook 'group' page remained consistently more popular than its 'fan' page, counting more than 17,000 members in 2016. The use of a Facebook group page bestowed great pluralistic potential upon DPAC's social media presence. Unlike Facebook 'fan' pages, Facebook group pages are managed jointly by a set of users who are identified through their personal screen-names rather than represented collectively by a faceless administrator account. This enhances accountability and facilitates communication between page administrators and supporters (Kavada 2012). In contrast, both the other groups examined here run a Facebook 'fan' page, which Facebook itself identifies as a tool for 'marketing' and 'brand growth' rather than community building.[5]

Furthermore, DPAC had set up 'virtual protest' pages and 'protest maps' on its website and Facebook pages to complement its own street demonstrations and other events it endorsed, such as the march of the Trades Union Congress (TUC) against public expenditure cuts on 26 March 2011. Virtual protest pages provided users unable to attend protests in person with opportunities to post messages and pin their location as alternative ways to take part. While arguably unsophisticated from a technical point of view, virtual protest pages enabled disabled users who were prevented from attending a protest in person by transport, financial or other barriers to voice their opposition to welfare changes and, more generally, feel part of a collective movement. The inclusion of these tools in DPAC's online repertoire was a testimony to the determination of this group to use new media technologies to boost disabled people's political agency. As one of DPAC's founders explained:

> [P]articipation online and in person are of equal value, [. . .] in fact it may even be more important to participate online as the [news media] coverage of the 26th of March [TUC] march did not even show disabled people.
>
> (DPAC founder, June 2011)

Strategically, DPAC considered online and in-person participation to be on the same level. This kind of statement was remarkable considering that only a couple of years earlier the consensus among disability organisations was that online media were inferior campaign and communication tools compared to more traditional channels (Trevisan 2014).

It is interesting to note that, while the Welfare Reform Bill was already at its final parliamentary reading in early 2012, DPAC did not mention personal disability stories on any of its Web outlets, which also did not feature customisable template messages for supporters to contact policy-makers (Table 3.2). This was at odds with the approach to personal stories taken by both The Hardest Hit, which was discussed previously, and The Broken of Britain, which is discussed later in this chapter. Some disability scholars have long called for disability activism to 'give voice' to disabled people's personal experiences (Morris 1992) and expose the political nature of 'everyday' oppression (Fawcett 2000). However, activists have tended to be wary of promoting the use of individual narratives for fear that these could be interpreted or re-elaborated in ways that support disabled people's victimisation instead of empowerment. Although this has always been an issue of framing rather than a blanket 'ban' on personal stories *per se*, DPAC started off its anti-welfare reform campaign by sticking to tradition and, at least at first, avoided customisable campaign resources that would encourage disabled supporters to contribute personal stories in their own words. This choice seemed to suggest that e-advocacy can be shaped by pre-existing principles just as much as online communications promise to change activism.

However, DPAC's position on the inclusion of personal stories in campaign material evolved after the Welfare Reform Act was passed in March 2012. Towards the end of summer 2012, DPAC organised a series of high-profile protests against Atos Origin, the information technology (IT) firm that at that time was in charge of carrying out the controversial Work Capability Assessments on Employment and Support Allowance (ESA) claimants and that had been contracted by the U.K. government to carry out PIP eligibility assessments starting in April 2013. These protests were timed to occur in conjunction with major events in the calendar of the London Paralympic Games – of which Atos was an official sponsor – and, for this reason, were dubbed the 'Atos Games'. This was a strategic move from DPAC designed to capitalise on unprecedented levels of mass media interest for disability issues during the 'home turf' Paralympics (Hodges et al. 2014) by exposing the dissonance between the celebratory atmosphere of the Games and the harsh reality of disabled people's everyday lives at a time of austerity. This choice paid off, as the 'Atos Games' received far more coverage in the British news media than any previous DPAC event. This coverage included a series of personal stories that resonated with the overarching narrative of discrimination and oppression sponsored by DPAC (Pearson & Trevisan 2015; Trevisan 2015).

More recently, DPAC launched a campaign against the closure of the ILF in March 2013. As part of this effort, DPAC posted a series of disabled people's personal stories of poverty, discrimination and loss of independence on one of its blog sites.[6] This was consistent with the approach taken by several other disability groups, from Scope to the Spartacus Network, which also included personal stories on their Web pages discussing the closure of the ILF. Although this is not the place for an in-depth examination of the content, tone and style of personal stories, this episode represents an important shift in DPAC's e-advocacy strategy. While all of DPAC's ILF stories were posted by the site's administrators, suggesting that core activists were in control of the frames used to describe disabled people's experiences, the experimentation with this new tactic confirmed that the action repertoire of British disability groups is indeed in flux. Disability rights self-advocates, including those with past experience in the disability rights movement and rooted in social model principles, appear willing to consider new and possibly controversial approaches in order to harness the full potential of digital advocacy.

DPAC in Context

The results of snowball link analysis with IssueCrawler (Figure 3.5) also corroborated the impression of DPAC as a 'digitised' successor of the participatory spirit of member-led disabled people's organisations. In particular, one of DPAC's protest blog sites (www.disabledpeopleprotest. wordpress.com) linked to the websites of several other anti-austerity groups. These included the Trade Unions, online petition platforms such as Beyond Clicktivism and 38Degrees, as well as grassroots collectives such as Women Against the Cuts, Right to Work and Benefits Claimants Fightback. Although some of these links were indirect (chiefly routed through www. marchforthealternative.org.uk, the website of the TUC anti-cuts march), they nonetheless showed that DPAC was surrounded by a fairly homogeneous network in which a majority of nodes was inspired by progressive ideals and sought to promote solidarity among the different social groups affected by welfare reforms and reductions in public spending more generally. This was important, as in the past British disability groups had overlooked opportunities to connect with other under-represented social groups despite there being scope for coordinated advocacy efforts (Priestley

Figure 3.5 Online network immediately surrounding DPAC.

2002). Furthermore, this was also in contrast with The Hardest Hit's network that is discussed above, which did not connect to the other components of the anti-austerity movement.

In addition, none of the websites of established disability organisations featured in DPAC's network except for those of specialised disability news providers such as www.disabilitynow.org.uk and www.disabilitynewsservice. com. This was in line with DPAC's strained relationship with many of the organisations that sponsored The Hardest Hit campaign, as well as with its overarching criticism of disability non-profits. More broadly, and again in stark contrast to The Hardest Hit's network, the websites of state actors were peripheral in the network that surrounded DPAC. Only two such websites featured in this map (www.dwp. gov.uk; www.parliament. uk), neither of which was directly connected to DPAC's pages.

Altogether, these findings highlighted a clear separation between DPAC on one side and established disability pressure groups and state institutions on the other. This not only confirmed the breakdown in communications between DPAC activists and 'professional' disability advocates emphasised by the refusal of the former to endorse The Hardest Hit coalition in March 2011, but suggested also a sceptical attitude towards representative institutions and the routine of policy-making. Instead, DPAC were part of a wider activist community that included women's groups, the Trade Unions and several other anti-cuts groups that exhibited some typical traits of a dissent network. In particular, most interconnected anti-cuts groups strongly preferred a contentious action repertoire to lobbying channels such as consultations and briefings with policy-makers.

Finally, it is also important to discuss the prominent position that social media platforms occupied in this network. Twitter received the highest number of in-links out of all the websites retrieved in this hyperlink crawl, with Facebook coming third behind DPAC's own blog (www.disabled-peopleprotest.wordpress.com). This reflected DPAC's intention to stretch its Web presence across multiple online spaces simultaneously, as was discussed above. In addition, it was interesting to note that the links to Twitter in this network focused specifically on an account that belonged to one of the founders of The Broken of Britain (www.twitter.com/Bendy-Girl). Although hyperlinks do not necessarily express endorsement (Rogers 2010a), the amount of connections to this Twitter account that were found in this network certainly indicated a high level of interest for the person behind it. At the same time, this also suggested that DPAC, despite being opposed to formal disability organisations, was not isolated from the broader context of disability activism, and instead entertained relation-ships with emerging actors in this area.

In light of these considerations and given its self-advocacy grassroots nature, DPAC appeared to be the group among those explored in this book that most closely fitted Tilly's (1999) classic definition of a social move-ment group, which:

> [C]onsists of a sustained challenge to power holders in the name of a population living under the jurisdiction of those power holders by means of repeated public displays of that population's worthiness, unity, numbers, and commitment.
>
> (p. 257)

In particular, DPAC's use of online media to support street protest, as well as its roots in the social model of disability and conflicted relationship with 'household' disability non-profits, was reminiscent of some key historic traits of the British disabled people's movement. That said, DPAC also engaged with a wider range of social media platforms than, for example, The Hardest Hit as shown by its simultaneous approach to Facebook, Twitter, YouTube and Flickr. The inclusion of personal disability stories in its 2012 and 2013 campaigns was part of this trend too, although DPAC cautiously adopted this tactic only after other groups had experimented with it successfully. Furthermore, the use of digital protest pages as alternative channels for disabled Internet users to express dissent was a testimony to DPAC's deter-mination to take advantage of the participatory features of social media in order to open up its initiatives to as many supporters as possible, both disabled and non-. This traced a picture of DPAC's 'digitised' activists as open to considering new tactics, but at the same time also committed to using new media in ways consistent with a pre-existing repertoire of contention primarily centred on protest and disruption. An in-depth discussion of DPAC's use of Facebook sheds more light on this point in the next two chapters.

Digital Action Networks: The Broken of Britain

The Broken of Britain (Figure 3.6) was an anti-austerity campaign launched in October 2010. Three main elements set this campaign apart from both The Hardest Hit and DPAC. First, The Broken of Britain's founders were a small group of disabled self-advocates who were too young to have participated in the anti-discrimination campaigns of the 1980s and 1990s. Second, many of them had blogged about their daily lives and experiences with the welfare system for a number of years prior to 2010. Their blogs included intimate accounts told in the first person, which somewhat preceded the incorporation of personal stories of disability in e-advocacy strategies. However, this was the first time that they leveraged their familiarity with new media technologies and digital storytelling to mount a coordinated effort. For many, the U.K. welfare reform was the first major experience of advocacy and collective action altogether. Third, The Broken of Britain operated exclusively online. Although this group occasionally endorsed offline initiatives promoted by others (for example, some of

Figure 3.6 The Broken of Britain's homepage.

The Hardest Hit's events as is discussed in detail later), it never organised any in-person events of its own. The fundamental role that the Internet played, not only in this group's action repertoire but also in its very existence, made The Broken of Britain a truly 'digital native' campaign. As one of its founders said in an interview for this book:

> [I]t was all down to social media: most of us have never met and when this [The Broken of Britain] started off nobody had met in person.
> (The Broken of Britain founder, July 2011)

For these reasons, it could be argued that The Broken of Britain's founders represented a new generation of disabled activists, which traced its roots in the enthusiastic avant-garde of early disabled technology-adopters that Sheldon (2004) identified just over a decade ago and has since developed the skills and determination to embark on high-profile political campaigning. The Broken of Britain was a relatively short-lived campaign, as it effectively ceased to operate in November 2011, when the debate on the U.K. Welfare Reform Bill was still on-going. While some of the reasons for this sudden stop are explored in the next chapters, it is important to note that this campaign left behind an influential legacy. As the first-ever online-only disability rights campaign in the U.K., The Broken of Britain introduced new tactics to the repertoire of disability advocacy that were then copied by other groups. In addition, many of The Broken of Britain's founders continued to be involved in other prominent online disability rights collectives such as the Spartacus Network and Where's the Benefit. This suggested that, although The Broken of Britain exhausted its course as a coherent campaign within about a year, its experience went on to influence British disability advocacy in the longer term through what Chadwick (2007) has defined as 'sedimentary networks', i.e. those links between e-activists that are created during moments of particularly intense activity and can re-emerge at a later stage in conjunction with other catalysing events.

The Broken of Britain's technology-savvy disabled Millennials displayed an originally pragmatic approach to both new media platforms and disability activism compared to the other groups that campaigned against changes to disability welfare. This was recognised by one of the representatives of formal disability organisations interviewed for this book, who explained that:

> Groups like this one [The Broken of Britain] are leading the way in terms of online campaigning.
> (Campaigns officer, U.K. charity, September 2011)

Crucially, The Broken of Britain's founders were a progressive-minded set of individuals who, under different circumstances, might have joinied a group such as DPAC. Yet, the Internet provided them with the space and tools to set up a separate campaign, capitalising on their direct experience with blogging about disability, the NHS, the welfare system and personal life to experiment with novel advocacy tactics. One of the core organisers interviewed for this book emphasised the pivotal role that technology played in providing disabled citizens with a voice, explaining that:

> Five years ago disabled people didn't have the ability to communicate this freely - if you wanted to meet other disabled people you had to go to a day [care] centre whereas with the internet and social media we can reach out to each other in other ways. [...] No-one sees it [an Internet connection] as a luxury payment, it's a lifeline, literally a lifeline.
>
> (The Broken of Britain founder, July 2011)

At the same time, technology was praised for providing a viable alternative to established disability organisations, in particular professionally run non-profits, which:

> [H]ave let us [disabled people] down, they are still not doing their jobs properly and it was about time that a new generation [of self-advocates] came forward and took charge [of representing disabled people].
>
> (The Broken of Britain founder, July 2011)

The Broken of Britain maintained a strict focus on disability welfare issues throughout its entire lifespan as a campaign. One of the founders explained that the anger sparked by the then coalition government's plans to overhaul DLA had prompted them to mobilise other people, as:

> [I]f they [the government] hadn't gone this far [with disability welfare changes], the reaction wouldn't have been there but people immediately realised that this [opposing the welfare reform], over-dramatic though it seems, is fighting to carry on existing because the more support [money] is taken away, the more of us will find it impossible to carry on [living]. David Cameron makes a lot of his Big Society and pulling everyone together and the reality is that he's done an amazing job at pulling everyone together, absolutely amazing: we're united against him!
>
> (The Broken of Britain founder, July 2011)

Thus, The Broken of Britain sought neither to expand into a more organic movement with a broader agenda, nor to formalise its governance structure. Indeed, the issue-focused nature of this campaign raised doubts with regard to its sustainability in the long term. Nevertheless, this approach was consistent not only with a general tendency for contemporary activism to be increasingly issue-driven, as was discussed in the introductory chapters, but also with Earl and Kimport's (2011) idea of 'lone-wolf organisers' (p. 205), according to which digital media have diminished the importance of having a shared identity and strong ideological ties for grassroots advocacy. The innovative character of this group was reflected in its online media repertoire, which sought to combine new ways for supporters to take part in the campaign while catering to a range of users with different needs.

Inclusivity Meets Grassroots Innovation

Through their choice of online media, The Broken of Britain's founders demonstrated profound awareness of accessibility issues and a clear determination to help fellow disabled users to overcome barriers to online advocacy. This group's website, which incidentally was set up as a blog, explicitly stated that the aim of this approach was to cater for the diverse needs of disabled Internet users by providing multiple online options for them and their non-disabled supporters to voice their concerns. This was achieved in several ways.

In addition to keeping both its website and Facebook page open to contributions from any user, The Broken of Britain also took advantage of social media to promote participatory lobbying tactics that enabled supporters to co-create the campaign narrative by sharing their individual stories and opinions on selected dates during the welfare reform debate. While customisable template messages addressed to policymakers similar to the ones used by The Hardest Hit were indeed part of this strategy (see Table 3.2 above), The Broken of Britain's online repertoire stretched well beyond these and provided greater choice, personalisation and accessibility in online advocacy. Typical examples of innovative tactics included a 'blog swarm' organised to coincide with the conclusion of the public consultation on DLA reform in February 2011. This asked users to 'broadcast' their experiences of the welfare system in personal blog posts. With another strategic move, The Broken of Britain launched specific Twitter hashtags such as #TwitterStories and #ProjectV, which were designed to create a sense of commonality while also capturing the attention of policy-makers and journalists on key dates throughout the welfare reform's legislative process. Again, these Twitter campaigns sought to exploit the persuasive power of personal stories of disability while at the same time accommodating the needs of disabled Internet users:

> [W]ith debilitating conditions that impair their ability to concentrate on standard long-form blog posts.
> (The Broken of Britain's website, February 2011)

In addition, another distinctive feature of The Broken of Britain's approach to online advocacy was the lack of virtual protest pages from their action repertoire. This corroborated the impression that this group was less interested than groups such as DPAC in extending traditional repertoires of contention online and instead focused on developing more novel forms of disability rights advocacy.

In light of this, The Broken of Britain constituted the most innovative group among those examined in this book. Its online action repertoire demonstrated both the ability to be creative with new media technologies and a profound awareness of the need to diversify e-advocacy options in order to engage disabled Internet users with a range of needs. At the same time, this also revealed a lack of qualms in breaking with some traditional aspects of disability activism. Again, personal stories emerged as an increasingly important trademark of multi-platform disability advocacy that used blogs, Twitter and customisable messages to connect personal narratives to a political struggle. This was without doubt a controversial approach. However, The Broken of Britain handled this element of its e-action repertoire in a fundamentally different way from The Hardest Hit's 'Your Stories' web page and even DPAC's ILF stories blog posts in 2013.

In this online-only campaign, the use of personal stories of disability was not centrally coordinated and narratives were not edited to fit a single campaign message. Instead, The Broken of Britain invited its supporters to post their stories on their own social media profiles and used a hashtag to link all this content together and back to the campaign. This approach provided opportunities for personalisation within a group effort. These personalised action frames (Bennett & Segerberg 2011) were especially relevant for users who might feel uncomfortable with traditional contentious action tactics such as those promoted by DPAC, but at the same time were distrustful also of mainstream disability organisations such as those involved in The Hardest Hit coalition. This suggested that The Broken of Britain operated in an intermediate space between more militant social movement groups on one side and 'professional' advocates on the other. Crucially, this afforded the young self-advocates behind The Broken of Britain opportunities to capture and engage new audiences, both disabled and non-, as is explained in detail in Chapters 4 and 5, which discuss The Broken of Britain's use of Facebook.

The promotion of less disruptive digital alternatives to traditional protest politics had three main benefits. First, this online repertoire had the potential to attract a larger number of supporters than those who tend to identify with the typical tactics of the disabled people's movement. Second, online participation could help this group shake off the image of self-advocates as 'troublemakers'. Third, it supported the empowerment of disabled Internet users by advocating in favour of disabled people's direct representation free from intermediary organisations. By pursuing these strategies, The Broken of Britain sought to position itself as a legitimate stakeholder, representative group and 'responsible' counterpart in the policy-making process. This stance was explicitly reiterated in Facebook discussions between this group's core-organisers and its online supporters, as is explained in detail in Chapter 5.

This attempt to appear as a moderate, no-nonsense self-advocacy group was well received by traditional news outlets such as *The Guardian*, *The Independent* and the BBC's website, which ran feature stories on The Broken of Britain between late 2010 and early 2011. Given that established news media organisations continue to command great influence over the policy-making process, especially in conjunction with very controversial issues (Koch-Baumgartner & Voltmer 2010, p. 223), this provided The Broken of Britain with a strategic advantage over other disability rights groups. In comparison, DPAC was virtually ignored by the news media until it organised its 'Atos Games' in conjunction with the London Paralympics between August and September 2012 (Trevisan 2015). Overall, this made for a pragmatic and original use of online media by The Broken of Britain, which had the potential to channel outrage and dissent into initiatives aimed at strengthening this group's visibility, reputation and therefore influence over public decision-makers (Burstein et al. 1995).

The Broken of Britain in Context

Unfortunately, the way in which The Broken of Britain's website was designed prevented Web crawling software from operating on it. For this reason, a detailed map of the online networks surrounding this group could not be generated. However, the way in which this group interacted with the events sponsored by other campaigns and organisations provided useful insights that suggested that it was far from isolated. Instead, its relationships with other disability groups seemed driven by pragmatism. In particular, The Broken of Britain formally endorsed The Hardest Hit's first march against the disability benefits changes that took place on 11 May 2011 in London. True to its ethos as an online-only initiative, The Broken of Britain did not take part in organising the march directly. Instead, it helped by publicising the event on its Web outlets and by pleading with its network of supporters to take part. This demonstrated that, despite expressing dissatisfaction with disability charities in the interviews carried out for this book, this group's founders were not necessarily prejudiced towards other disability groups. Instead, The Broken of Britain was likely to assess any external initiatives on a case-by-case basis and consider their potential contribution to a common cause. At the same time, the decision to lend 'external' support to The Hardest Hit and avoid any direct involvement in street demonstrations signalled this group's intention to preserve its independence and protect its reputation as a 'responsible' campaign and credible counterpart in negotiations with government.

In light of this, it could be argued that The Broken of Britain's founders exploited their familiarity with new media technologies – in particular blogging – and personal experience as disabled individuals to launch a new 'genre' in British disability activism. While this group's online action repertoire incorporated elements typical of both social movement groups and professional lobbying organisations, it also represented more than a mere 'hybrid' between those two. This is because The Broken of Britain's online repertoire provided supporters with choice and flexibility in a similar fashion to the Web presence of more established advocacy organisations, both digital-native and non-, operating in other areas, which foster a range of different participatory styles and an expanded notion of 'membership' (Bimber et al. 2012, pp. 170–1). Thus, The Broken of Britain promoted self-advocacy for disabled people, but in a very different form from how we have known it so far. This group's online initiatives were underpinned by a pragmatic attitude that encouraged its founders to disregard customary approaches to disability rights activism in order to exploit the full potential of online media to try and stop what was seen as an extraordinary, long-term threat to the livelihoods and fundamental rights of disabled people in the U.K.

That said, it should be noted that, just as Internet usage is not a predictor of online civic engagement in itself (Nisbet et al. 2012; Norris 2001), providing online participatory tools does not necessarily guarantee that disabled users can become empowered through them. This raised the question of whether The Broken of Britain's innovative approach effectively enabled ordinary users to become meaningful participants in the policy process or, instead, generated what Schudson (Schudson 2011) has defined as 'monitorial' citizenship, i.e. the ability to 'keep an eye on the scene' and, possibly, discuss it with others, while at the same time considering the political 'game' to be the prerogative of 'experts' (Schudson 2006), in this case core campaigners. For example, it was particularly interesting to note that access to The Broken of Britain's forum was restricted to authorised forum members (Table 3.2). This was a notable exception in what otherwise constituted a participatory online repertoire and suggested that core campaigners felt the need to limit and control user-input to specific discussions. While in itself the idea of monitorial citizenship does not have disempowering connotations, this attempt to restrict the ability of ordinary supporters to take part in certain intra-group discussions was at odds with the ethos of inclusive citizenship as defined in Chapter 1, which calls for 'participatory parity' as a fundamental pre-requisite for the attainment of full citizenship. This called for a deeper investigation of how The Broken of Britain's supporters used the e-participation channels provided by the campaign founders, as well as the need to shed light on the relationship between core campaigners and 'ordinary' supporters.

Conclusions

The British disability movement appeared substantially revitalised in the wake of the welfare reform debate that took place between 2010 and 2012. Both technology and the intense atmosphere of crisis that surrounded disability benefit changes played crucial roles in this process as it was the combination of these two elements that lay the foundations for some important renewal in British disability politics. This brought change across the entire spectrum of disability advocacy in the U.K. By supporting a campaign such as The Hardest Hit, online media made temporary unity possible for a broad range of disability non-profits and established membership groups that had tended to act individually over the previous two decades. In addition, new media technologies also aided the formation of new groups, some of which were centred around experienced self-advocates, while others were launched by a new generation of disabled activists who took a pragmatic approach to e-advocacy more generally.

Broadly speaking, the Web presence of all these groups stretched across many of the same platforms, most notably Facebook and Twitter. This signalled a general tendency for disability rights advocates to move away from websites and custom-built forums in order to embrace readily available social media platforms, thus lowering the costs of digital activism and reaching a greater number of potential supporters across the country. At the same time, however, subtle but important differences separated the case studies discussed in this chapter, which supported three specific styles of grassroots digital advocacy. The Hardest Hit favoured a somewhat 'minimalist' approach to technology while also promoting the use of personal stories in customisable messages to policymakers. DPAC sought to import the traditional repertoire of contention online but at the same time was open to learning from the innovations introduced by others too. The Broken of Britain's core organisers capitalised on their familiarity with technology to design targeted campaigns for supporters with different needs to join through multiple types of social media (see Figure 3.7 for a summary of online features unique to each group/network).

Such a combination of platforms, tools and tactics contributed additional pluralism to the online initiatives that opposed changes to the disability welfare system in the U.K. between 2010 and 2012. In particular, it expanded the range of options available to the potential supporters of these groups, who were presented with multiple ways to participate in advocacy efforts. Some of these options were fairly demanding while others less so, but nearly all of them required some type of original input and were never restricted to simply 'pushing a button' to send out a standardised message. This was consistent with a broader trend in contemporary advocacy, which emphasises choice for supporters and promotes an 'entrepreneurial' participatory style (Bimber et al. 2012).

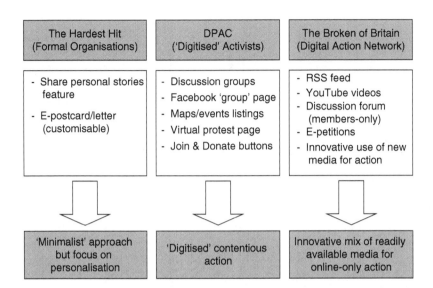

Figure 3.7 Online features unique to each U.K. group/network at the peak of the welfare reform controversy.

The relationship between British disability advocacy and new media technologies is in flux. All types of groups, including those most closely aligned with traditional forms of activism, have shown to be both capable and willing to learn from the experience of others, as well as their own, to renew their actions. The group typology illustrated in this chapter provides a useful matrix to understand the grassroots actors that populate the struggle for disability rights and their relationship with technology. Yet, new groups – or even new types of groups – may emerge and others may lose relevance as time passes. Despite the amount of choice that e-advocacy offers to potential online supporters of disability rights groups, this evolutionary dynamic raises some important questions. Most crucially, did the online strategies of groups such as The Hardest Hit, DPAC and The Broken of Britain effectively deliver on their potential for interactivity and user-participation? This question is intimately tied to two other issues, namely: the distribution of power and decision-making opportunities within each of these groups; as well as the ways in which their supporters used the e-advocacy platforms that were made available to them. These issues are discussed in the next two chapters through the analysis of conversation threads drawn from the Facebook pages of each of the three case studies examined here. This type of analysis opened a direct window onto naturally-occurring conversations between core organisers and the 'rank-and-file' supporters of these groups, generating valuable insights into their nature and ability to promote inclusive citizenship for disabled Internet users.

Notes

1 'Disabled', 'disability', 'welfare', 'cuts', 'reform', 'DLA/disability living allowance', 'ESA/employment and support allowance', 'consultation', 'protest', 'demonstration', 'campaign', 'activist' and 'advocate' were searched in different combinations.
2 See: www.issuecrawler.net (accessed 10 June 2016).
3 The DBC brings together over 60 disability organisations, including both member-led disabled people's organisations (DPOs) and traditional charities. Although member organisations generally run their own individual campaigns, the consortium facilitates discussion on disability welfare and occasionally acts on behalf of its members. The vast majority of the groups and organisations involved in The Hardest Hit were DBC affiliates. For more information, see: www.disabilitybenefitsconsortium.wordpress.com.
4 DPAC set up a Facebook 'fan' page in addition to its existing 'group' page in the second half of 2011.
5 See: www.facebook.com/create/pages (accessed 10 June 2016).
6 See: www.campaigndpac.wordpress.com (accessed 12 March 2016).

References

Barnes, C., 1992. *Disabling Imagery and the Media: An Exploration of the Principles for Media Representations of Disabled People*, Halifax: BCODP with Rayburn.

Barnes, C. & Mercer, G., 2001. The Politics of Disability and the Struggle for Change. In L. Barton, ed. *Disability Politics and the Struggle for Change*. London: David Fulton Publishers, pp. 11–23.

Barnett, J. & Hammond, S., 1999. Representing Disability in Charity Promotions. *Journal of Community & Applied Social Psychology*, 9(4), pp. 309–314.

Baulieu, A., 2005. Sociable Hyperlinks: An Ethnographic Approach to Connectivity. In C. Hine, ed. *Virtual Methods: Issues in Social Research on the Internet*. Oxford/NY: Berg, pp. 183–198.

Bennett, W.L. & Segerberg, A., 2011. Digital Media and the Personalization of Collective Action. *Information, Communication & Society*, 14(6), pp. 770–799.

Bimber, B., 2003. *Information and American Democracy: Technology in the Evolution of Political Power*, Cambridge: Cambridge University Press.

Bimber, B., Flanagin, A.J. & Stohl, C., 2012. *Collective Action in Organizations: Interaction and Engagement in an Era of Technological Change*, Cambridge: Cambridge University Press.

Briant, E., Watson, N. & Philo, G., 2013. Reporting Disability in the Age of Austerity: The Changing Face of Media Representation of Disability and Disabled People in the United Kingdom and the Creation of New 'Folk Devils'. *Disability & Society*, 28(6), pp. 874–889.

Burstein, P., 1999. Social Movements and Public Policy. In M. Giugni, D. McAdam, & C. Tilly, eds. *How Social Movements Matter*. Minneapolis/London: University of Minnesota Press, pp. 3–21.

Burstein, P., Einwohner, R. & Hollander, J., 1995. The Success of Political Movements: A Bargaining Perspective. In C. J. Jenkins & B. Klandermans, eds. *The Politics of Social Protest: Comparative Perspectives on States and Social Movements*. Minneapolis: University of Minnesota Press, pp. 275–294.

Campbell, J.L., 2005. Where do we stand? Common Mechanisms in Organizations and Social Movements Research. In G.F. Davis, D. McAdam, W.R. Scott & M.N. Zald, eds. *Social Movements and Organization Theory*. Cambridge: Cambrige University Press, pp. 41–68.

Chadwick, A., 2007. Digital Network Repertoires and Organizational Hybridity. *Political Communication*, 24(3), pp. 283–301.

―――― 2012. Web 2.0: New Challenges for the Study of E-Democracy in an Era of Informational Exuberance. In S. Coleman & P. Shane, eds. *Citizenship and Vulnerability*. Cambridge, MA: The MIT Press, pp. 45–73.

Dahlberg, L., 2004. Net-Public Sphere Research: Beyond The 'First Phase'. *Javnost-The Public*, 11(1), pp. 27–43.

della Porta, D., 2005. Deliberation in Movement: Why and How to Study Deliberative Democracy and Social Movements. *Acta Politica*, 40(3), pp. 336–350.

Doddington, K., Jones, R.S.P. & Miller, B.Y., 1994. Are Attitudes to People with Learning Disabilities Negatively Influenced by Charity Advertising? *Disability & Society*, 9(2), pp. 207–222.

Earl, J. & Kimport, K., 2011. *Digitally Enabled Social Change: Activism in the Internet Age*, Cambridge, MA: The MIT Press.

Fawcett, B., 2000. *Feminist Perspectives on Disability*, Harlow: Pearson Education Limited.

Fossato, F., Lloyd, J. & Verkhovsky, A., 2008. *The Web That Failed: How Opposition Politics and Independent Inititiatives Are Failing on the Internet in Russia*. Available at: http://reutersinstitute.politics.ox.ac.uk/publication/web-failed (accessed 28 February 2016).

George, A. & Bennett, A., 2004. *Case Studies and Theory Development in the Social Sciences*, Cambridge, MA: MIT Press.

Gibson, R.K. & Ward, S., 2000. A Proposed Methodology for Studying the Function and Effectiveness of Party and Candidate Web Sites. *Social Science Computer Review*, 18(3), pp. 301–319.

Gibson, R.K., Margolis, M., Resnick, D. & Ward, S., 2003. Election Campaigning on the WWW in the USA and UK: A Comparative Analysis. *Party Politics*, 9(1), pp. 47–75.

Gibson, R.K., Gillan, K., Greffet, F., Lee, B.J. & Ward, S., 2013. Party Organizational Change and ICTs: The Growth of a Virtual Grassroots? *New Media & Society*, 15(1), pp. 31–51.

Gillan, K., 2009. The UK Anti-War Movement Online. *Information, Communication & Society*, 12(1), pp. 25–43.

Gillan, K., Pickerill, J. & Webster, F., 2008. *Anti-War Activism in the Information Age*, Basingstoke: Palgrave Macmillan.

Hindman, M., 2009. *The Myth of Digital Democracy*, Princeton, NJ: Princeton University Press.

Hodges, C., Jackson, D., Scullion, R., Thompson, S. & Molesworth, M., 2014. *Tracking Changes in Everyday Experiences of Disability and Disability Sport Within the Context of the London 2012 Paralympics*, Bournemouth: Bournemouth University.

Jansen, B.J. & Spink, A., 2005. An Analysis of Web Searching by European Alltheweb.com Users. *Information Processing & Management*, 41(2), pp. 361–381.

———— 2006. How Are We Searching the World Wide Web? A Comparison of Nine Search Engine Transaction Logs. *Information Processing & Management*, 42(1), pp. 248–263.

Kavada, A., 2012. Engagement, Bonding, and Identity Across Multiple Platforms: Avaaz on Facebook, YouTube, and MySpace. *MedieKultur: Journal of Media and Communication Research*, 28(52), p. 21.

Koch-Baumgartner, S. & Voltmer, K., 2010. Conclusion: The Interplay of Mass Communication and Political Decision Making – Policy Matters! In S. Koch-Baumgartner & K. Voltmer, eds. *Public Policy and the Mass Media: The Interplay of Mass Communication and Political Decision Making*. London: Routledge, pp. 215–227.

Lilleker, D. & Jackson, N., 2011. *Political Campaigning, Elections, and the Internet: Comparing the UK, U.S., France and Germany*, London: Routledge.

Mager, A., 2012. Algorithmic Ideology. *Information, Communication & Society*, 15(5), pp. 769–787.

McMillan, S.J., 2002. A Four-Part Model of Cyber-Interactivity Some Cyber-Places Are More Interactive Than Others. *New Media & Society*, 4(2), pp. 271–291.

Meikle, G., 2010. Intercreativity: Mapping Online Activism. In J. Husinger, L. Klastrup, & M. M. Allen, eds. *International Handbook of Internet Research*. Dordrecht: Springer, pp. 363–377.

Morris, J., 1992. Personal and Political: A Feminist Perspective on Researching Physical Disability. *Disability, Handicap & Society*, 7(2), pp. 157–166.

Mosca, L. & della Porta, D., 2009. Unconventional Politics Online: Internet and the Global Justice Movement. In D. della Porta, ed. *Democracy in Social Movements*. Basingstoke: Palgrave Macmillan, pp. 194–216.

Nisbet, E.C., Stoycheff, E. & Pearce, K.E., 2012. Internet Use and Democratic Demands: A Multinational, Multilevel Model of Internet Use and Citizen Attitudes About Democracy. *Journal of Communication*, 62(2), pp. 249–265.

Norris, P., 2001. *The Digital Divide: Civic Engagement, Information Poverty and the Internet Worldwide*, Cambridge: Cambridge University Press.

Oates, S., 2012. Political Challengers or Political Outcasts?: Comparing Online Communication for the Communist Party of the Russian Federation and the British Liberal Democrats. *Europe-Asia Studies*, 64(8), pp. 1460–1485.

———— 2013. *Revolution Stalled: The Political Limits of the Internet in the Post-Soviet Sphere*, New York: Oxford University Press.

Olsson, T., 2008. The Practises of Internet Networking – A Resource for Alternative Political Movements. *Information, Communication & Society*, 11(5), pp. 659–674.

Pearson, C. & Trevisan, F., 2015. Disability Activism in the New Media Ecology: Campaigning Strategies in the Digital Era. *Disability & Society*, 30(6), pp. 924–940.

Pickerill, J., 2004. Rethinking Political Participation: Experiments in Internet Activism in Australia and Britain. In R. Gibson, A. Römmele, & S. Ward, eds. *Electronic Democracy: Mobilisation, Organisation and Participation via New ICTs*. London: Routledge, pp. 170–193.

Pointon, A., 1999. Out of the Closet: New Images of Disability in the Civil Rights Campaign. In B. Franklin, ed. *Social Policy, the Media and Misrepresentation*. London: Routledge, pp. 222–237.

Priestley, M., 2002. Whose Voices? Representing the Claims of Older Disabled People Under New Labour. *Policy & Politics*, 30(3), pp. 361–372.

Qin, J., Zhou, Y., Reid, E., Lai, G. & Chen, H., 2007. Analyzing Terror Campaigns on the Internet: Technical Sophistication, Content Richness, and Web Interactivity. *International Journal of Human-Computer Studies*, 65(1), pp. 71–84.

Rogers, R., 2010a. Mapping Public Web Space with Issuecrawler. In B. Reber & C. Brossaud, eds. *Digital Cognitive Technologies: Epistemology and the Knowledge Economy*. London/Hoboken, NJ: John Wiley and Sons, pp. 89–99.

——— 2010b. Internet Research: The Question of Method – A Keynote Address from the YouTube and the 2008 Election Cycle in the United States Conference. *Journal of Information Technology & Politics*, 7(2–3), pp. 241–260.

Schudson, M., 2006. The Trouble with Experts – And Why Democracies Need Them. *Theory and Society*, 35(5–6), pp. 491–506.

——— 2011. *The Good Citizen: A History of American Civic Life*, New York: The Free Press.

Sheldon, A.2004. Changing Technology. In J. Swain, S. French, C. Barnes & C. Thomas, eds. *Disabling Barriers – Enabling Environments*. London: SAGE, pp. 155–160.

Shirky, C., 2008. *Here Comes Everybody*, New York: Penguin.

Stromer-Galley, J., 2007. Measuring Deliberation's Content: A Coding Scheme. *Journal of Public Deliberation*, 3(1), pp. 1–35.

Tilly, C., 1999. From Interaction to Outcomes in Social Movements. In M. Giugni, D. McAdam, & C. Tilly, eds. *How Social Movements Matter*. Minneapolis/London: University of Minnesota Press, pp. 253–270.

Trevisan, F., 2012. ICTs for Empowerment? Disability Organizations and the Democratizing Potential of Web 2.0 in Scotland. In A. Manoharan & M. Holzer, eds. *E-Governance and Civic Engagement: Factors and Determinants of E-Democracy*. Hershey: IGI Globa, pp. 381–404.

——— 2014. Scottish Disability Organizations and Online Media: A Path to Empowerment or 'Business as Usual?' *Disability Studies Quarterly*, 34(3).

——— 2015. Contentious Disability Politics on the World Stage: Protest at the London 2012 Paralympics. In D. Jackson, C. Hodges, M. Molesworth & R. Scullion, eds. *Reframing Disability? Media, (Dis)empowerment and Voice in the 2012 Paralympics*. London: Routledge, pp. 145–171.

Turbine, V., 2007. Russian Women's Perceptions of Human Rights and Rights-Based Approaches in Everyday Life. In R. Kay, ed. *Gender, Equality, and Difference During and After Socialism*. Basingstoke: Palgrave Macmillan, pp. 167–186.

Witschge, T., 2008. Examining Online Public Discourse in Context: A Mixed Method Approach. *Javnost-The Public*, 15(2), pp. 75–92.

Woliver, L., 1993. *From Outrage to Action: The Politics of Grassroot Dissent*, Urbana & Chigago: The University of Illinois Press.

Wright, S., 2012a. Politics as Usual? Revolution, Normalization and a New Agenda for Online Deliberation. *New Media & Society*, 14(2), pp. 244–261.

——— 2012b. From 'Third Place' to 'Third Space': Everyday Political Talk in Non-Political Online Spaces. *Javnost-The Public*, 19(3), pp. 5–20.

4 Policy Issues and Storytelling on Facebook

This is the first of two chapters that discuss the use of Facebook in the British disability rights advocacy groups examined in this book: The Hardest Hit; Disabled People Against Cuts (DPAC); and The Broken of Britain. This analysis has three main aims. First, it clarifies how each of these groups used Facebook and in particular whether this platform was merely a venue for conversation and community formation, or it also promoted agency and collective action in a more direct fashion. Second, it investigates the way in which 'rank-and-file' supporters of these three groups made sense of complex policy issues in conversations with others. Third, it provides detailed insights into the structure and power dynamics within these groups by shedding light on the relationship between core organisers and online supporters to better understand whether the use of social media granted the latter real influence within the renewed British disability movement that emerged from the opposition to the welfare reform plans discussed in 2010–12.

After a brief section that illustrates why this investigation focused on Facebook and how conversation threads were analysed, this chapter focuses in particular on explaining the main trends that cut across all three case studies. Three main factors determined the ability of a given group's Facebook page to attract a high volume of user-generated content and conversations. These included: 'real world' catalysing events; the ability of core campaigners to build momentum around specific issues and events; and the centrality of seemingly non-political discussion topics – especially personal stories – in enabling disabled supporters to articulate very complex policy issues in 'everyday' terms. These results provide a useful overview of the 'rules of engagement' on the Facebook pages maintained by contemporary disability rights groups in the U.K. More importantly, these findings demonstrate that, provided that certain conditions are met, conversations on Facebook facilitate the engagement of citizens unfamiliar with politics who would normally sit at the margins of the civic arena, including disabled Internet users, in discussions about salient policy issues. The next chapter elaborates on these findings by bringing each group into the spotlight and exploring its specific perspective on Facebook.

Why Facebook?

As was discussed in Chapter 3, each of the groups considered in this study engaged in multiple interactive platforms. These included blogs, forums, social networking sites such as Facebook and Twitter, as well as picture- and video-sharing services such as Flickr and YouTube. However, different interactive platforms lend themselves to the pursuit of different communicative and advocacy outcomes. For example, Twitter can be viewed as an outward-oriented medium to 'broadcast' one's opinions and share content rather than engaging in intra-organisational conversations (Marwick & boyd 2011). Conversely, discussion forums with regulated access can be seen as more 'private' spaces where information is shared with a certain degree of confidentiality, which may in turn foster a sense of community and belonging. Activists are alert to these differences and increasingly skilled in combining the use of multiple online media in order to reach different 'audiences' and support a range of different outcomes (Carty 2010; Lievrouw 2011). This kind of approach demonstrates the complementariness of different interactive platforms in the context of political campaigning.

Facebook has by far the highest number of active users of any social networking platform, both worldwide and in the U.K. This makes it a prime tool for advocacy groups to reach a critical mass of people, including those who typically are not interested in politics. While Twitter tends to be the domain of technology-savvy and politically-experienced activists, Facebook is more relevant to the vast majority of citizens who have little or no civic experience – including disabled people – to whom it provides a familiar venue to articulate connections in ways that blur the lines between private and public (Gerbaudo 2012, p. 146). Research with advocacy organisations has shown that they tend to favour Facebook over any other social media platform for engaging and mobilising supporters (Obar et al. 2012). Approaching Facebook as a space for genuine dialogue between core organisers and ordinary supporters has been proved to foster supporter retention and network growth (Bortree & Seltzer 2009).

As Chadwick (2012) noted, on Facebook 'politics [. . .] aligns itself with broader repertoires of self-expression and lifestyle values. Politics in Facebook goes to where people are, not where we would like them to be' (p. 59). In other words, Facebook is a flexible platform capable of accommodating the preferences of a range of users by blurring the distinction between private and public, and offering a variety of options for participating in online activities, from less demanding forms of 'clicktivism' such as 'liking' someone else's post and sharing content, to more articulated contributions such as content creation and participating in ongoing conversations. Recent work on the use of Facebook as a deliberative space to 'democratise' policy-making at the local level also showed that this platform's 'affordances seem biased towards a more dialogic, open-ended mode of discourse' (Bendor et al. 2012, p. 82), while its 'support of conversation threads seems to especially promote less purposive and more rhizomatic forms of conversation' (ibid.). In light of this, studying the conversation threads posted on the Facebook pages of The Hardest Hit, DPAC and The Broken of Britain constituted the most useful way of clarifying the role played by online supporters in each group, their interaction with one another and their relationship with core organisers.

All the groups examined in this book had set up their Facebook pages so that any follower could start a conversation thread. This suggested a level of openness to user contributions that should not be taken for granted in contemporary action networks as other Facebook pages associated with recent grassroots movements – for example those at the centre of the Egyptian revolution that toppled Hosni Mubarak in 2011 – restricted the ability to start new conversations to administrators only (Poell et al. 2016). Instead, the idea of Facebook as a venue for open discussion was reflected in interviews with representatives from all the groups investigated here. As a campaigns officer from a British disability non-profit involved in The Hardest Hit explained:

> Facebook is there to let people comment and have a conversation, to build a community.
>
> (Campaigns officer, U.K. disability charity,
> September 2011)

Instead:

> Twitter was used to broadcast, update people with simple messages to keep them up to date with what is happening [in the campaign], especially people who can't be there [in person].
>
> (Communications officer, U.K. disability charity,
> July 2011)

Therefore, the analysis of Facebook conversations also provided a useful way of verifying whether core campaigners practiced exactly what they preached when it came to engaging in meaningful conversations with 'ordinary' users.

Furthermore, Facebook stood out among other interactive online platforms for two more reasons. First, its asynchronous nature and the unrestricted length of user-posts make it a less fast-paced and volatile discussion board than, for example, Twitter. This is particularly relevant for disabled Internet users who may have complex needs and find it difficult to take part in real time conversations or summarise their thoughts in very short messages. Second, core campaigners from each group explained in the interviews carried out for this book that they moderated Facebook posts only for profanity and when they contained discriminatory or aggressive remarks directed towards private individuals. Core campaigners considered comment moderation to be 'poor social media practice', which could have raised suspicion among online supporters and ultimately damaged the online reputation of their respective groups. As such, analysing Facebook conversations afforded an unprecedented view into natural and un-filtered intra-group dynamics that may otherwise have been impossible to capture.

Having said that, it is important to note that visually impaired people can find accessing Facebook independently difficult because it combines different types of content and employs software as well as templates that might not work well with screen readers. This example demonstrates how researchers of disability and new media can find themselves trapped between the rock of inaccessible online platforms and the hard place of needing to assess the relevance of those platforms for disabled users. Responsible researchers in both disability studies and communication should approach this issue as an opportunity to reflect on the importance of including the lived experiences of disabled Internet users in their analyses of new media and disability (Ellis & Kent 2011, p. 93). The most useful solution to this impasse seems to be to carry on with the empirical investigation in order to expand our understanding of the relationship between disabled users and specific online applications, while at the same time clearly acknowledging the limitations that derive from focusing on platforms that are not fully accessible to users with certain impairments.

In-Depth Content Analysis

The analysis of Facebook conversations tackled a series of complex questions, including: who talked and who set the topics of discussion? To what extent, if at all, did core organisers take part in Facebook conversations? Did discussions focus on policy issues, whether explicitly or implicitly? What other types of issues, if any, were discussed? How did users frame their contributions? Did core organisers use Facebook to encourage political action among supporters? And, finally, did supporters use Facebook to self-organise and set up their own initiatives?

A lot of recent work on social media and collective action has employed 'big data' analysis. In short, big data analysis relies on automated or semi-automated coding of massive amounts of data – often drawn from Twitter – to identify key social trends and emerging public opinion patterns. This is a powerful approach that has enabled scholars to investigate evolving dynamics of mobilisation and online political discussion in the early twenty-first century (for instance, Bastos & Mercea 2015; Freelon et al. 2015). However, given the complexity of the issues at the centre of this book and the need to account for the nature of discussants (core organisers or rank-and-file supporters, disabled and non-disabled), as well as their interaction in Facebook, a 'small data' approach was more valuable in this case. As boyd and Crawford (2012) noted in their considerations on the methodological turn to big data analysis, 'researchers [...] need to understand [...] the limits of which questions they can ask of a [big data] data set and what interpretations are appropriate. [...] The size of data should fit the research question being asked; in some cases, small is best' (p. 669–70).

Big data analysis looks at manifest content that can be 'counted'. Thus, it considers the explicit meaning of online artefacts, mainly textual communication. Instead, the questions listed above called for the investigation of implicit meanings and conversational dynamics. This involves a deeper layer of analysis, which considers also latent content by focusing on a targeted sample of highly salient material rather than exploring a great amount of content at a more superficial level. Furthermore, Facebook content is also less 'standardised' than Twitter content, at least in terms of length, which strengthens the need for a more flexible approach than that offered by exclusively computational methods. For these reasons, the analysis focused on a purposively selected sample of Facebook content that was drawn from the most intense period of the U.K. welfare reform debate. Obviously, this approach has some limitations, the most important being that results reflect a very specific moment in time. While it is essential to keep this in mind in reviewing the findings discussed in this chapter, as well as the next one, the small data approach was particularly suited for investigating the use of Facebook at a moment in which all the groups examined here were involved in some of their most high-profile initiatives, both online and offline.

Having considered the welfare reform timeline (see Table 2.1 in Chapter 2 for a detailed overview), as well as fluctuations in online interest for disability-related topics as expressed in Google Trends (see Figure 2.1), the period comprised between mid-February and mid-May 2011 was chosen. This also ensured that sufficient time had passed from the foundation of the groups examined in this book in order for them to reach the level of visibility and gather the critical mass of supporters needed to sustain a fair amount of regular conversation on Facebook. This period was marked by a series of key initiatives that defined the campaign style and online repertoire of each group. The first part of the analysis looked at fluctuations in the amounts of content posted daily on Facebook over the course of these three months with a view to uncovering participation catalysts. Thereafter, a further sample of Facebook content was selected and analysed in greater depth. This part of the analysis focused on three weeks in which particularly salient events connected with the reform of British disability welfare occurred, namely: the closure of the Disability Living Allowance (DLA) reform public consultation and the introduction of the Welfare Reform Bill to the House of Commons (12–19 February); the Trades Union Congress (TUC) march against cuts to public services (23–29 March); and The Hardest Hit's demonstration that brought thousands of people to the streets of London (8–14 May). One-week periods were chosen to accommodate for both the build-up and wind-down of participation around each event in a technological context where the fast speed of communication can create discussion hype very rapidly, but also make conversations vanish just as quickly.

In total, 2,126 Facebook posts were generated in these three weeks. A total of 602 of these posts were 'orphans', i.e. potential conversation starters that had failed to attract at least one comment from another user. Given that conversation was the primary focus of this investigation, orphan posts were excluded from the in-depth analysis. Analysing orphan posts – virtually all of which had been generated by page administrators – would have shifted the analysis towards the use of Facebook as a platform to 'broadcast' messages rather than interacting. Thus, 1,524 Facebook posts were analysed in detail through the coding scheme discussed in the next section. These included 201 Facebook posts from The Hardest Hit, 153 from DPAC and 1,170 from The Broken of Britain.

These numbers signalled a strong disparity between the amount of content that featured on The Broken of Britain's Facebook page during this period and the volume of posts on The Hardest Hit and DPAC's pages, as is discussed in detail below. At the same time, this was also a consequence of the sampling strategy's purposive nature, which aimed at capturing and making sense of online conversations exactly as seen by users on days of particular relevance to each group, without interfering with the natural flow of discussion. Furthermore, it provided opportunities for complementing the analysis of online data with additional information drawn from the offline context in a fashion that would not have been possible with a representative random sample.

Coding Facebook Content

Facebook posts can include multiple forms of content (text, pictures, videos, hyperlinks, etc.). They can also be long and complex. Some scholars have proposed that, in order to code lengthy messages (in this case Facebook posts), content be broken down into 'thoughts', defined as 'unique ideas signalled by orienting talk from the speaker' (Stromer-Galley & Muhlberger 2009, p. 181). However, this process asks researchers to consider content units outside the broader conversational context in which they are generated, which can have potentially distortive effects on results. For these reasons, a working compromise was struck here between maximising the amount of detailed information obtained from coding and avoiding the excessive manipulation of Facebook content in order to preserve validity. Two different coding units were adopted: the first part of the coding scheme focused on entire Facebook conversation threads, while the second one analysed individual posts. The first part of the coding scheme was designed to obtain basic information about the nature of online discussions and assess whether any particular topics were more likely than others to spark extended discussions. Thereafter, a second set of variables was used to acquire detailed knowledge of how users had articulated their arguments and interacted with others, including both core organisers and ordinary supporters.

While a complete copy of the coding scheme is included in Appendix C, it is useful to summarise briefly how this tool was developed, as well as the main areas it covered. Methodological literature in the area of online deliberation has flourished in recent years (for instance, Black et al. 2011; Graham 2008; Stromer-Galley 2007; Stromer-Galley & Martinson 2009; Stromer-Galley & Muhlberger 2009). This work suggested some useful variables. However, given that this was the first in-depth study of discussions in online disability rights networks and looked at content in which 'personal' and 'political' were expected to be interwoven (Vergeer & Hermans 2008, pp. 42–6), many other variables were developed inductively by familiarising with a sub-sample of Facebook posts ($n=277$) and optimising the coding scheme through four successive iterations.

The first part of the coding scheme adopted entire discussion threads as both coding and analysis units. A series of basic elements were registered, including the sponsor/owner of the thread, start and end dates, the total number of posts (thread length), as well as the number of unique contributors to each thread. In addition, each thread was scanned also for its 'structural focus' and 'structural topic'. While 'structural focus' aimed at establishing whether each thread revolved primarily around a political issue (e.g. a political party or ideology, a politician, a political process such as elections, etc.), a matter of policy (e.g. a specific policy issue or measure, a bill, etc.), or something of an altogether different nature, 'structural topic' went further and sought to determine whether each thread focused on welfare reform or, rather, on a different topic. This approach was inspired by Stromer-Galley and Martinson's (2009) work on internal coherence in online discussions. This gradually revealed that most Facebook conversations tended to start with an explicit reference to either specific institutional actors or policy-related issues, as discussed in detail further on in this chapter.

The second section of the coding frame adopted individual posts as coding units. This included both fairly straightforward variables and more complex ones that required a careful process of refinement before coding could begin in earnest. In particular, it was possible to code for date, time, function (conversation starter vs. secondary comment), length (number of words) and type(s) of media used in each post, together with user type (page owner, admin/central blogger, individual user, other organisation, or other) fairly straightforwardly. In addition, two other variables were developed to account for the 'content of post' and 'political action mentions' respectively. Both these variables allowed for multi-coding in order to cater for posts spanning more than one topic and ensure that any references to different types of 'action' be registered.

Variables that had a more complex genesis included those accounting for the presence of personal disability stories in Facebook posts and seeking to establish the frames employed by users to present their arguments. Empirical deliberation studies (Black et al. 2011; Ryfe 2007) have shown that citizens often refer to their personal experiences when they try to articulate complex issues in public debates. In the case of disability advocacy, assessing the role of personal stories in online talk was particularly important due to the controversial nature of individual narratives in the disability rights movement, as discussed in Chapter 3. In particular, the issue of 'voice' came to the fore here. Did disabled Internet users tell their own stories on Facebook, or did others 'talk' for them? Telling one's own story can be empowering, while the appropriation of a narrative by third party speakers can generate opposite outcomes (Alcoff 1991). Detecting personal stories in Facebook posts was fairly straightforward, but identifying their authors was less so. Some users clarified that they were reporting their own experiences, while others did not. For this reason, authorship of personal stories was recorded only when those who had posted them had explicitly stated whether they spoke for themselves or reported someone else's experience (e.g. a friend, family member, client, patient, etc.). As with any investigation of user-generated social media content, the authenticity of these stories was presumed. This approach was supported by recent work showing that social media that support peer-networks tend to encourage users to share with others personal stories typically associated with stigma, which otherwise would remain untold (Page 2012, pp. 64–5).

A final set of variables explored the ways in which users had framed their Facebook posts. As Snow and Benford (1992) noted, 'frames [. . .] provide the interpretive medium through which collective actors associated with different movements within a cycle assign blame for the problem they are attempting to ameliorate' (p. 139). This can fundamentally influence a group's sense of agency and its ability to influence public decision-makers (Benford & Snow 2000). Individualistic frames that present issues as isolated and 'personal' problems can be particularly detrimental to advocacy efforts (Cooper 2004). As such, the coding scheme accounted for whether substantive posts framed core discussion topics as either 'collective' or 'individual' (Baldez 2003, pp. 256–7; Zhongdang & Kosicki 2003, pp. 39–40). In addition, a second 'framing' variable explored whether users inscribed their individual grievances within broader themes, including the rights-based components of inclusive citizenship (Fraser 2003) as defined in Chapter 1 (socio-economic rights, political rights and civil/human rights), as well as issues of 'moral panic', 'personal tragedy', 'irony' and 'media propaganda' that emerged during coding. Given that any one post can involve multiple frames, this variable allowed multi-coding. This approach followed a consolidated practice in research that deals with messages that contain multiple, overlapping or even opposite frames (Chong & Druckman 2011, p. 251; Iyengar 1990, pp. 17–18).

Ethical Considerations

Given that no other study has focused on disability-related Facebook content on this scale before this one, it is useful to reflect for a moment on the ethical challenges involved in this type of work. Despite its purely observational nature, this project raised two main ethical issues. First, is it at all appropriate to analyse user-generated content drawn from a semi-public platform such as Facebook (Burkell et al. 2014; Neuhaus & Webmoor 2012) where 'personal' and 'political' are tightly interwoven? Contrary to a popular assumption, the mere fact that Facebook content is publicly available does not necessarily make its analysis ethical (boyd & Crawford 2012; Zimmer 2010). Second, if the analysis was to go ahead, how should the anonymity of individual Facebook users be protected?

In previous work on new media and disability, other researchers categorically ruled out naturalistic discourse analysis of user-generated content due to the perceived level of risk for unaware participants (Bowker & Tuffin 2004). However, this choice is at odds with the principle for which:

> [R]esearch should attend to what disabled people say and think [...] researchers and activists alike should be attentive to the ways in which people wish to define their own experience, to what matters to individuals, to the perspectives and choices which people make in their everyday lives.
>
> (Shakespeare & Watson 2010, p. 72).

Similarly, the consolidated practice of considering disabled adults as 'vulnerable subjects' by default, which still features in some ethical review processes, unduly limits opportunities for the 'voices' of disabled people to inform research. In contrast with traditional approaches and given the controversial nature of the U.K. welfare reform, the view prevailed here that analysing naturally-occurring Facebook conversations provided the supporters of disability right groups with an opportunity to shape research outcomes directly. This was consistent with the principle for which 'researchers must balance the rights of subjects [...] with the social benefits of research' (Markham et al. 2012, p. 4). Thus, a decision was taken to proceed with the analysis while implementing a strategy to minimise risk for (unaware) participants. One key element of this strategy was to devise a way to present Facebook data in a way that would contextualise and illustrate content analysis results while also preserving the anonymity of individual Facebook users, both now and in the future.

Previous research has suggested that the redaction or removal of usernames and online aliases may not ensure confidentiality. The verbatim reproduction of text in research reports might enable the original post to be located via the use of search engines, leading to the identification of individual users (Markham 2012). Personally Identifiable Information (PII) may also be inadvertently revealed by the researcher through the use of content that refers to the economic, social or cultural identity of the poster (Zimmer 2010). The risk of identification with social media material makes it difficult to present research findings effectively. One innovative practice that draws upon user-generated content without the need for verbatim quotes is the 'fabrication' strategy proposed by Markham (2012). This solution requires the researcher to create composite accounts that convey key themes from a data set without reproducing the text as provided by participants. This is a bold and unconventional approach that builds on the idea that qualitative research identifies patterns and trends that can be represented just as successfully through fictional narratives as they would be by verbatim quotes. However, 'fabrication' also presents a particular problem in the context of disability studies and research concerned with under-represented social groups more in general. As the perspectives of disabled people remain an essential component of this type of research, 'fabrication' may ultimately distort their online 'voices' because it works on the premise that the researcher can elaborate 'proxy' accounts in order to prove rhetorical points.

The working solution implemented here was to avoid the use of direct quotes when information on 'sensitive' topics (e.g. daily routines, financial details, detailed accounts of impairment or chronic illness, etc.) was included in Facebook posts as this could facilitate user-identification through Internet search (Trevisan & Reilly 2014). This was not, however, a blanket ban on direct quotes altogether. Instead, direct quotes were useful when the identification of the author was not possible or would not cause specific ethical problems (i.e. sensitive topics were not involved). Furthermore, a distinction was also made between Facebook content generated by ordinary users and that posted by page administrators and core organisers. This is because, while the former may not realise the full implications of publishing personal information on publicly-available online forums, the latter can be regarded as public figures. In this way, this study took an 'agile' approach to online research ethics (Markham 2012; Neuhaus & Webmoor 2012; Whiteman 2012). This strategy fell in the category of 'medium cloaked' approaches as described by Kozinets (2010, pp. 154–5), for which verbatim quotes are admissible under carefully controlled circumstances.

Offline Catalysts and Discussion on Facebook

The first step in the analysis of Facebook data was to compare the distribution of posts over time on each of the pages under scrutiny. This focused on the entire three-month period between mid-February and mid-May

2011. Two important findings emerged from this process. First, as expected, talk on Facebook did not flow steadily. Instead, it fluctuated widely throughout the entire period on all three Facebook pages (Figure 4.1). Second, The Broken of Britain's Facebook page included a much greater amount of user-generated content than any of the other pages for the entire three months, except for a handful of days towards mid-May. This was no surprise given that The Broken of Britain's Facebook posts made up the majority of the sample selected for in-depth analysis. However, it was interesting to note that, on an average day, the volume of content posted to The Broken of Britain's Facebook substantially surpassed that of the other two pages combined together (Table 4.1). This positioned The Broken of Britain's Facebook page as a leading online space for talking about disability welfare issues at a crucial time for the U.K. welfare reform process. What factors, both internal and external to The Hardest Hit, DPAC and The Broken of Britain, could explain these trends?

A reasonable assumption was that fluctuations in the volume of conversation on Facebook could be connected to significant events. In particular, recent work has suggested that there is a strong relationship between events 'on the ground' and the volume of protest-related social media content generated at any one time (Bastos & Mercea 2015, p. 12). Indeed, comparing the Facebook timeline to that of the U.K. welfare reform (see Table 2.1 for details) showed that most discussion 'peaks' tended to concentrate on or around dates that were marked by specific catalysing

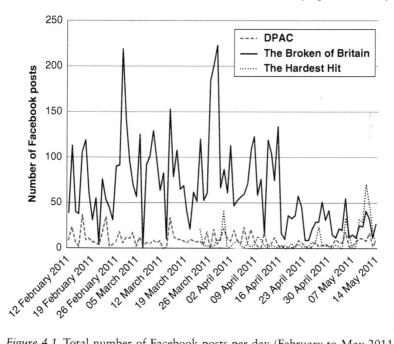

Figure 4.1 Total number of Facebook posts per day (February to May 2011).

Table 4.1 Average number of Facebook posts per day (including orphan posts)

Group	Posts-per-day ratio (mean)	Posts-per-day ratio (median)	Range
DPAC	8.75	7	0–37
The Broken of Britain	65.06	56	0–223
The Hardest Hit	9.28	3	0–71

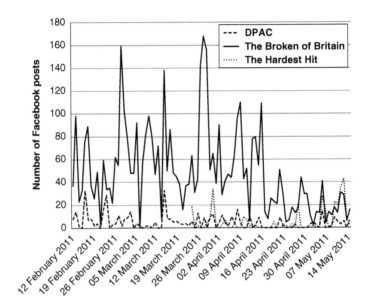

Figure 4.2 Total number of Facebook posts per day, excluding orphan posts (February to May 2011).

events. Thus, fluctuations in the volume of Facebook conversation were connected to 'real world' events in a similar fashion to the way in which the welfare reform timeline influenced levels of interest in disability-related information among Google users, as discussed in Chapter 2. Interestingly, taking out orphan posts from the Facebook timeline did not affect the location of discussion 'peaks' (Figure 4.2). This corroborated the impression that these peaks constituted genuine outbursts of discussion rather than increases in the quantity of failed conversation starters.

Most of the catalysts associated with discussion peaks on Facebook were external to the groups considered in this book. These were major events ignited by third party actors – often government departments and parliamentary procedures – that cut across all the case studies. For example, the first week (12–18 February) featured two major peaks of Facebook discussion for both The Broken of Britain and DPAC (The Hardest Hit did not set up a Facebook page until March 2011). One of these occurred on the day before the closing date for the public consultation on DLA reform (13 February, then unexpectedly extended to 18 February at the last minute). The other one took place on the same day on which the Welfare Reform Bill was introduced to the House of Commons for the first time (16 February). In addition, another day on which discussion peaks coincided with a major external catalyst was the 23 March, when the Chancellor of the Exchequer presented the government's budget in parliament, which included further important details about the reform of disability welfare.

Furthermore, the period between 26–28 March, which started with the TUC march against the cuts in Westminster, was particularly interesting. Overall, these three days registered the biggest discussion outburst for the entire three months under examination, with 466 contributions between 'starters' and 'comments' posted to The Broken of Britain's page alone. It was interesting to note that, although The Broken of Britain had not endorsed or publicised the TUC initiative, a major discussion peak still occurred on its Facebook page on the day of the march (26 March). In stark contrast, DPAC's Facebook page was completely 'silent' on that day and featured only a handful of posts in the days that followed. This was surprising in consideration of the fact that DPAC supported the TUC protest and many of its activists even took part in it. Why did the same event coincide simultaneously with opposite levels of Facebook discussion for groups that were indeed different but nonetheless pursued similar objectives with regard to disability welfare?

One possible explanation could be that each group understood online discussion as having a specific function under these circumstances and therefore approached social networking platforms with different aims in mind. While the TUC march provided The Broken of Britain with an opportunity for intense online conversation, DPAC may have steered off of Facebook on the very same day in order to concentrate on participating in the event, both in person and through Web outlets associated with the march such as the virtual protest pages hosted on its own website (but not on Facebook), which were discussed in Chapter 3. As the analysis progressed, this impression was corroborated by the results of in-depth content coding. Thus, the idea that each group had carved a distinct role for Facebook discussion within its overall advocacy and mobilisation strategy emerged as a key finding from the examination of user-generated content. This issue is discussed in detail in the next chapter, which looks at each group's specific approach to Facebook.

In addition to external catalysts, the volume of Facebook content appeared to be connected also to activities internal to the groups. Two of these are particularly worthy of a mention. First, The Broken of Britain's page registered a remarkable spike between 8–10 March. This came immediately after the launch of its second round of campaign initiatives, which kicked off on 7 March and was dubbed 'Left Out in the Cold'.

Second, The Hardest Hit's Facebook page experienced a substantial discussion surge around 11 May, when this issue-focused coalition held its first street demonstration against disability welfare cuts in London. Both these examples demonstrated the importance of 'internal catalysts' for clarifying the origin of discussion spikes that otherwise would appear to be unconnected to offline events. Having said that, not every single surge in the number of Facebook posts was explained by either 'external' or 'internal' catalysts. Furthermore, as many external catalysts were equally relevant to all the groups examined in this book, their influence did not explain the striking difference between The Broken of Britain and the other two groups in terms of overall Facebook content.

One possible explanation for the high volume of content hosted on The Broken of Britain's Facebook page could be that it had more 'fans' than those of the other groups. However, this was simply not the case. In fact, between February and May 2011 The Broken of Britain had the smallest cohort of Facebook followers among the groups examined in this study (Table 4.2). It was interesting to note though that only The Broken of Britain's page included a substantial amount of posts generated by 'regulars' (i.e. users who posted more than five contributions during the three-week period). More broadly, more than 13 per cent of The Broken of Britain's Facebook supporters had posted on its page at least once within the same timeframe. Although 13 per cent may not sound like a great proportion in absolute terms, it is worth noting that both DPAC and The Hardest Hit had substantially fewer 'active' fans during the same period (Table 4.2). Taken altogether, these results were consistent with previous work that showed that typically it is only a minority of the 'followers' of a given social media account who interact with one another (Huberman et al. 2008). Yet, at the same time these data suggested also that online supporters of The Broken of

Table 4.2 Levels of activity among Facebook 'fans' of U.K. disability groups

Number of Facebook posts	Number of unique users		
	The Broken of Britain	DPAC	The Hardest Hit
1	81	22	71
2–5	71	10	29
6–10	12	5	2
11–20	13	—	—
21+	4	—	—
'Active' Facebook fans	181	37	102
Total number of Facebook fans (as of 31 May 2011)	1,357	1,761	3,086
'Active' fans as share of total Facebook fans	13.4%	2.1%	3.3%

Britain were much more likely than those of other groups to express their point of view and share their thoughts and experiences through Facebook, rather than merely 'lurking' over the content generated by others. The next section starts to explore more in detail what contributed to this trend.

Turning 'Likes' into Discussion

Examining authorship was particularly useful to better understand why The Broken of Britain's Facebook page hosted a much greater amount of content and attracted many more 'active' users than DPAC and The Hardest Hit's. In particular, it was useful to focus on starter posts as they set the topic of discussion in each conversation thread, as well as the overall pace of discussion. This immediately revealed some important differences between groups. On the one hand, ordinary supporters were the type of users most likely to kick-start a conversation on both DPAC and The Hardest Hit's Facebook pages. On the other hand, nearly 90 per cent of the starter posts on The Broken of Britain's page had been generated by the page administrator (Table 4.3). In addition, the respective shares of 'starter', 'comment' and 'orphan' posts featured on The Broken of Britain's Facebook page had remained virtually constant throughout the entire period (Figure 4.3). This meant that the number of comment posts, most of which had been generated by ordinary supporters, had increased or decreased in similar measure to that of variations in the levels of conversation starters, most of which had been created by the page administrator.

These results prompted two main observations with regard to the mechanisms that regulated conversation on Facebook. First, the core organisers of both DPAC and The Hardest Hit favoured a relatively less proactive approach to this platform and often left it up to ordinary supporters to initiate new discussion threads. Arguably, this pattern could be seen as a way for organisers to step back, avoid monopolising online talk

Table 4.3 Facebook posts authorship

Group	Post function	Author			
		Page administrator	Other core organiser	Supporter	Other organisation
DPAC	Starter	—	38.46%	58.97%	2.56%
	Comment	—	50.00%	48.25%	1.75%
The Broken of Britain	Starter	86.64%	1.84%	11.52%	—
	Comment	21.03%	—	78.97%	—
The Hardest Hit	Starter	39.40%	12.12%	45.45%	3.03%
	Comment	3.09%	2.47%	93.21%	1.23%

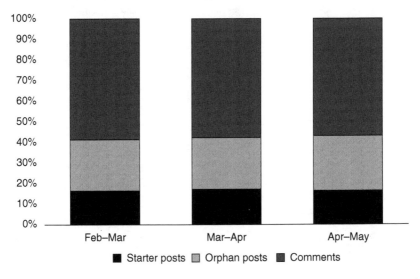

Figure 4.3 Ratio of starter, comment and orphan posts over time (The Broken of Britain).

and encourage pluralism. Yet, whatever the intention of those in charge of these groups, their 'hands off' approach was met with consistently low levels of Facebook conversation throughout the entire period under examination here. This suggested that supporters, despite the motivation and sense of urgency generated by the welfare reform crisis, did not simply 'flock' to and start contributing to whatever social networking page campaigners had set up, confirming that the mere availability of interactive channels does not necessarily ensure that users engage with them, let alone become empowered along the way.

In contrast, the data collected for The Broken of Britain proved that a more 'hands-on' approach by lead organisers can foster a substantial – if highly variable – amount of discussion on Facebook. The content posted by The Broken of Britain's core campaigners, as well as the frequency with which it was updated, were crucial for persuading ordinary users to 'join in' the discussion. This is corroborated also by the small drop in Facebook conversations on The Broken of Britain's page around mid-May, which can be explained by the fact that the administrator was unable to attend to the page for some time due to personal reasons, as she explained in personal correspondence with the author. Thus, it could be argued that attracting potential supporters is only the first step in a multi-stage 'activation' process in which online followers are more likely to become discussants if core organisers deploy a consistent effort to stir the conversation.

Overall, these results were in line with those of previous work that showed that online discussion in politically-oriented forums does not drive itself, but instead relies on constant stimulation from a 'core' group to reach 'peripheral' supporters who otherwise can limit themselves to being mere observers (Anstead 2009; Lilleker 2011). Thus, The Broken of Britain's Facebook page administrators played a similar role to that of the lead activists who stimulated online participation in the Egyptian revolution and the Spanish *Indignados* movement (Gerbaudo 2016). Indeed, less than 40 per cent of potential starter posts had actually generated discussion threads on The Broken of Britain's Facebook page. Yet, this apparent lack of efficiency did not detract from the overall effectiveness of this group's 'hands-on' approach, which ultimately led its Facebook page to becoming the most popular discussion space among those examined for this project. In addition, it could be hypothesised also that The Broken of Britain had attracted supporters who were naturally more inclined towards interaction with others. Although proving this point was not possible with content analysis alone, it was still interesting to note that only a handful of Facebook users had posted on more than one of the pages examined here and none of them was a 'regular' contributor. This corroborated the impression that each group addressed a somewhat different 'audience' and interacted with a different set of Facebook supporters within the British disability community.

Another important factor that differentiated The Broken of Britain's Facebook page from those of DPAC and The Hardest Hit was the type of media included in starter posts. In particular, conversation starters that included a link to the websites of traditional mass media organisations such as national newspapers and the BBC seemed to generate a high volume of discussion. On The Broken of Britain's page, over a quarter of starter posts included a link to traditional media content (Table 4.4). In addition, another 10 per cent of starters linked to emergent and activist media websites. This raised the share of opening contributions

Table 4.4 Types of media used in Facebook starter posts

Medium	DPAC	The Broken of Britain	The Hardest Hit
Text only	46.2%	26.3%	50.00%
Photo	5.1%	1.8%	15.6%
Video	—	2.3%	6.3%
Link to traditional mass media	10.3%	26.7%	12.5%
Link to emergent/activist media	2.6%	10.1%	—
Link to group's own website	7.7%	1.8%	—
Link to group's official blog	—	1.8%	—
Link to other blog	2.6%	9.2%	—
Link to other disability org.	10.3%	6.9%	12.5%
Other	15.4%	12.4%	3.1%
Not classifiable	—	0.5%	—

that included links to 'news' content to nearly 38 per cent of starter posts on this page. Conversely, the proportion of starter posts that included a link to news content – whether on traditional or emergent/activist media websites – on the Facebook pages of DPAC and The Hardest Hit was only about 10 per cent. Starter posts on these pages were dominated instead by plain text almost twice as often as on The Broken of Britain's.

Although it was unclear whether the inclusion of so many links to traditional news media sites in starter posts was part of a deliberate strategy with which The Broken of Britain tried to spark discussion on Facebook, these data outlined a connection between this type of content and a high volume of conversation. This resonated with the findings of recent work that showed that, during crises, social networking platform users are more likely to respond to and share content put out by traditional news media outlets than any other type of content (Procter et al. 2013).

The inclusion of so many links to traditional news content in Facebook conversation starters clashed with the high levels of cynicism and anger expressed by supporters of all groups towards major British media outlets with the possible exception of *The Guardian* and Channel 4. Distrust of journalists and mass media conglomerates was so widespread in the conversations examined for this study that a 'media propaganda' frame emerged inductively during the coding process (Table 4.5). Interestingly, the 'media propaganda' frame was used on The Broken of Britain's Facebook page more than on the other two pages.

Supporters who framed their contributions around the theme of 'media propaganda' often argued that the most:

> [P]revalent attitudes amongst the [news] media [are] that we [disabled people] are all either 'full time useless' drains on society or lead-swinging fraudsters.
>
> (Facebook post, The Hardest Hit supporter, 12 May 2011)

Table 4.5 Arguments used to frame Facebook posts

Argument	DPAC	The Broken of Britain	The Hardest Hit
Socio-economic rights	9%	9.5%	16.7%
Political rights	57.7%	29.6%	29.6%
Civil/Human rights	9%	5.7%	2.5%
Moral panic	8.1%	23%	24.1%
Personal tragedy	1.8%	3.6%	4.3%
Media propaganda	—	10.4%	6.2%
Irony	4.5%	6.9%	4.3%
Other	2.7%	0.3%	1.2%
Not classifiable	7.2%	10.9%	11.1%

Another supporter of The Hardest Hit also explained that:

[T]he media, like the 'caring' general public don't care, to them we [disabled people] are all just benefit scroungers living a life of luxury at their expense.

(Facebook post, The Hardest Hit supporter, 24 March 2011)

This sense of frustration with news media representations of disabled people resonated strongly with the findings of recent work that showed that negative stereotypes – especially references to benefit fraud – have become increasingly prevalent in coverage of disability issues in the British press, particularly with tabloid newspapers (Briant et al. 2013). In hindsight, the very level of controversy that surrounded news media representations of disabled people may help to explain the role of traditional media content as a driver of conversation on The Broken of Britain's Facebook page.

'Big P' Politics, 'Small P' Politics or no Politics?

In addition to authorship and the types of media included in each post, the topics covered in conversations were another element that fundamentally influenced the ability of each Facebook page to become a lively discussion venue during the debate on disability welfare reform. Did people talk politics, policy, both or neither? Did they share their personal experiences? If so, were personal stories associated with any particular types of issues and framed in specific ways? The rest of this chapter addresses these complex questions.

Results for the 'structural focus' variable, which looked at whether each conversation revolved primarily around a political issue (e.g. a political party or ideology, a politician, a political process such as elections, etc.), a matter of policy (e.g. a specific policy issue or measure, a bill, etc.), or something of an altogether different nature were especially relevant. Overall, the majority of discussion threads examined for each case study started with an explicit reference to either institutionalised politics or a specific policy measure/area (Table 4.6). This was hardly surprising, given that these conversations were

Table 4.6 Structural focus of Facebook discussion threads

Structural focus	DPAC	The Broken of Britain	The Hardest Hit
Politics	58.3%	39%	45.5%
Policy	16.7%	26.3%	33.8%
Both politics and policy	8.3%	7.5%	3.9%
Other non-political issues	8.3%	23.9%	11.7%
Not classifiable	8.3%	3.3%	5.2%

hosted on the social networking pages of three groups for which the most immediate goal was to block changes to disability welfare. However, on closer inspection, more subtle and revelatory differences emerged behind this common trend. In particular, while nearly 60 per cent of DPAC's threads focused on 'big P' politics, the conversations hosted on the Facebook pages of the other two groups were less intensely dominated by broad political themes and drew more often on specific policy issues, as well as topics of another nature.

This was an important result that fitted the overarching nature of each group as discussed in Chapter 3. In addition, the direct involvement of many of DPAC's core organisers in the early 1990s disability rights protests, their commitment to social model and independent living principles, as well as their familiarity with traditional repertoires of contention also underpinned the high concentration of explicitly 'political' talk on this group's Facebook page. Instead, both The Broken of Britain and The Hardest Hit took a more pragmatic issue-focused approach, meaning that although they were:

> [Q]uite passionate about wider disability rights as a civil rights movement, the cuts are [were] so damaging and are [were] being brought in so urgently that we have [they had] to concentrate on that.
> (Interview, The Broken of Britain founder, July 2011)

Crucially, crossing-checking these data with those for the total volume of user-generated content discussed above revealed that the two Facebook pages on which policy and 'other' non-political issues were more popular – i.e. The Hardest Hit and The Broken of Britain's – tended to host a considerably greater number of comments from supporters. This suggested that favouring an issue-based approach to discussion and reducing the number of explicitly ideological, institutional or party political discussion topics constituted a further determinant of 'Facebook success' among emerging British disability rights online networks. Using social media platforms to disseminate and discuss content that is not overtly political and to which ordinary citizens can relate easily has been shown to promote the growth of action networks (Zuckerman 2015). In contrast, privileging explicitly political topics on social media can lead activists to become isolated in their own bubble (Gerbaudo 2012, p. 148). For these reasons, DPAC trailed behind the other groups in terms of online conversation volume not simply because a lot of its Facebook discussions drew explicitly on 'big P' politics, but rather because quintessentially political content outweighed other types of talk in a very decisive manner.

As was discussed in Chapter 2, people who are unfamiliar with the public arena and are only just discovering political discussion through social media generally struggle to engage in explicitly political conversations centred on parties, ideologies and other formal institutions. These kinds of conversations tend to favour participants who have a strong ideological commitment to campaigning and 'speak the same language'. In light of this, it is reasonable to assume that the strong focus on 'big P' politics that characterised DPAC's Facebook page may have discouraged users who were not already versed in political conversations from joining in the same fashion as government-sponsored e-democracy initiatives, which typically have marginalised minority voices (Albrecht 2006; Vedel 2006). By emphasising the overtly political nature of discussion, DPAC's Facebook page somewhat offset a major benefit of online discussion, which is to lower the participation threshold by removing the distinction between private and public talk (Bimber et al. 2005).

In contrast, results for The Broken of Britain revealed that conversations focused on issues that apparently had nothing to do with institutionalised politics or specific policy measures may have contributed to the intensification of the discussion on this group's Facebook page. It was interesting to note that more than a quarter of the conversation threads hosted on the busiest page among those investigated for this book had been set up to discuss 'other' topics, including arguably mundane ones such as music and sports (Table 4.6). In addition, conversation threads that revolved primarily around non-political or policy topics tended to include more posts than average (Table 4.7).

These trends were consistent with the findings of recent work that explored the deliberative potential of online discussions in 'a-political' spaces, which flagged the importance of conversations on seemingly mundane topics as training grounds for citizenship and, possibly, collective action (Graham 2012; Graham et al. 2015). In this respect, The Broken of Britain's Facebook page was similar to those managed by Egyptian activists at the start of the 2011 revolution, which promoted a sense of inclusion by strategically avoiding discussion topics that were overtly ideological, partisan or more simply political (Poell et al. 2016). Testing for the existence of a user 'flow' from threads discussing 'other' issues towards those explicitly focused on political or policy-related matters was not possible in this study. Yet, it is realistic to assume that The Broken of Britain's Facebook fans would stumble upon politically-relevant content in their personal newsfeeds and when they browsed the group's page directly. Therefore, conversations centred on 'other' non-political issues could be considered 'magnets' capable of attracting and engaging civically inexperienced users

Table 4.7 Average length of Facebook discussion threads (The Broken of Britain)

Thread structural focus	Mean number of posts	Median number of posts	Range
Other non-political issues	5.41	4	2–43
Overall average	4.40	3	2–43

who otherwise may have continued to be disconnected and disenfranchised. More generally, these results also reflected a tendency for social media to make boundaries between private and public more permeable (Papacharissi 2010). This was particularly apparent in the Facebook posts that mentioned personal stories of disability, which constituted an important tool for the supporters of these groups to articulate and make sense of complex policy issues.

Personal Stories as Filters to Understand Policy

Personal stories of disability appeared in a sizeable amount of Facebook posts on all the pages examined for this study (Table 4.8). Given the controversial role of individual disability narratives in the history of the British disability movement (Corbett & Ralph 1995; Pointon 1999), the presence of personal stories in Facebook posts was particularly interesting. As The Hardest Hit, DPAC and The Broken of Britain had different histories and ethos, it was reasonable to assume that each group adopted a different approach to the practice of sharing personal stories on social media. Interviews with core organisers demonstrated that these groups were aware of the contentious nature of individual narratives. As a participant from The Broken of Britain explained:

> [W]e shouldn't have to do this [publicising personal stories], but unfortunately the situation is so serious that the only way that we can move away from this established round of rhetoric [focused on benefit fraud] is to use real people's stories […] pitiful stories […] it is not to degrade or use people in any way, we felt the most powerful tool we had as individuals was our own voices.
> (Interview, The Broken of Britain founder, July 2011)

This and other similar interview statements pointed out two fundamental issues connected to personal stories. First, British disability rights groups were alert to the value of storytelling tactics for contemporary social media-driven advocacy as demonstrated by the successes of story-focused campaigns in other areas such as mental health advocacy and environmentalism (Vromen & Coleman 2013). Second, young self-advocates in particular believed that projecting personal stories constituted the best

Table 4.8 Share of Facebook posts that contained personal stories of disability

Group	Posts that contained personal stories
DPAC	7.8%
The Broken of Britain	9.6%
The Hardest Hit	26.2%

strategy for disabled people's own voices to be heard in the U.K. welfare debate. Therefore, to assess the role of personal stories in Facebook conversations correctly, it was crucial to establish whose 'voices' narrated them.

Content analysis revealed that the vast majority of the Facebook posts containing personal stories on each of the pages under examination was narrated in the first person by users who self-identified as disabled (Figure 4.4). This suggested that the personal narratives posted on Facebook represented the un-mediated 'voices' of those disabled Internet users who followed these groups online. This impression was strengthened also by the fact that, in the interviews carried out for this study, all the groups stated that they did not edit or moderate user-generated Facebook posts. This trend marked a clear departure from the centralised editing practices applied to personal stories of disability that were uncovered in previous work on the use of new media technologies among disability non-profits in the U.K. (Trevisan 2012, 2014).

Several factors may have underpinned this shift, ranging from a process of mere 'domestication' of technology (Baym 2010, pp. 45–9) to a growing awareness of the benefits of surrendering some level of control over Web content to users in e-advocacy. Overall, these findings also resonated with the expectation that, during a crisis, ordinary users would look for opportunities to vent their frustration and voice their anger by means of personal terms in an inadvertent but effective attempt to build a community based on common experiences and interests (Rainie & Wellman 2012, p. 218).

A second and possibly even more important finding was that a very large number of personal stories were included in Facebook posts that drew on

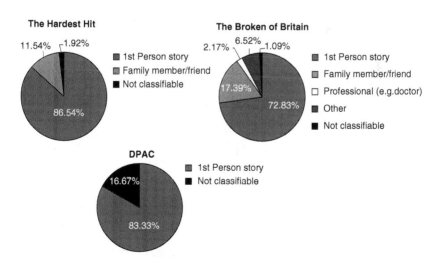

Figure 4.4 Authorship of personal stories of disability on Facebook.

specific policy issues, mainly to do with the welfare system. This tendency was particularly strong on The Broken of Britain and The Hardest Hit's Facebook pages (Table 4.9). Overall, personal stories came to the fore when specific policy measures were discussed, while they moved out of the limelight when conversations centred on other topics. This suggested that personal experiences provided disabled Internet users with a lens to interpret the effects of policy issues, facilitating their understanding of complex technicalities and encouraging user-participation in relevant online conversations.

In addition, the longitudinal distribution of personal stories on both The Hardest Hit and The Broken of Britain's Facebook pages (Table 4.10) indicated that the online supporters of these groups had shared their experiences more frequently in the initial stages of the welfare reform crisis and then moved away from this type of narrative as they became increasingly mobilised and geared up towards a particular event. Most of the personal stories on The Broken of Britain's page were posted in February and became increasingly infrequent in March and May, both months that were marked by major protest events. Similarly, nearly half of the user contributions posted to The Hardest Hit's page included a personal story of disability when this was launched in March. Yet, these were replaced by other content in May as the main demonstration against disability cuts organised by this coalition became closer.

In light of these findings, it can be argued that talking about personal circumstances on Facebook represented more than just an opportunity for disabled citizens to vent their frustration during a time of crisis. Instead, it provided a filter capable of enhancing the relevance of policy issues for ordinary people, enabling them to articulate the impact of controversial policy measures in a way that made such complex topics more accessible and possibly drew disengaged users into politically-relevant debates

Table 4.9 Topics of Facebook posts that contained personal stories of disability

Topic of posts that contained personal stories of disability	The Broken of Britain	The Hardest Hit
Welfare reform and public cuts	20.7%	17.65%
Other issues with the welfare system	19.54%	62.75%
Other government policy	4.49%	—
Disability group's own initiatives	4.4%	11.76%
Other group's initiatives	3.26%	—
Institutionalised politics (e.g. elections)	1.08%	—
Politicians' attitudes to disability/inequality	5.34%	1.96%
Other barriers and discrimination issues	15.21%	—
Media representations of disability	10.86%	1.96%
Other	8.6%	—
Not classifiable	6.43%	3.92%

Table 4.10 Longitudinal distribution of personal stories of disability in Facebook

| | Posts including personal stories of disability as share of total Facebook content | | |
	Feb	Mar	May
The Broken of Britain	14.5%	6.2%	4.03%
The Hardest Hit	—	49.23%	14.73%

(Bimber et al. 2005). This was also a testimony to the fact that welfare policy, while a seemingly dry, technical and 'geeky' topic, had touched a special chord with disabled citizens. For these reasons, British disability activism appeared to have become involved in what Bennett and Segerberg (2011) have described as the ever expanding 'personalisation of collective action', for which the centrality of interactive media to participation and the lack of a clear distinction between private and public are fostering the growth of politics inspired by individual experiences.

Due to its apparent lack of ideological grounding and to the loose ties it promoted, it could be tempting to dismiss this turn to personal factors in British disability advocacy as just a 'fashionable' and ephemeral trend or, worse, a slippery slope towards more individualism and fragmentation. This seems particularly relevant for disability rights advocacy, which has been affected by internal divisions for a long time, as was discussed in Chapter 1. Thus, there is a risk that the growing emphasis placed on personal experiences may compromise opportunities for collective action and endanger the overall strength of advocacy groups (Tilly 2004). However, in this case the impression was that disability activists had not simply 'jumped on the bandwagon' of the latest campaign innovation. This is because, despite the prominence of personal stories in policy talk, the majority of Facebook posts on each one of the pages examined here had framed the problems it discussed as 'collective' instead of 'individual' (Figure 4.5). In addition, the most prevalent frame adopted across all the Facebook pages considered in this book was that of 'political rights', which characterised nearly a third of the posts on The Hardest Hit and The Broken of Britain's pages respectively, as well as almost 60 per cent of the content on DPAC's page. By comparison, the idea of 'personal tragedy', which supports the understanding of disability as a 'private' matter and was used in the past by disability charities, appeared only in 1.8 to 4.3 per cent of posts (for details, see Table 4.5).

In this context, the negative potential of 'personalised' participation for division was mitigated by an overarching sense of commonality that seemed to bind together individuals based on their feelings and experiences. This demonstrated that sharing personal stories of disability on social media sites should not be classed *a priori* as a disempowering process. Depending on circumstances, its outcome can be quite the opposite. In this instance, the majority of personal stories provided a channel for disabled

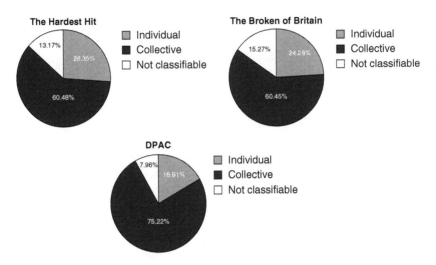

Figure 4.5 Problem framing in Facebook content.

online supporters to counter feelings of isolation and powerlessness, ushering in a better understanding of complex policy issues and thus providing the common ground that is an essential pre-requisite for collective action (Benford & Snow 2000). More broadly, this practice echoed the arguments put forward by feminist disability writers who highlighted the 'political' nature of seemingly 'private' experiences (Crow 1996; Fawcett 2000; Morris 1992) and supports the work of scholars who called for the re-evaluation of the role of personal experiences and impairment in order to better understand disability as a whole (Corker 1999; Shakespeare 2006; Thomas & Corker 2002).

Recent work on how people with serious illnesses or chronic conditions use Facebook has found that they avoid telling personal stories in individual status updates because this may lead to their stigmatisation (Page 2012, p. 91). In contrast, the stories of disability examined for this study showed that posting personal narratives on collective and peer-oriented Facebook pages can encourage disclosure and conversation. This resonates with the arguments put forward by some disability theorists who emphasised that sharing personal experiences with peers remains fundamental to the formation of group identity and, therefore, the enhancement of disabled people's political citizenship (Watson 1998). As shown here, group Facebook pages can facilitate this process.

Conclusions

The analysis of conversations drawn from the Facebook pages of The Hardest Hit, DPAC and The Broken of Britain at the height of the U.K.

welfare reform debate revealed that this type of interaction was governed by four main 'rules' of online engagement. In particular:

1   Offline catalysts, both internal and external to each group, performed an important role as drivers of Facebook discussion, which was characterised by rapid peaks and equally rapid drops throughout the entire period;
2   Conversations were not self-sustaining; instead, core organisers needed to display proactive efforts to build momentum and encourage participation among rank-and-file supporters;
3   Starter posts that included links to news coverage or focused on non-political topics tended to generate longer and richer discussions; and, finally,
4   Personal stories provided a powerful tool for disabled Internet users to articulate complex policy proposals as 'everyday' issues and simultaneously build a community based on shared interests and experiences.

Both the inclusion of topics that were not overtly political, as well as the frequent use of personal stories as vehicles for discussing complex policy measures lowered the threshold of participation in these conversations. This had positive implications for disabled Internet users as it provided more easily approachable and potentially more inclusive opportunities for talking about U.K. welfare reforms at a time of acute crisis. Personal stories, most of which were expressed in the first person, facilitated the emergence of disable Internet users' own un-mediated voices. As such, these groups' Facebook pages fostered participatory parity for disabled Internet users, as described by Lister (2003). Having said that, it ought to be noted also that the key role played by administrators and other core organisers in building momentum on Facebook pages appeared to be somewhat at odds with the idea that social media platforms are naturally oriented towards the promotion of horizontal, self-supporting and possibly leader-less networks (Bennett 2003; Scholz 2010). The next chapter looks further into Facebook content and interview data to better understand the role of ordinary supporters and core organisers in the groups under scrutiny, as well as their respective approach to social media. In particular, The Broken of Britain is brought into the spotlight to investigate its internal structure and establish whether the ways in which it used new media technologies contributed to the emergence of a concealed leadership based on the control of communication flows (Gerbaudo 2012, p. 135; Hands 2011, pp. 110–11).

References

Albrecht, S., 2006. Whose Voice Is Heard in Online Deliberation?: A Study of Participation and Representation in Political Debates on the Internet. *Information, Community and Society*, 9(1), pp. 62–82.

Alcoff, L., 1991. The Problem of Speaking for Others. *Cultural Critique*, 20, pp. 5–32.

Anstead, N., 2009. The Evolving Relationship between Core and Periphery of Political Campaigns in the Internet Era. In ECPR General Conference, Potsdam, 10–12 September.

Baldez, L., 2003. Women's Movements and Democratic Transition in Chile, Brazil, East Germany, and Poland. *Comparative Politics*, 35(3), pp. 253–272.

Bastos, M.T. & Mercea, D., 2015. Serial Activists: Political Twitter Beyond Influentials and the Twittertariat. *New Media & Society*, doi: 10.1177/1461444815584764.

Baym, N.K., 2010. *Personal Connections in the Digital Age*, Cambridge: Polity Press.

Bendor, R., Lyons, S.H. & Robinson, J., 2012. What's There Not To 'Like'? *eJournal of E-Democracy*, 4(1), pp. 67–88.

Benford, R.D. & Snow, D.A., 2000. Framing Processes and Social Movements: An Overview and Assessment. *Annual Review of Sociology*, 26, pp. 611–639.

Bennett, W.L., 2003. Communicating Global Activism: Strengths and Vulnerabilities of Networked Politics. *Information, Communication & Society*, 6(2), pp. 143–168.

Bennett, W.L. & Segerberg, A., 2011. Digital Media and the Personalization of Collective Action. *Information, Communication & Society*, 14(6), pp. 770–799.

Bimber, B., Flanagin, A.J. & Stohl, C., 2005. Reconceptualizing Collective Action in the Contemporary Media Environment. *Communication Theory*, 15(4), pp. 365–388.

Black, L.W., Burkhalter, S., Gastil, J. & Stromer-Galley, J., 2011. Methods for Analyzing and Measuring Group Deliberation. In E. P. Bucy & R. L. Holbert, eds. *The Sourcebook for Political Communication Research*. New York/London: Routledge, pp. 323–345.

Bortree, D.S. & Seltzer, T., 2009. Dialogic Strategies and Outcomes: An Analysis of Environmental Advocacy Groups' Facebook Profiles. *Public Relations Review*, 35(3), pp. 317–319.

Bowker, N. & Tuffin, K., 2004. Using the Online Medium for Discursive Research About People With Disabilities. *Social Science Computer Review*, 22(2), pp. 228–241.

boyd, D. & Crawford, K., 2012. Critical Questions for Big Data: Provocations for a Cultural, Technological, and Scholarly Phenomenon. *Information, Communication & Society*, 15(5), pp. 662–679.

Briant, E., Watson, N. & Philo, G., 2013. Reporting Disability in the Age of Austerity: The Changing Face of Media Representation of Disability and Disabled People in the United Kingdom and the Creation of New 'Folk Devils'. *Disability & Society*, 28(6), pp. 874–889.

Burkell, J., Fortier, A., Wong, L.L.Y.C. & Simpson, J.L., 2014. Facebook: Public Space, or Private Space? *Information, Communication & Society*, 17(8), pp. 974–985.

Carty, V., 2010. *Wired and Mobilizing: Social Movements, New Technology, and Electoral Politics*, London: Routledge.

Chadwick, A., 2012. Web 2.0: New Challenges for the Study of E-Democracy in an Era of Informational Exuberance. In S. Coleman & P. Shane, eds. *Citizenship and Vulnerability*. Cambridge, MA: The MIT Press, pp. 45–73.

Chong, D. & Druckman, J., 2011. Identifying Frames in Political News. In E. P. Bucy & R. L. Holbert, eds. *The Sourcebook for Political Communication Research.* New York/London: Routledge, pp. 238–267.

Cooper, D., 2004. *Challenging Diversity: Rethinking Equality and the Value of Difference,* Cambridge: Cambridge University Press.

Corbett, J. & Ralph, S., 1995. UK: The Changing Image of Charity Advertising. *British Journal of Special Education,* 22(4), pp. 155–160.

Corker, M., 1999. Differences, Conflations and Foundations: The Limits to 'Accurate' Theoretical Representation of Disabled People's Experience? *Disability & Society,* 14(5), pp. 627–642.

Crow, L., 1996. Including All of Our Lives: Renewing the Social Model of Disability. In C. Barnes & G. Mercer, eds. *Exploring the Divide: Illness and Disability.* Leeds: The Disability Press, pp. 55–72.

Ellis, K. & Kent, M., 2011. *Disability and New Media,* London: Routledge.

Fawcett, B., 2000. *Feminist Perspectives on Disability,* Harlow: Pearson Education Limited.

Fraser, N., 2003. Social Justice in the Age of Identity Politics: Redistribution, Recognition and Participation. In N. Fraser & A. Honnoeth, eds. *Redistribution or Recognition? A Political-Philosophical Exchange.* London/New York: Verso, pp. 7–109.

Freelon, D., Lynch, M. & Aday, S., 2015. Online Fragmentation in Wartime: A Longitudinal Analysis of Tweets about Syria, 2011–2013. *The ANNALS of the American Academy of Political and Social Science,* 659(1), pp. 166–179.

Gerbaudo, P., 2012. *Tweet and the Streets: Social Media and Contemporary Activism,* London: Pluto Press.

———— 2016. Rousing the Facebook Crowd: Digital Enthusiasm and Emotional Contagion in the 2011 Protests in Egypt and Spain. *International Journal of Communication,* 10, pp. 254–273.

Graham, T., 2008. Needles in a Haystack: A New Approach for Identifying and Assessing Political Talk in Nonpolitical Discussion Forums. *Javnost-The Public,* 15(2), pp. 17–36.

———— 2012. Beyond 'Political' Communicative Spaces: Talking Politics on the Wife Swap Discussion Forum. *Journal of Information Technology & Politics,* 9 (1), pp. 31–45.

Graham, T., Jackson, D. & Wright, S., 2015. From Everyday Conversation to Political Action: Talking Austerity in Online 'Third Spaces'. *European Journal of Communication,* 30(6), pp. 648–665.

Hands, J., 2011. *Is For Activism: Dissent, Resistance And Rebellion In A Digital Culture,* New York: Pluto Press.

Huberman, B., Romero, D.M. & Wu, F., 2008. Social Networks That Matter: Twitter Under the Microscope. *First Monday,* 14(1).

Iyengar, S., 1990. *Is Anyone Responsible? How Television Frames Political Issues,* Chicago: University of Chicago Press.

Kozinets, R.V., 2010. *Netnography: Doing Ethnographic Research Online,* London: SAGE.

Lievrouw, L.A., 2011. *Alternative and Activist New Media,* Cambridge: Polity Press.

Lilleker, D., 2011. Politics as Usual and Politics of the Unusual: Political Communication Coproduction and the Harnessed Crowd. In Transforming Audiences 3 Conference. 1–2 September, University of Westminster.

Lister, R., 2003. *Citizenship: Feminist Perspectives*, Basingstoke: Palgrave Macmillan.

Markham, A., 2012. Fabrication as Ethical Practice. *Information, Communication & Society*, 15(3), pp. 334–353.

Markham, A., Buchanan, E., AoIR Ethics Working Committee, 2012. *Ethical Decision-Making and Internet Research: Recommendations from the AoIR Ethics Working Committee (Version 2.0)*. Available at: http://aoir.org/reports/ethics2.pdf (accessed 28 February 2016).

Marwick, A.E. & boyd, D., 2011. I Tweet Honestly, I Tweet Passionately: Twitter Users, Context Collapse, and the Imagined Audience. *New Media & Society*, 13(1), pp. 114–133.

Morris, J., 1992. Personal and Political: A Feminist Perspective on Researching Physical Disability. *Disability, Handicap & Society*, 7(2), pp. 157–166.

Neuhaus, F. & Webmoor, T., 2012. Agile Ethics for Massified Research and Visualization. *Information, Communication & Society*, 15(1), pp. 43–65.

Obar, J.A., Zube, P. & Lampe, C., 2012. Advocacy 2.0: An Analysis of How Advocacy Groups in the United States Perceive and Use Social Media as Tools for Facilitating Civic Engagement and Collective Action. *Journal of Information Policy*, 2, pp. 1–25.

Page, R., 2012. *Stories and Social Media: Identities and Interaction*, London: Routledge.

Papacharissi, Z., 2010. *A Private Sphere: Democracy in a Digital Age*, Cambridge: Polity.

Poell, T., Abdulla, R., Rieder, B., Woltering, R. & Zack, L., 2016. Protest Leadership in the Age of Social Media. *Information, Communication & Society*, 19(7), pp. 994–1014.

Pointon, A., 1999. Out of the Closet: New Images of Disability in the Civil Rights Campaign. In B. Franklin, ed. *Social Policy, the Media and Misrepresentation*. London: Routledge, pp. 222–237.

Procter, R., Vis, F. & Voss, A., 2013. Reading the Riots on Twitter: Methodological Innovation for the Analysis of Big Data. *International Journal of Social Research Methodology*, 16(3), pp. 197–214.

Rainie, L. & Wellman, B., 2012. *Networked: The New Social Operating System*, Cambridge, MA: The MIT Press.

Ryfe, D.M., 2007. Narrative and Deliberation in Small Group Forums. *Journal of Applied Communication Research*, 34(1), pp. 72–93.

Scholz, T., 2010. Infrastructure: Its Transformations and Effects on Digital Activism. In M. Joyce, ed. *Digital Activism Decoded: The New Mechanics of Change*. New York: International Debate Education Association, pp. 17–31.

Shakespeare, T., 2006. *Disability Rights and Wrongs*, London: Routledge.

Shakespeare, T. & Watson, N., 2010. Beyond Models: Understanding the Complexity of Disabled People's Lives. In G. Scambler & S. Scambler, eds. *New Directions in the Sociology of Chronic and Disabling Conditions*. London: Palgrave Macmillan, pp. 57–77.

Snow, D. & Benford, R., 1992. Master Frames and Cycles of Protest. In A. Morris & C. McClurg Muller, eds. *Frontiers in Social Movement Theory.* New Haven, CT: Yale University Press, pp. 133–155.

Stromer-Galley, J., 2007. Measuring Deliberation's Content: A Coding Scheme. *Journal of Public Deliberation,* 3(1), pp. 1–35.

Stromer-Galley, J. & Martinson, A.M., 2009. Coherence in Political Computer-Mediated Communication: Analyzing Topic Relevance and Drift in Chat. *Discourse & Communication,* 3(2), pp. 195–216.

Stromer-Galley, J. & Muhlberger, P., 2009. Agreement and Disagreement in Group Deliberation: Effects on Deliberation Satisfaction, Future Engagement, and Decision Legitimacy. *Political Communication,* 26(2), pp. 173–192.

Thomas, C. & Corker, M., 2002. A Journey Around the Social Model. In M. Corker & T. Shakespeare, eds. *Disability/Postmodernity: Embodying Disability Theory.* London/New York: Continuum, pp. 18–31.

Tilly, C., 2004. *Social Movements: 1768–2004,* Boulder, CO: Paradigm.

Trevisan, F., 2012. ICTs for Empowerment? Disability Organizations and the Democratizing Potential of Web 2.0 in Scotland. In A. Manoharan & M. Holzer, eds. *E-Governance and Civic Engagement: Factors and Determinants of E-Democracy.* Hershey: IGI Globa, pp. 381–404.

——— 2014. Scottish Disability Organizations and Online Media: A Path to Empowerment or 'Business as Usual?' *Disability Studies Quarterly,* 34(3).

Trevisan, F. & Reilly, P., 2014. Ethical Dilemmas in Researching Sensitive Issues Online: Lessons From the Study of British Disability Dissent Networks. *Information, Communication & Society,* 17(9), pp. 1131–1146.

Vedel, T., 2006. The Idea of Electronic Democracy: Origins, Visions and Questions. *Parliamentary Affairs,* 59(2), pp. 226–235.

Vergeer, M. & Hermans, L., 2008. Analysing Online Political Discussions: Methodological Considerations. *Javnost-The Public,* 15(2), pp. 37–55.

Vromen, A. & Coleman, W., 2013. Online Campaigning Organizations and Storytelling Strategies: GetUp! in Australia. *Policy & Internet,* 5(1), pp. 76–100.

Watson, N., 1998. Enabling Identity: Disability, Self and Citizenship. In T. Shakespeare, ed. *The Disability Reader.* London: Continuum, pp. 147–162.

Whiteman, N., 2012. *Undoing Ethics: Rethinking Practice in Online Research,* London: Springer.

Zhongdang, P. & Kosicki, G.M., 2003. Framing as a Strategic Action in Public Deliberation. In S. Reese, O. Gandy, & A. Grant, eds. *Framing Public Life: Perspectives on Media and Our Understanding of the Social World.* Mahwah, NJ: Lawrence Erlbaum Associates, pp. 35–65.

Zimmer, M., 2010. 'But the Data Is Already Public': On the Ethics of Research in Facebook. *Ethics and Information Technology,* 12(4), pp. 313–325.

Zuckerman, E., 2015. Cute Cats to the Rescue? Participatory Media and Political Expression. In D. Allen & J. Light, eds. *Web Search: Information Science and Knowledge Management.* Chicago: University of Chicago Press, pp. 131–154.

5 Communication Flows, Leadership and The Emergence of 'Peer-Mediated' Citizenship

This chapter includes a detailed examination of the relationship between core organisers and rank-and-file supporters in The Hardest Hit, Disabled People Against Cuts (DPAC) and The Broken of Britain. By combining the analysis of Facebook content with data obtained from semi-structured interviews with core organisers, crucial differences are exposed with regard to the internal structure and perspective on social media of British disability advocacy groups. The chapter then goes on to consider the implications of these findings for the citizenship levels of disabled Internet users. Three distinct approaches to discussion on Facebook are delineated below. In particular, the limits of 'tactical' success, represented primarily by the ability to generate a high volume of conversation on Facebook, are explored. This illustrates that the amount of posts, in itself, was not a sign of meaningful participation or empowerment for 'ordinary' disabled Internet users. More broadly, this also provides the opportunity to discuss whether conversations that took place on Facebook were responsible for shaping group interaction or merely reproduced relationships and power differentials that were primarily negotiated in other venues, both online and offline. The chapter reflects also on the specific combinations of ideological ethos and strategic planning that led each group to champion a different approach to Facebook.

Overall, the result was one of tentative innovation in which change in the ecology of British disability activism was coupled with some potential for micro-empowerment at the individual level. However, political *talk*, and not collective *action*, represented the norm on Facebook in the vast majority of cases. Among the case studies considered in this book, The Broken of Britain's organisational structure stood out as surprisingly centralised and unstable, but also potentially empowering. Facebook played a key role in this process by enabling a new generation of tech-savvy disabled self-advocates to communicate with and 'represent' other disabled Internet users. This opened up new opportunities for disabled people's political citizenship to be mediated by a group of peers versed in the practice of digital advocacy instead of formal organisations with layers of bureaucracy and professionalised leaderships, or experienced activists that privileged a more traditional and arguably less effective repertoire of contention.

The Hardest Hit: 'Advocacy as Usual' Meets Micro-Empowerment

While Chapter 6 examines the perspective of The Hardest Hit on social media in the context of a comparison between U.K. and U.S. formal disability organisations, it is useful to reflect here on two ways in which this collaborative campaign approached Facebook at a time of crisis and heightened political debate. These include the prominence of personal stories on The Hardest Hit's Facebook page and the broader tendency for this coalition to focus its online endeavours on specific events. Although it could be argued that both these trends replicated advocacy tactics long established among British disability non-profits, a closer look at the data revealed that old practices had in fact been adjusted in significant ways.

In particular, the examination of the Facebook posts that contained personal stories of disability showed that the majority of these – roughly 60 per cent – had been posted in response to an explicit request from The Hardest Hit's Facebook page administrators to:

> Tell us [The Hardest Hit] what DLA [Disability Living Allowance] means for you and your family.
>
> (Facebook post, The Hardest Hit page administrator, 23 March 2011)

Undoubtedly, it is possible that publicly sharing these stories on Facebook boosted a sense of community among the supporters of this coalition. Personal narratives were regularly charged with emotional references and filled with intimate details, which arguably characterised them as 'hyper-personal' computer-mediated communication (Walther 1996). At the same time, however, the fact that these accounts had been requested directly by the organisers was reminiscent of the longstanding tendency for U.K. disability non-profits to elicit personal stories from supporters in order to include them in mediated campaign material (e.g. publicity, consultation documents, position papers, etc.).

As such, it could be argued that The Hardest Hit used Facebook in a way that supplemented the 'Your Stories' page featured on its main website (see Chapter 3 for details) in order to expand a tried and tested advocacy tactic. This generated a tension between the voluntary nature of user-contributions and the way in which personal narratives could in theory be edited for 'advocacy as usual'. This also created an ambiguous situation for which, potentially, digital channels could support both the emergence of new 'voices' and the use of pre-existing practices of indirect representation at the same time. In other words, the effect of these contributions on the empowerment of disabled Internet users was unclear as online stories were simultaneously mediated (on The Hardest Hit's website and other campaign material) and un-mediated (on Facebook and in personalised 'clicktivism plus' messages that individual supporters could send directly to policy-makers, as is discussed in Chapter 3).

A range of activist groups have used Facebook to ask their supporters to supply both personal stories and pictures in recent years. For example, the administrators of one of the main Facebook pages associated with the 2011 Egyptian revolution – *Kullena Khaled Said* – directly invited these types of contributions from supporters and curated this material to present a coherent online narrative. This created a 'looping process' between page administrators and Facebook users that combined 'a creative form of user participation' with 'the growing centrality of marketing techniques in contemporary protest' (Poell et al. 2016, p. 1005), granting ordinary citizens a greater level of engagement than the one provided by a traditional advocacy organisation. In light of this, it is interesting to note that the request for personal stories on The Hardest Hit's Facebook page generated some of the most popular conversations on it. This suggested that disabled Internet users, who were directly responsible for most of these posts, welcomed this kind of invitation as an opportunity to share their experiences, vent frustration and, possibly, find others in a similar situation. Furthermore, most of the personal stories on this page were framed in a positive way. In particular, personal stories were cast primarily as matters of 'socioeconomic citizenship' (Table 5.1). This detracted, at least partially, from the impression that disability non-profits may try to gather 'tragic' narratives to use in support of their agendas.

A second practice that The Hardest Hit 'inherited' from pre-existing advocacy repertoires was that for which interaction on Facebook was primarily driven by specific campaign events, clustering around the days of specific initiatives with almost completely 'silent' intermissions between them. As noted in Chapter 4, the high concentration of content on The Hardest Hit's Facebook page around the date of this group's London demonstration (11 May 2011) was a clear example of this practice.

Table 5.1 Arguments used to frame posts that included personal stories on The Hardest Hit's Facebook page

Arguments used to frame posts containing personal stories of disability (The Hardest Hit)	
Socio-economic citizenship	46.94%
Political citizenship	12.24%
Civil/human rights	2.04%
Moral panic	16.33%
Personal tragedy	14.28%
Media propaganda	—
Irony	—
Other	—
Not classifiable	8.17%

During that week, The Hardest Hit's Facebook page briefly replaced The Broken of Britain's as the busiest online discussion space in terms of user-contributions among those examined in this book. While this was in line with the strategies that other established advocacy organisations employed in the past to re-vitalise their mobilisation processes and reach new audiences (Chadwick 2007; Kenix 2007; Lusoli & Ward 2006), this nevertheless amounted to 'retro-fitting' the Web in order to support more traditional methods of participation. This suggested that The Hardest Hit coalition was more interested in short-term mobilisation than long-term engagement. As an advocacy specialist from one of The Hardest Hit's sponsor organisations stated in an interview:

> [The disability] organisations [involved in The Hardest Hit] lack[ed] a strategy to create momentum and sustain engagement in the long term.
> (Interview, Campaigns officer, U.K. charity,
> September 2011)

In some ways, it was underwhelming that this coalition had built its online endeavours on familiar tactics. While in fact some of its sponsor organisations took a more daring approach on their own social networking pages, The Hardest Hit coalition as a whole stuck to a fairly standard online repertoire. That said, it would be unfair to label its use of Facebook as simply 'advocacy as usual'. This is because the interviews with those who were directly in charge of The Hardest Hit's Facebook page revealed that:

> [M]essages received through Facebook influenced decision-making, for example the local marches organised for [the 22] October [2011] came out of this [a suggestion made by Facebook supporters].
> (Interview, Communications officer, U.K. charity,
> July 2011)

Ordinary users were able to advance suggestions directly to seemingly responsive leaders, who listened to requests for more accessible and de-centralised campaign events. At the same time, this channel also enabled leaders to 'harness' the potential of the crowd, capture its mood and interpret its needs. While decisional power remained the prerogative of few people, ordinary users had an indirect opportunity to shape the campaign through contributions such as Facebook comments. Supporter-generated requests resulted in new events being added to the campaign calendar that contributed to the continuation of this coalition past its first demonstration on the streets of London. This represented again a form of mediated participation, yet one that was different from the 'appropriation' of disabled people's personal stories seen in the past. It was more about co-defining paths to participation than supporting pre-arranged initiatives.

For these reasons, this process could be described as a form of 'micro-empowerment', which is less about directly participating in decision-making and organisational agenda setting, and more about informing the opinion of representative leaders (Davey 1999, p. 38). Overall, this was acknowledged by the disability organisations involved in this coalition, which stressed that:

> [B]ecause of changes in people's expectations as their familiarity with technology advances, organisations necessarily have to lessen their input in campaigning.
>
> (Interview, Campaigns officer, U.K. charity,
> September 2011)

Undoubtedly, this represented only a partial step towards the establishment of more inclusive and empowering models of online participation. Yet, for disabled Internet users, this could provide an opportunity to become what Coleman (2005) has defined as 'directly represented citizens' (p. 211–12). This means that, while direct representation remains an unrealistic and impractical utopia, technology could reform the relationship between ordinary supporters and campaign organisers. On balance, this could be seen as evidence of the 'normalised revolution' introduced by Web 2.0 platforms (Wright 2012), for which the expansion of the interactive Internet and two-way communication channels update and enhance, but do not overturn, the representative system typical of liberal democracies. As a severe limit to this process, however, it remains that micro-empowerment for ordinary Internet users depends entirely on the existence of a responsible leadership willing to listen to their digital grassroots and act accordingly.

Disabled People Against Cuts: Protest in Flux

Among the groups examined for this project, DPAC was the one that hosted the smallest amount of discussion on its Facebook page. Nevertheless, it would be misleading to interpret this as proof of a social media failure. Instead, scratching beneath the surface revealed that DPAC had adopted an approach to online communications that was very coherent with its collective ethos, albeit limited in its potential for innovation and anchored to an understanding of activism that sees traditional protest tactics as the main forms of participation. Three main elements contributed to this outcome, including: the relationship between online talk on Facebook and offline direct action; the care that went into setting up a Facebook space that would promote inclusiveness and equality (within the limits set by Facebook templates); and, finally, the limited number of personal disability stories found on DPAC's page.

Very nearly half of the content posted to DPAC's Facebook page during the period examined here mentioned some form of political action

Table 5.2 Share of Facebook posts that mentioned political action explicitly

Group	Posts that mentioned action	Posts that did not mention action
The Broken of Britain	19.4%	80.6%
DPAC	49%	51%
The Hardest Hit	39%	61%

Table 5.3 Types of political action mentioned in Facebook posts

Types of political action	As percentage of posts containing action		
	The Hardest Hit	The Broken of Britain	DPAC
Individual action (e.g. email politician)	9.2%	8.9%	5.3%
Collective online (e.g. e-protest page)	5.3%	6.9%	8.0%
Collective in person (e.g. street protest)	51.3%	45.5%	57.3%
Spread the word online	13.2%	14.9%	13.3%
Contact the news media	3.9%	2.0%	2.7%
Oust politicians at elections	1.3%	3.5%	2.7%
Mandate core organisers to represent supporters	—	8.9%	—
Unspecified action	1.3%	9.4%	10.7%

(Table 5.2). In addition, the majority of these posts referred directly to traditional protest initiatives and other collective 'in-person' actions endorsed or co-organised by DPAC such as the Trades Union Congress (TUC) demonstration in London (Table 5.3). Typically, these posts were dedicated to arranging practicalities or sharing useful information for those who wished to participate in street protests. Furthermore, the less frequent Facebook conversations that discussed online collective action focused primarily on promoting the virtual protest pages set up on DPAC's website for the benefit of people who were unable to attend demonstrations in person.

In light of these results, DPAC's Facebook page functioned as a useful channel to mobilise supporters towards a specific goal. This demonstrated that lower levels of activity on Facebook are not necessarily connected to smaller amounts of collective action and vice-versa. In addition, given that many of this group's core organisers were directly involved in the disabled people's movement of the 1980s and early 1990s, this could be interpreted as further evidence that experienced disability activists have started to integrate digital tools into a campaigning repertoire in which street protest continues to occupy a central role. Further evidence of this trend was provided by DPAC's Atos Games campaign during the 2012 London Paralympics, which

Table 5.4 Share of Facebook posts that mentioned any political institution

	Posts that mentioned institutions	Posts that did not mention institutions
DPAC	19.6%	80.4%
The Broken of Britain	44.6%	55.4%
The Hardest Hit	46.2%	53.8%

used social media but continued to revolve also around physical protest (Pearson & Trevisan 2015).

Interestingly, only one in five DPAC Facebook posts referred to a politician or a democratic institution. Instead, these figures were mentioned more than twice as frequently on the Facebook pages maintained by The Hardest Hit and The Broken of Britain (Table 5.4). This corroborated the impression that DPAC privileged direct action over institutionalised forms of representation. In other words, conversations on DPAC's Facebook page suggested that its supporters saw this group as collateral, or altogether alternative to the representative system (Tilly 2008), and believed that the most effective way for it to put its message across was:

> [T]o take a stance, 'outside' Parliament, rather than inside.
>
> (Facebook post, DPAC supporter, 29 March 2011)

In light of these considerations, the traditional repertoire of contention continued to represent the main priority for both this group's core organisers and its online supporters. This is not to say that DPAC failed to appreciate the growing importance and opportunities offered by online advocacy in contemporary movements. At the same time, however, it was strongly influenced by previous experiences of disability activism, which favoured the use of electronic media as extensions of street protests rather than spaces for the promotion of radically new forms of political action. These findings were consistent with observations made in previous work on social movement groups and the Internet (Lievrouw 2011, pp. 174–6). What, then, lay at the origin of such a cautious approach to e-advocacy?

Two of DPAC's founders talked extensively about the rationale that underpinned their approach to digital media when they were interviewed for this book. In particular, they seemed fully aware of the ambivalent nature of platforms such as Facebook for disabled Internet users. As such, while they claimed that:

> [V]irtual protest at least makes disabled users feel less useless.
>
> (Interview, DPAC founder, June 2011)

They were also:

> [C]oncern[ed] for disabled people without Internet access [...] and for Facebook's nature as a 'gated community'.
> (Interview, DPAC founder, June 2011)

This confirmed that DPAC's leading members, who were rooted both personally and ideologically in the history of the British disabled people's movement, were in fact positively inclined towards a 'participatory' approach to social media that is respectful of the needs of both disabled users and non-users. Inevitably, this quest for inclusiveness required DPAC to avoid some of the digital tactics employed by other groups, including the pursuit of high volumes of Facebook discussion. This was reflected in DPAC's choice to set up a Facebook group page with multiple administrators identified by their personal screen-names as opposed to a 'fan' page with a single, anonymous profile owner. More importantly, this also meant that DPAC's organisers:

> adopt[ed] a selective approach to posting material on Facebook because many disabled users cannot cope with information overload.
> (Interview, DPAC founder, June 2011)

These principles explained the relatively small number of starter contributions posted by DPAC's core organisers to their Facebook page and consequently the low volume of discussion that this hosted. This revealed an entirely different approach to Facebook compared to the one adopted by The Broken of Britain. Not only did DPAC understand 'quantity' and 'quality' of online content to be separate from one another but it also clearly preferred the latter to the former. Furthermore, these findings also resonated with those that identified concerns with regard to the inclusiveness of new media technologies as one of the key reasons for the 'conservative' views on interactive platforms held by Scottish member-led disability organisations (Trevisan 2014).

Finally, another element that revealed DPAC's commitment to the creation of an inclusive online environment was the relatively low number of personal stories retrieved on its Facebook page compared to those of other groups. Indeed, the mere presence of personal narratives on a page maintained by a group committed to reinforcing disabled people's collective identity constituted a reminder of the need for disability theorists to re-evaluate the importance of individual lived experiences. In particular, future research should investigate how disabled Internet users 'framed' their experiences in contributions to online conversations about relevant policy issues with a view to assessing the role of impairment in identity formation, which has too often been overlooked due to its historical association with the medical model of disability (Crow 1996;

French 1993; Shakespeare 1994). That said, the limited frequency with which individual stories appeared on DPAC's Facebook page was underpinned by a deliberate choice to:

[T]ake personality out of DPAC because we are different from personal blogs [such as those run by The Broken of Britain], we want to be a united voice, and not speak only for one person at a time.

(Interview, DPAC founder, June 2011)

Similarly, DPAC actively discouraged its supporters from posting personal stories on Facebook in an effort to:

[P]romote intersectionality that reflects the differences that exist among disabled people, and prevent individualism and stigmatisation.

(Interview, DPAC founder, July 2011)

These arguments mirrored those advanced previously by the disabled people's movement and social model scholars, who criticised the use of individual narratives of impairment for advocacy and fundraising by disability non-profits (Barnes 1992). At the same time, however, this attempt to avoid personal accounts on Facebook was not part of a 'blanket ban' on personal stories. As was discussed in Chapter 3, DPAC used personal stories in some of its more recent initiatives, most notably the campaign against the closure of the Independent Living Fund (ILF) launched in March 2013. However, in these cases the use of personal stories and private narratives was centrally coordinated. Although this approach may seem at odds with the ideals of participatory online activism proposed by DPAC, it can be reasonably assumed to reflect the determination of its founders to prevent the diffusion of disempowering stories of disability that focus primarily on impairment. In this context, it is useful to note that the stories used by DPAC in these more recent campaigns have tended to emphasise issues of poverty, discrimination and entitlement over illness and impairment (Trevisan 2015).

Overall, DPAC's approach to Facebook was strongly characterised by its commitment to inclusiveness. This led this group to use Facebook as a channel to support and expand the 'classic' protest repertoire of disability rights activism, with both positive and negative consequences. Undoubtedly, discussions on DPAC's Facebook page reflected a strong sense of collective identity, which in turn reinforced its credibility as a long-term movement in contrast to issue-focused and temporary coalitions. Yet, this space was primarily intended as an electronic extension of traditional protest initiatives, while creativity and experimentation were effectively held back. Despite originating from praiseworthy ideals, such reluctance to engage in more innovative areas of digital advocacy might in fact be detrimental to this group in the long run. This is because it could make it increasingly difficult for experienced self-advocates to keep up with the ever-changing political and technological landscape, thus limiting opportunities for rejuvenating the disabled people's movement as a whole. In particular, a generational gap seems to be looming, with young energies channelled into other forms of participation, as demonstrated by The Broken of Britain's rapid ascent. As one of DPAC's founders noted in an interview carried out for this book:

> [Y]oung disabled people don't come to us, not even through electronic media.
>
> (Interview, DPAC founder, June 2011)

While better ways to fully conciliate inclusiveness with innovative trends in digital advocacy may indeed emerge as activists become more familiar with political uses of technology, this situation provided a powerful reminder of the potential ambivalence of social media for disability advocates as both an opportunity for renewal and a source of concern.

The Broken of Britain and the Emergence of 'Peer-Mediated' Citizenship

Compared to the other two groups considered here, The Broken of Britain was somewhat of a trendsetter. This group introduced an innovative, online-only action repertoire and was very popular with online supporters. At the height of the welfare reform debate in 2011, its Facebook page hosted an amount of conversation up to ten times higher than those of the other groups considered in this book. Yet, was this 'tactical' success ultimately linked to meaningful user-participation? In other words, did Facebook conversation contribute to the empowerment of those involved? To answer these questions, it is useful to examine in detail three crucial issues, including: this group's vision of online advocacy as a more effective alternative to traditional forms of protest and dissent; the relationship between online *talk* and political *action* on its Facebook page; and, finally, what Facebook conversations revealed about The Broken of Britain's internal structure and its implications for internal pluralism and long-term sustainability. The picture that emerged from this analysis diverged in various ways from the idea of a horizontal network promoting online dialogue with ordinary Facebook users. Nevertheless, this structure also enabled The Broken of Britain to promote new ways to exercise political citizenship in less contentious and arguably more effective ways for disabled Internet users.

A Third Way Between 'Corrupt' and 'Contentious' Politics

While a widespread sense of wariness and frustration with 'politics as usual' was evident on all the Facebook pages examined in this study, these feelings were especially prominent on The Broken of Britain's page. Those who had posted on this page not only expressed profound distrust in politicians, but also felt 'abandoned' by society more generally, including institutions such as British news media organisations and even other anti-cuts groups that allegedly brushed disabled people's concerns aside to paint a broader picture. For example, during the TUC march against the cuts, one supporter of The Broken of Britain wrote on Facebook that:

> [T]he old 'Invisible me' thing is going on! [. . .] Heartening to see us [disabled people] there [at the march], but saddened by the lack of public & Union Support.
>
> (Facebook post, The Broken of Britain supporter,
> 26 March 2011)

Similarly, another supporter posted to say that:

> [L]ike most other people, they [the TUC march organisers] thought we [disabled people] would go away and have nothing to say. Just how wrong can they be?
>
> (Facebook post, The Broken of Britain supporter,
> 26 March 2011)

Furthermore, mentions of politicians – whether specific members of the government, parliamentarians or local representatives – on this page were charged with expletives and emotional language in greater measure compared to the Facebook pages run by DPAC and The Hardest Hit. This was interesting because the use of this kind of expressive rhetoric has been found to be a mark of low quality online political talk (Graham 2010). While this is not the place for a detailed linguistic analysis of these Facebook posts, it useful to note that negative characterisations applied equally to political figures of any ideological persuasion with the sole exception of Green Party representatives, who were described positively but mentioned in only four posts.

In particular, there was a large amount of Facebook content that criticised the Labour Party. This was surprising as conventional wisdom indicates Labour as a 'guardian' of the welfare state and therefore a natural ally of disabled people's organisations. For example, several supporters of The Broken of Britain had posted on Facebook to claim that there was no distinction between Labour and the government, observing that:

> They [Labour] are letting political alliance cloud their judgement. No better than the [Conservative–Liberal Democrat] Coalition [government]!
>
> (Facebook post, The Broken of Britain supporter,
> 26 March 2011)

Another supporter used Facebook to question the motives for which Labour had become involved in initiatives such as the TUC march against the cuts, pointing out that:

> [A]llowing the protest [TUC march] to be hijacked by [then Labour leader Ed] Miliband was a failure of purpose.
> (Facebook post, The Broken of Britain supporter, 26 March 2011)

These sentiments were reflected in interviews with The Broken of Britain's founders, who unambiguously branded the Labour leadership as:

> Rats fighting on a sinking ship: all they [Labour leaders] care about is themselves and getting back into power.
> (Interview, The Broken of Britain founder, July 2011)

In fact, Labour was mentioned more frequently than any other British political party on The Broken of Britain's Facebook page (Table 5.5). This was surprising given that Labour was in opposition and anger was naturally expected to be directed at government parties, in particular the Conservatives. Furthermore, the then Labour leader Ed Miliband was the second most talked about politician, behind only Prime Minister David Cameron. Typically, Miliband was criticised for being 'too soft' about disability welfare cuts or even a 'traitor' of disabled people.

Table 5.5 Share of Facebook posts that mentioned specific politicians or institutions

Institution	DPAC	The Broken of Britain	The Hardest Hit
David Cameron (Prime Minister)	3.3%	9.5%	3.3%
Ed Miliband (Leader of the opposition)	—	6.6%	—
Maria Miller (Minister for Disabled People)	—	1.9%	17.8%
George Osborne (Chancellor of the Exchequer)	—	2.7%	—
Iain Duncan Smith (Work and Pensions Secretary)	—	1.2%	—
Other ministers	—	5.6%	2.2%
Conservative Party	3.3%	5.8%	4.4%
Liberal Democrats	3.3%	2.7%	2.2%
Labour Party	3.3%	6.4%	—
Government	13.3%	9.9%	22.2%
Parliament	16.7%	5.8%	6.7%
Department for Work and Pensions (DWP)	10.0%	4.5%	7.8%
National Health Service (NHS)	—	2.3%	1.1%
DWP/NHS contractors	10.0%	5.0%	6.7%
Traditional mass media (e.g. BBC, Guardian, etc.)	3.3%	11.4%	4.4%

This clearly illustrated the high levels of distrust in all politicians among The Broken of Britain's supporters and core organisers.

Growing distrust of politicians and strong criticism of party politics are certainly not new and well documented in Western democracies (Franklin 2004). Traditionally, these trends are seen as co-determinants of a widespread decline in political participation. In this case, however, the negative rhetoric that was applied to politicians did not transfer over to the institute of representative democracy itself, which instead was regarded as a legitimate decision-making system. Discussions on Facebook showed that The Broken of Britain's founders were keen on joining institutionalised participation channels. Their supporters seemed to approve of this type of approach. The Broken of Britain's core organisers actively pursued opportunities to meet with government representatives. As they explained in a Facebook post:

> [T]he meeting at the [House of] Commons on Monday [28 March 2011 was] ... achieved without having to throw [at the government] anything beyond well-researched, intelligently written and substantiated arguments.
>
> (Facebook post, The Broken of Britain page
> administrator, 27 March 2011)

Similarly, some of The Broken of Britain's founders participated in the Labour Party conference in September 2011, putting questions to Ed Miliband in one of the sessions. Although this may seem at odds with the sentiment of extreme frustration towards politicians expressed on this group's Facebook page, episodes like these signalled its determination to advocate for the rights of disabled people within the system of representative democracy. While groups like DPAC protested outside political party conferences, The Broken of Britain had tried to find a way in. More generally, the decision to engage with formal political arenas set The Broken of Britain apart from other examples of networked activism that have emerged in recent years, including the Occupy movement, which found it difficult to influence public decision-making while rejecting the legitimacy of elected representatives and democratic processes as we know them (Castells 2012, pp. 235–6).

In this context, the scorn poured over 'evil' politicians on Facebook could be seen as a perverse consequence of the broader tendency for British politics to become increasingly personalised and mediated (Langer 2010, 2011). As individual personalities have taken centre stage in politics, the blame for the welfare crisis was placed on 'morally corrupt' individuals. These attacks seem to discredit the person, but not the institution they represent. These patterns were reflected in the way in which arguments were framed on this group's Facebook page, which, as was discussed in the previous chapter, combined the idea of 'moral panic' with a strong belief in disabled people's 'political rights' (see Table 4.5 in Chapter 4). As The Broken of Britain's page administrator explained on Facebook, these circumstances led this group to the realisation that:

> [T]here doesn't seem to be anyone fighting our [disabled people's] corner these days [...], [and therefore] we [they] need to fight our [their] own corner and not give up!
>
> (Facebook post, The Broken of Britain page administrator, 27 March 2011)

This, in turn, raised the issue of what repertoire should be employed in order to ensure the efficacy of representation for disabled people. This issue was particularly challenging for The Broken of Britain, which was openly opposed to traditional protest and contentious tactics. The reason for this dislike was primarily strategic. As one of The Broken of Britain's founders explained in a Tweet:

> Shouting/screaming doesn't work. [...] There's real desire to understand out there, but fear to ask. [...] Explaining the reality of our lives calmly & rationally does [work].
>
> (Tweet, The Broken of Britain founder, June 2011)

In other words, digital advocacy was seen as a viable and more effective form of participation than traditional protest. Online actions had the added benefit of reaching out to and possibly engaging other disabled Internet users who felt uncomfortable with contentious action. When the perceived reluctance of Labour to assuming a strong position against the then coalition government's welfare reform created a 'representation void' for disabled people, The Broken of Britain turned to new media technologies to fill that gap in ways compatible with representative democracy. This is not to say that this group's core organisers were naïve about the dynamics of institutionalised politics. On the contrary, their strategy derived from the awareness that:

> The digital age has completely changed the nature of activism. [...] Older methods like demos work but to reach a lot of people in a short time you need the web.
>
> (Tweet, The Broken of Britain founder, June 2011)

More generally, this showed that online media can make an original contribution to the existing repertoire of disability activism, especially in times of crisis. The picture emerging from these considerations was therefore consistent with the expectation formulated in Chapter 3 that The Broken of Britain would be using social media to provide politically-isolated disabled users with a 'moderate' option for direct participation where previously there would not have been one. On the one hand, this confirmed the impression of this group as one that sought to reach out to new online 'audiences' by positioning itself as the promoter of a different form of advocacy for those disappointed by the efforts of formal disability organisations but at the same time also reluctant to take part in direct actions such as street protests, sit-ins or occupations. On the other hand, however, this also raised the question of whether platforms such as Facebook were in fact used to support digital advocacy efforts directly. The next section focuses on this issue in detail.

Facebook 'Talk' Versus 'Action'

Coding for explicit mentions of political action in Facebook posts clearly showed that the percentage of posts openly discussing action on The Broken of Britain's page was substantially lower than those for the other two case studies (see Table 5.2). Having said that, these data revealed also that the frequency with which specific types of action were discussed was strikingly similar among the three groups. In particular, traditional protest tactics (e.g. rallies and street demonstrations) were the type of collective action discussed most frequently on all the Facebook pages under examination, followed at a considerable distance by invitations to 'spread the word' by sharing content online (see Table 5.3). On The Broken of Britain's page, a striking 69 per cent of all references to traditional collective action focused directly on the TUC march. This means that, if the TUC march had been included in the coding scheme as a separate category, it would have accounted for 6.8 per cent of all the Facebook content coded for this group. These patterns were expected for both DPAC and The Hardest Hit due to the important role that street demonstrations played in their respective repertoires, as discussed in Chapters 3 and 4. Yet, the prominence that these types of tactics had in discussions on The Broken of Britain's page was rather surprising.

At first, this high level of interest for street demonstrations may seem paradoxical for the supporters of a group that was fully committed to digital advocacy. However, it was interesting to note that these conversations consisted entirely of event commentary. The Broken of Britain's supporters used Facebook to talk about what happened at events such as the TUC march, which they experienced through news coverage or social media feeds. Yet, they almost never asked for or provided logistical details for these kinds of events in Facebook conversations. Similarly, ways to participate in protests remotely through new media platforms were not mentioned either. A close look at starter posts – including orphans – revealed that, although the page administrator posted links to The Broken of Britain's own digital initiatives numerous times during the period under examination, only a small percentage of these posts attracted comments. Therefore, the posts that focused on the TUC march fell under two broad categories, including: contributions that reported the events almost in real-time; and threads that discussed the episodes of vandalism that surrounded the march. In particular, the discussion of politically-motivated violence was exclusive to The Broken of Britain, as this topic failed to generate extended conversations on the Facebook pages of the other groups.

While a detailed examination of the content of these conversations about collective action is beyond the scope of this book, it is crucial to note that their commentary nature fitted entirely with Facebook's role as an open discussion forum for The Broken of Britain, as discussed in Chapter 4. As one of the founders explained in an interview, this group believed that:

> [Facebook] is a hub for people to go and get information from, [...] which is what it is designed and set up for and that's why people go to it. [...] People are angry and disenfranchised and frightened [...]; what they need is a space to air those fears and a group of people who can put it together in some sort of coherent narrative that they can then support.
>
> (Interview, The Broken of Britain founder, July 2011)

Facebook was designated as a space for *talk* and not a venue for *action* or a platform for organising mass mobilisation. The Broken of Britain's founder went on to explain that, on Facebook, users enjoyed the:

> [F]reedom to come and go, and the freedom to express themselves more clearly.
>
> (Interview, The Broken of Britain founder, July 2011)

Yet, key decisions as well as political action remained in the hands of a restricted group of people, whose self-discerned:

> job is [was] to go through the information, to find the bits that we [they] can use and put them into a narrative on one side to the public and the media, and on the other side to the politicians.
>
> (Interview, The Broken of Britain founder, July 2011)

As explained here, this strategy was consistent with the one adopted by other emerging advocacy networks such as GetUp!, which have collected the experiences and opinions of supporters through new media technologies and then used this material as the basis for building coherent messages aimed at influencing both public opinion and policy-makers (Vromen & Coleman 2013). These findings cemented The Broken of Britain's place among those organisations whose 'campaign strategies are built around the Internet' (Karpf 2012, p. 156), but at the same time 'are far different from the "organising without organisations" often heralded in public discourse' (ibid.). In light of these considerations, it is important to reflect on the internal structure of this group. What kind of relationship did The Broken of Britain's innovative and moderate repertoire promote between core organisers and rank-and-file supporters? What implications did that have for their levels of citizenship?

Nothing About us Without (the Five of) us

As was discussed in Chapter 4, The Broken of Britain's core organisers fulfilled an essential role in building momentum and stimulating Facebook discussion around specific catalysts. A closer look at the content of the online exchanges between core organisers and their supporters revealed more important details about the structure of this network. First, the centrality of core organisers did not occur by chance. Instead, it was the result of a deliberate effort by this group's founders to establish a clear structure and carve out a strong leadership position that would enable them to control key decisions. In particular, a series of Facebook posts that The Broken of Britain's page administrator contributed to a discussion about the TUC demonstration on the 26 March was especially illuminating. In these posts, The Broken of Britain explicitly invited its supporters to:

> [N]ot do anything in #TBofB's [The Broken of Britain's] name w/o [without] consulting us [the founders] first, however well-intentioned it might be.
>
> (Facebook post, The Broken of Britain page administrator, 26 March 2011)

In addition, these posts clarified also that supporters should publicise the campaign only:

> [A]s long as no-one outside of the core TBofB [The Broken of Britain] team of 5 does something in an official capacity . . . and [not] without clearing it with us [the founders] beforehand. Particularly anything to do with our branding and photos.
>
> (Facebook post, The Broken of Britain page administrator, 26 March 2011)

These Facebook posts were generated in response to an episode in which a small group of individuals was seen using the The Broken of Britain's logo and name at the TUC march in ways that core organisers deemed unauthorised. By publishing these 'guidelines' on Facebook, The Broken of Britain was unusually transparent about its desire to keep the ability to act on behalf of the group limited to its core 'team'. This approach is typical of many activist groups, although most are less open about it or try to hide it from supporters (della Porta 2005; della Porta & Diani 2006). In this instance, an incident that the group's founders saw as a potential threat to the coherence of their message exposed the inherent tension between the participatory nature of online advocacy and the strategic need for a group to protect its 'brand'. In addition, these posts could be interpreted also as an attempt to ensure that The Broken of Britain did not become involved directly in street protests or other direct action tactics, which can cause online organisers to lose both their relevance and ability to steer the movement (Gerbaudo 2012; Poell et al. 2016). Thus, at times, core organisers may feel forced to curb some of the spontaneity of their supporters in order for their strategy to work effectively. Other action networks, much larger than The Broken of Britain, have struggled with this in recent years. This includes Occupy and the groups that spearheaded the Egyptian revolution in 2011. All of these have strived to project a collective image online while setting an extensive list of guidelines for the use of social media in order to ensure they projected a coherent message (Gerbaudo 2012; Kavada 2015; Poell et al. 2016). Previously, a similar trend had been identified in the peace movement (Olsson 2008).

This approach certainly addressed some of the key weaknesses of digital activist networks, including the lack of a clear leadership (Bennett 2003). However, this also introduced some of the typical drawbacks of more established advocacy organisations to The Broken of Britain, including structural rigidity and difficulties in adapting to changing circumstances (Taylor & Burt 2005). This lack of flexibility in particular had the potential to seriously compromise this group's resilience in the long term. This very limit became apparent on several occasions, both during the period examined in detail here and later in 2011. As is discussed in Chapter 4, the days on which The Broken of Britain's Facebook account manager was not very active were characterised by a virtual 'silence' on the page. This happened on 21 February and again on 6 March, as well as 13 March (see Figure 4.1 in the previous chapter for details). Moreover, the data for May, when the page administrator was unable to attend to it due to personal reasons, identified a similar – albeit more gradual – pattern. Finally, discussion came to a sudden halt in November 2011, when the organisers posted a notice on the group's website to inform supporters that they needed to 'take a break' from campaigning. Almost immediately, the number of posts on the Facebook page shrunk drastically and stopped altogether in April 2012. Although in their notice the organisers said that they hoped to put the campaign on hold for only about a month, The Broken of Britain as a whole rapidly lost momentum and never returned to its previous levels of activity.

Since then, other digital disability action networks have emerged in the U.K., which represent a 'legacy' of The Broken of Britain. Examples include the Spartacus Network and Where's the Benefit. As was discussed in Chapter 3, some of the founders of The Broken of Britain have been involved in these new initiatives, which arguably demonstrates the idea of 'sedimentary' networks put forward by Chadwick (2007). By remaining committed to social media activism over a number of years, these individuals defy traditional assumptions that see online activists as short-term oriented and ephemeral (Bastos & Mercea 2015). Yet, the decline of The Broken of Britain as a group also provides a useful reminder of the fact that online initiatives centred on a small set of very active organisers are at risk of disappearing as rapidly as they can acquire prominence. Whatever the reasons for The Broken of Britain's sudden stop, its disappearance points to its lack of flexibility and inability to stabilise its supporter-base in order to set itself up for the long term, possibly shifting organising responsibilities to new members. Whether because of internal disagreements or more simply because the group's founders felt unable to keep up with what is required to run a successful campaign, this showed that the importance of core organisers in digital disability activism cannot be overstated. Such visionary leadership is a fundamental driver of innovation in digital advocacy, but can also be a source of great vulnerability if it is not able to distribute responsibility more broadly once a network has grown.

These findings clashed with the conventional wisdom about social media, which sees them as tools for promoting horizontal networks in which power is diffused rather than concentrated among few people. At the same time, they also outlined a structure that was arguably capable of legitimising a new generation of disabled self-advocates and boosting their visibility. The analysis suggested that The Broken of Britain's founders, similarly to the leaders of traditional non-profits (Kenix 2008), believed in the potential of social media to provide advocates with credibility in the public arena. Having said that, the central role played by The Broken of Britain's small and inflexible core 'team' generated two main limitations. First, there was a basic resilience problem, for which this group rapidly entered a declining spiral when core organisers suspended their activity. Second, there was also an issue with the accountability of said organisers. This undoubtedly had implications for the levels of citizenship of those who supported The Broken of Britain. Although it may be tempting to assume that this kind of group structure could only provide ordinary disabled Internet users with the illusion of empowerment, it is important not to rush to conclusions. Considering these findings in the context of citizenship theory as discussed in Chapter 1 and the levels of user-engagement on Facebook presented in the previous chapter revealed the situation to be more complex and nuanced than it looked at first.

De Facto *Leadership and 'Peer-Mediated' Citizenship*

As was illustrated in Chapter 4, three different types of users had clustered around The Broken of Britain's Facebook page. These included:

1   The five disabled bloggers responsible for launching The Broken of Britain. They adopted a particularly 'hands on' approach to online

activism and therefore were central not only to the very existence of this group but also to its continued growth until its sudden stop in November 2011.

2   Nearly 200 supporters who actively contributed to the Facebook page, interacting with one another and with core organisers. Around 100 of these users participated in multiple Facebook discussions at the height of the welfare reform debate. That said, their involvement remained largely confined to political *talk* rather than *action*. Thus, their role in shaping the campaign only went as far as core organisers were willing to act upon their suggestions and follow up on their requests submitted through Facebook.

3   A majority of supporters – ca. 1,400 on Facebook and 5,000 on Twitter – who more simply followed The Broken of Britain's updates on different social media platforms, as well as its website.

The different communicative styles adopted by the first two of these subgroups set them at different lengths along the continuum between digital 'residents' and 'visitors' envisaged by White and Le Cornu (2011). In turn, this could be stretched even further to account for the large group of 'observers' whose main contribution to The Broken of Britain was to boost its following on social media and, possibly, share its posts with other social media users. As communication practices have a fundamental role in defining the very structure of contemporary networked activism (Castells 2012, p. 229; Gerbaudo 2012, p. 139), it is possible to draw a parallel between these practices and different citizenship profiles. As Nakamura (2004) wrote, this helps to:

> [E]nvision various *categories* of online citizens rather than thinking in terms of gaps and divides. Just as on airplanes [. . .] this metaphor can be useful because it dodges the problematics of the binary digital divide by envisioning Internet use as subject to several gradations.
>
> (p. 80)

In the case of advocacy networks such as The Broken of Britain, different Internet users perform different roles, which in turn are associated with different citizenship styles, some more intense than others.

In the case of The Broken of Britain, it was possible to identify three such citizenship categories. First, the group's founders could be described as 'digital residents' and therefore 'connected citizens'. They capitalised on their familiarity with technology, knowledge of the policy context and personal experience of disability to broadcast alternative and un-mediated views on disability welfare. At the same time, they also devised opportunities for others to contribute to the campaign by adding their own personalised content through a combination of readily available online media (e.g. 'blog swarms', targeted Twitter hashtags, etc.) that accounted as much as possible for the needs of users with different impairments. Second, supporters who regularly contributed to Facebook discussions were 'digital visitors' and 'monitorial citizens' (Schudson 2011). They used online media to keep up to date with and comment on the course of events, informing the positions of core organisers with their opinions and personal accounts, especially disabled supporters. Yet, they also took a back seat when it came to political action. As Prior (2008) noted, 'monitorial' tasks are encouraged and facilitated by the hyperlinked nature of online information. Third, the position of the large group of 'observers' who followed The Broken of Britain on social media but only very rarely, if ever, contributed original content was somewhat ambiguous. In some ways, it could be tempting to class these users as 'slacktivists' who limited themselves to 'liking' the campaign on Facebook and lurking on its Web presence more generally. Yet, their role as 'observers' suggested it may be unfair to automatically consider them as passive free-riders. This is because, in theory, these followers could at any point use the knowledge they had accumulated by keeping up with the campaign and the welfare reform progress on social media to join the ranks of monitorial citizens. Thus, their perceived lack of agency might have been only temporary, expressing an embryonic form of participation, which arguably characterised them as 'latent citizens'.

While in order to verify whether 'latent citizens' do in fact transform into 'monitorial citizens' and, if so, for what reasons and in what numbers requires longitudinal research that follows these 'observers' over a greater period of time, it is useful to visualise the three citizenship profiles listed here as a series of concentric circles (Figure 5.1). At the centre of this model are core organisers, from which opportunities for others to become involved – and thus accrue political rights – radiate. This representation evokes the tendency for core (professional) and periphery (volunteer) agents in political campaigns to be increasingly connected and interdependent (Anstead 2009), as well as the idea of citizenship as a series of consecutive concentric stages outlined by Turner (1986). Intuitively, this categorisation may look at odds with the definitions of participatory parity and inclusive citizenship in feminist theory (Fraser 2003; Lister 2004, 2007). Yet, it ought to be pointed out that participatory parity does not postulate the achievement of the most sophisticated levels of participation by everyone. Rather, it more simply predicates that all are given fair opportunities to participate in politics. What truly matters is equality of opportunity and freedom from barriers, with the understanding that, while everyone can benefit from these conditions, some will take a more proactive approach to politics than others and become more intensely involved in advocacy initiatives.

Given the central role played by equality of opportunity and freedom from barriers in enabling inclusive citizenship, the key question here is how permeable the boundaries between communicative styles – and thus citizenship profiles – really are and how likely it is for online supporters to move across them to become more or less directly involved in advocacy

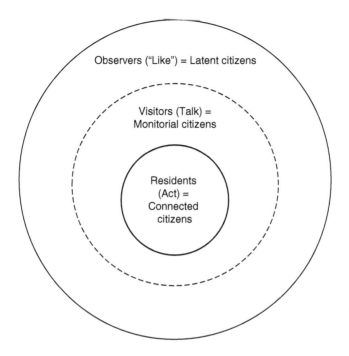

Figure 5.1 Communicative styles and citizenship profiles in peer-mediated citizenship.

work. This is a complex issue that is determined by a variety of factors including, for example, the types of issues at stake at any one moment and the motivation for people to act that derives from them, the specific online platforms involved in a given campaign and the technological know-how of potential supporters. One element that stands out among others for having a deep influence on the opportunity for supporters to move from one citizenship profile to another and is particularly useful to discuss here is the style of 'leadership' exercised by core organisers. The adoption of a more open and participatory style of leadership by core organisers can enhance opportunities for the online supporters of a given group to play a more meaningful role. Did those at the centre of The Broken of Britain perform their role in a way that facilitated or inhibited the transition of online supporters to a more active behaviour and thus a more meaningful citizenship profile?

From the onset of this investigation, it was clear that different participatory styles were likely to coexist within each of the British groups examined in this book. This can be seen as a function of the 'customised' participation model promoted by online media through an ever-expanding range of options from which users can select those most suited to their preferences and/or needs (Bimber et al. 2012, p. 179; Prior 2008). For this reason, it would have been misleading to ever envisage The Broken of Britain as a perfectly horizontal network that grew spontaneously or just 'happened' online. As in all networks, different 'nodes' performed different functions and therefore a certain amount of disparity between core organisers and supporters was implicit and expected. However, a close look at the relationship between the five blogger-cum-activists who started this campaign and their online supporters revealed a surprisingly high degree of centralisation that was evident in how decisions were taken and The Broken of Britain's 'brand' was managed.

With hindsight, the presence of such a strong 'leadership' inscribed this group within a wider paradigm that covers both innovative advocacy organisations such as MoveOn.org (Carty 2010, p. 70), as well as recent movements such as Occupy, the Spanish *Indignados* and some of the groups responsible for the Arab uprisings of 2011 (Gerbaudo 2012). While online media in fact helped all of the above to project a 'leader-less' image (Castells 2012, p. 221), their ability to ignite mass mobilisation has invariably been linked to the existence of a 'concealed' leadership construed and exercised through social media by relatively small groups of core organisers (Gerbaudo 2012, pp. 143–4). Similarly, The Broken of Britain sought to project a collective image by devising a strong 'brand' and organising its social media presence around 'anonymous' pages with face-less administrators, but at the same time its communications were firmly in the hands of a very small team, which *de facto* constituted its leadership. More broadly, this also echoed the tendency for social media to be highly influenced by a minority of 'power users' who contribute a much larger proportion of content than the average user, especially on Facebook (Hampton et al. 2012).

Indeed, the role of The Broken of Britain's *de facto* leadership should not necessarily be interpreted in a negative way. Rather, recent work has found that 'super-users' perform crucial tasks as forum moderators and facilitators of online deliberation, especially in non-political online spaces (Graham & Wright 2014). Yet, an important difference separated The Broken of Britain from mass movements such as Occupy and the Spanish *Indignados*. While in fact the latter engaged in street demonstrations that somewhat mitigated the influence of their online leadership (Gerbaudo 2012), The Broken of Britain's founders actively shunned offline mass gatherings. Whether this was part of a deliberate strategy to enhance the credibility of their advocacy efforts in the eyes of policy-makers or more simply a choice dictated by disabling barriers and resource constraints, avoiding street demonstrations nevertheless strengthened the position of the core organisers, granting them more control over its message and the modes of engagement available to supporters.

These choices resonated with a view of Facebook as a platform for talking and gaining credibility for advocacy groups, rather than mobilising and organising supporters, as discussed earlier in this chapter. In addition, this strategy was consistent also with the approach to policy-making in this group, which saw itself as operating within the framework of representative democracy – unlike larger networked movements such as Occupy, which have challenged the legitimacy and efficacy of representative democracy in its current form (Castells 2012, p. 225) – and therefore benefited from the existence of clear leaders capable of liaising with elected representatives and other government officials in certain offline arenas. In sum, while the boundary between 'observers' and 'monitorial' citizens was a flexible one and The Broken of Britain's supporters were able to cross at their will, the line between supporters and core organisers in this group was rigid and contributed coherence to the campaign, at least in the short term.

In light of this, it would be legitimate to ask whether The Broken of Britain's founders did in fact constitute an emerging digital 'elite' (Hindman 2009) who used social media to construct a sense of community where there was in fact no physical 'community' along the lines of what organisations such as MoveOn.org have done using email (Eaton 2010). As compelling as this interpretation may seem, it disregards the role that core organisers played in this case in catalysing the attention of Internet users who had a deep, often personal, interest in the debate on disability welfare, but otherwise could have remained entirely disengaged from it, and providing them with a digitally-based alternative to existing forms of disability advocacy. This process afforded The Broken of Britain's supporters an opportunity to take some basic but very important steps in the direction of meaningful political participation.

As such, it is more appropriate to interpret the effects of the networked campaign promoted by The Broken of Britain on the sense of citizenship of those involved in it as an outcome of the connection between 'ordinary Internet users' on one side and disabled bloggers-cum-activists on the other. In other words, citizenship is not a function of the individual, but rather the product of a relationship between different actors who strive to defend and possibly expand the rights of a social group. From this perspective, The Broken of Britain's core organisers, given their role as self-advocates, did not represent an isolated elite. Instead, they acted as 'brokers' for the concerns of other disabled people in a process that could be described as 'peer-mediated' citizenship. New media technologies played a fundamental role in supporting this type of arrangement by enabling the emergence of a new generation of disabled activists and connecting them with a critical mass of potential supporters, especially disabled Internet users, who had a direct stake in the U.K. government's proposed changes to disability welfare.

Undoubtedly, the type of movement promoted by The Broken of Britain's founders was not without its drawbacks. Most notably, it was not a perfectly democratic arrangement. Core organisers were effectively self-appointed and not subjected to a clear accountability mechanism.

Nevertheless, this campaign did not foster 'citizenship by proxy' either because the voice of the disability community was not delegated to non-disabled 'others' with potentially distorting and disempowering effects (Alcoff 1991). Instead, it remained in the hands of a new generation of pioneering self-advocates who demonstrated advanced campaigning skills and sensitivity to the needs of disabled Internet users, both of which stemmed from their familiarity with blogging and personal experience of disability. Despite being imperfect, 'peer-mediated' citizenship could be seen as an important opportunity for disabled citizens to enhance their political rights that is uniquely supported by technology. This is not necessarily in contrast with, but rather complements, direct representation that is expressed through more established yet also more contentious activist tactics.

Conclusions

This chapter shed light on the strategic approaches to social media platforms that a range of British disability rights groups developed in the wake of austerity measures that followed the 2008 global financial crisis. This also helped to clarify the relationship between the online supporters and core organisers of these groups. By blending the analysis of Facebook conversations with in-depth interviews with the founders and core organisers of The Hardest Hit, DPAC and The Broken of Britain, this chapter showed that each of these groups took a distinct approach to Facebook. As was first mentioned in Chapter 4 and illustrated in greater detail here, The Broken of Britain took a particularly 'hands on' approach to its Facebook page, posting new content very frequently during the very intense period in the welfare reform debate comprised between February and May 2011. This helped it generate the highest volume of Facebook discussion among the groups examined in this book. At the same time, both The Hardest Hit and DPAC were substantially less active on Facebook and used it primarily to expand and support consolidated tactics that pre-dated social media, albeit for different reasons. This had important implications for the ability of these groups to foster political citizenship for their online supporters, especially disabled Internet users. In addition, the specific role that Facebook talk had in each group was strongly connected to internal institutional variables, including their structure and ethos, as well as their respective outlook on the broader political environment (Chadwick 2011).

DPAC approached Facebook in a way that was consistent with the history and previous experience of its founders in the disability rights movement of the 1980s and 1990s. Thus, it regarded it primarily as a channel for organising and paralleling street protest. Since 2011, this group appears to have expanded and diversified its action repertoire, as is discussed in Chapters 3 and 4. Yet, conventional protest remains at the core of its strategy, influencing the ways in which social media platforms are approached. Conversely, The Hardest Hit coalition of formal disability organisations was ambivalent towards Facebook. On the one hand, this group embraced suggestions that supporters had put forward in Facebook conversations as a way of enriching its campaign through 'crowdsourced' ideas. This openness on the part of campaign managers potentially expanded opportunities for supporters to use Facebook and other social media platforms to shape the campaign. At the same time, The Hardest Hit translated some of the 'trademark' practices of formal disability organisations into online advocacy. In particular, personal stories of disability were posted in an un-mediated and un-moderated fashion on the Facebook page of this joint campaign, but also appeared in a curated form in a dedicated section of its website. This blend of new and established tactics generated a strategy by which the organisations behind The Hardest Hit tried to preserve their role as democratic mediators of the disability community's interests while responding also to the request from supporters to become more 'entrepreneurially engaged' in advocacy work. Chapter 6 puts these findings into perspective by comparing the online advocacy practices of British formal disability organisations to those of their American counterparts.

DPAC's focus on traditional street protest on one side and The Hardest Hit's ambivalent approach to participatory campaigning on the other opened up an opportunity for new and emerging advocates to reach out to people who had a stake in the reform of disability welfare promoted by the U.K. government but were unconvinced by disruptive protest and similarly disillusioned with established organisations. New media technologies, in particular social media, provided an opportunity to connect these advocates to potential supporters. The Broken of Britain's founders were particularly successful at this, using the Internet to build a 'third way' between disruptive protest and seemingly ineffective advocacy. The result of this approach was a new type of online-only effort, which provided supporters with online outlets to discuss issues connected to the U.K. welfare reform, including protest. At the same time, however, this was also managed like a brand, meaning that supporters were encouraged to contribute to the online actions set up by core organisers, but could be reprimanded for engaging in more spontaneous initiatives. This revealed that this group had a less horizontal structure than was envisaged originally and instead benefited from having a *de facto* leadership that was legitimised by its online supporters and empowered by its centrality in communication flows.

Considering the role that concealed leaders played in digital action networks such as The Broken of Britain, one could be forgiven for assuming that this group's style of campaigning only enhanced the citizenship status of the people at its core. However, careful consideration of the relationship between core organisers and ordinary supporters as shown from Facebook conversations revealed that the potential impact of this arrangement was in fact more far reaching. Three communicative styles coexist within a group like The Broken of Britain, which in turn are associated with three citizenship profiles, including: 'observers' who are also 'latent citizens'; 'visitors' who are also 'monitorial citizens' (in the positive sense of the term); and 'residents' who are also 'connected citizens'. Indeed, this system does not fulfil the requirement of 'participatory parity' that is essential for the development of 'inclusive citizenship' because it precludes those in the outer layers of citizenship from reaching the innermost one. Nevertheless, the combination of self-advocacy by disabled bloggers-cum-activists with the use of technology to reach out to other disabled people created the conditions for political citizenship to be mediated by a small grassroots group of young peers instead of being delegated to bureaucratic and often professionalised organisations, or enacted within protest frameworks that often are not effective. While The Broken of Britain set an important precedent in disability politics, it remains for both researchers and future activists to understand whether its model is viable in the long term and, more importantly, if it is possible to inject more accountability into it without trading off the benefits associated with strong leadership.

References

Alcoff, L., 1991. The Problem of Speaking for Others. *Cultural Critique*, 20, pp. 5–32.

Anstead, N., 2009. The Evolving Relationship between Core and Periphery of Political Campaigns in the Internet Era. In ECPR General Conference, Potsdam, 10–12 September.

Barnes, C., 1992. *Disabling Imagery and the Media: An Exploration of the Principles for Media Representations of Disabled People*, Halifax: BCODP with Rayburn.

Bastos, M.T. & Mercea, D., 2015. Serial Activists: Political Twitter Beyond Influentials and the Twittertariat. *New Media & Society*, pp. 1–20.

Bennett, W.L., 2003. Communicating Global Activism: Strengths and Vulnerabilities of Networked Politics. *Information, Communication & Society*, 6(2), pp. 143–168.

Bimber, B., Flanagin, A.J. & Stohl, C., 2012. *Collective Action in Organizations: Interaction and Engagement in an Era of Technological Change*, Cambridge: Cambridge University Press.

Carty, V., 2010. *Wired and Mobilizing: Social Movements, New Technology, and Electoral Politics*, London: Routledge.

Castells, M., 2012. *Networks of Outrage and Hope: Social Movements in the Internet Age*, Cambridge: Polity Press.

Chadwick, A., 2007. Digital Network Repertoires and Organizational Hybridity. *Political Communication*, 24(3), pp. 283–301.

——— 2011. Explaining the Failure of an Online Citizen Engagement Initiative: The Role of Internal Institutional Variables. *Journal of Information Technology & Politics*, 8(1), pp. 21–40.

Coleman, S., 2005. The Lonely Citizen: Indirect Representation in an Age of Networks. *Political Communication*, 22(2), pp. 197–214.

Crow, L., 1996. Including All of Our Lives: Renewing the Social Model of Disability. In C. Barnes & G. Mercer, eds. *Exploring the Divide: Illness and Disability*. Leeds: The Disability Press, pp. 55–72.

Davey, B., 1999. Solving Economic, Social and Environmental Problems Together: An Empowerment Strategy for Losers. In M. Barnes & L. Warren, eds. *Paths to Empowerment*. Bristol: The Policy Press, pp. 37–49.

della Porta, D., 2005. Deliberation in Movement: Why and How to Study Deliberative Democracy and Social Movements. *Acta Politica*, 40(3), pp. 336–350.

della Porta, D. & Diani, M., 2006. *Social Movements: An Introduction*, Malden, MA: Blackwell Publishing.

Eaton, M., 2010. Manufacturing Community in an Online Activist Organization. *Information, Communication & Society*, 13(2), pp. 174–192.

Franklin, M., 2004. *Voter Turnout and the Dynamics of Electoral Competition in Established Democracies Since 1945*, Cambridge: Cambridge University Press.

Fraser, N., 2003. Social Justice in the Age of Identity Politics: Redistribution, Recognition and Participation. In N. Fraser & A. Honnoeth, eds. *Redistribution or Recognition? A Political-Philosophical Exchange*. London/New York: Verso, pp. 7–109.

French, S., 1993. Disability, Impairment, or Something in Between. In C. Barnes, J. Swain, S. French & C. Thomas, eds. *Disabling Barriers, Enabling Environments*. London: SAGE, pp. 17–25.

Gerbaudo, P., 2012. *Tweet and the Streets: Social Media and Contemporary Activism*, London: Pluto Press.

Graham, T., 2010. The Use of Expressives in Online Political Talk: Impeding or Facilitating the Normative Goals of Deliberation? In E. Tambouris, A. Macintosh, & O. Glassey, eds. *Electronic Participation*. Berlin, Heidelberg: Springer, pp. 26–41.

Graham, T. & Wright, S., 2014. Discursive Equality and Everyday Talk Online: The Impact of 'Superparticipants'. *Journal of Computer-Mediated Communication*, 19(3), pp. 625–642.

Hampton, K., Sessions, L.F., Marlow, C. & Rainie, L., 2012. *Why Most Facebook Users Get More Than They Give: The Effect of Facebook 'Power Users' on Everybody Else*, Washington, DC: Pew American Life and the Internet Project.

Hindman, M., 2009. *The Myth of Digital Democracy*, Princeton, NJ: Princeton University Press.

Karpf, D., 2012. *The MoveOn Effect: The Unexpected Transformation of American Political Advocacy*, New York: Oxford University Press.

Kavada, A., 2015. Creating the Collective: Social Media, the Occupy Movement and Its Constitution as a Collective Actor. *Information, Communication & Society*, 18(8), pp. 872–886.

Kenix, L.J., 2007. In Search of Utopia: An Analysis of Non-Profit Web Pages. *Information, Community and Society*, 10(1), pp. 69–94.

———— 2008. Nonprofit Organizations' Perceptions and Uses of the Internet. *Television & New Media*, 9(5), pp. 407–428.

Langer, A.I., 2010. The Politicization of Private Persona: Exceptional Leaders or the New Rule? The Case of the United Kingdom and the Blair Effect. *The International Journal of Press/Politics*, 15(1), pp. 60–76.

—— 2011. *The Personalisation of Politics in the UK: Mediated Leadership from Attlee to Cameron*, Manchester: Manchester University Press.

Lievrouw, L.A., 2011. *Alternative and Activist New Media*, Cambridge: Polity Press.

Lister, R., 2004. A Politics of Recognition and Respect: Involving People with Experience of Poverty in Decision-Making that Affects their Lives. In J. Andersen & B. Siim, eds. *The Politics of Inclusion and Empowerment: Gender, Class and Citizenship*. Basingstoke: Macmillan, pp. 116–138.

—— 2007. Inclusive Citizenship: Realizing the Potential. *Citizenship Studies*, 11(1), pp. 49–61.

Lusoli, W. & Ward, S., 2006. Hunting Protestors: Mobilisation, Participation and Protest Online in the Countryside Alliance. In S. Oates, D. Owen, & R. Gibson, eds. *The Internet and Politics: Citizens, Voters and Activists*. London: Routledge, pp. 52–71.

Nakamura, L., 2004. Interrogating the Digital Divide: The Political Economy of Race and Commerce in New Media. In P. Howard & S. Jones, eds. *Society Online: The Internet in Context*. London: SAGE, pp. 71–84.

Olsson, T., 2008. The Practises of Internet Networking – A Resource for Alternative Political Movements. *Information, Communication & Society*, 11(5), pp. 659–674.

Pearson, C. & Trevisan, F., 2015. Disability Activism in the New Media Ecology: Campaigning Strategies in the Digital Era. *Disability & Society*, 30(6), pp. 924–940.

Poell, T., Abdulla, R., Rieder, B., Woltering, R. & Zack, L., 2016. Protest Leadership in the Age of Social Media. *Information, Communication & Society*, 19(7), pp. 994–1014.

Prior, M., 2008. Are Hyperlinks 'Weak' Ties? In J. Turow & L. Tsui, eds. *The Hyperlinked Society: Questioning Connections in the Digital Age*. Ann Arbor: The University of Michigan Press, pp. 250–267.

Schudson, M., 2011. *The Good Citizen: A History of American Civic Life*, New York: The Free Press.

Shakespeare, T., 1994. Cultural Representation of Disabled People: Dustbins for Disavowal? *Disability & Society*, 9(3), pp. 283–299.

Taylor, J. & Burt, E., 2005. Voluntary Organisations as E-Democratic Actors: Political Identity, Legitimacy and Accountability and the Need for New Research. *Policy & Politics*, 33(4), pp. 601–616.

Tilly, C., 2008. *Contentious Performances*, Cambridge: Cambridge University Press.

Trevisan, F., 2014. Scottish Disability Organizations and Online Media: A Path to Empowerment or 'Business as Usual?' *Disability Studies Quarterly*, 34(3).

—— 2015. Contentious Disability Politics on the World Stage: Protest at the London 2012 Paralympics. In D. Jackson, C. Hodges, M. Molesworth & R. Scullion, eds. *Reframing Disability? Media, (Dis)empowerment and Voice in the 2012 Paralympics*. London: Routledge, pp. 145–171.

Turner, B.S., 1986. *Citizenship and Capitalism: The Debate over Reformism*, London: Allen & Unwin.

Vromen, A. & Coleman, W., 2013. Online Campaigning Organizations and Storytelling Strategies: GetUp! in Australia. *Policy & Internet*, 5(1), pp. 76–100.

Walther, J.B., 1996. Computer-Mediated Communication: Impersonal, Interpersonal, and Hyperpersonal Interaction. *Communication Research*, 23(1), pp. 3–43.

White, D.S. & Le Cornu, A., 2011. Visitors and Residents: A New Typology for Online Engagement. *First Monday*, 16(9).

Wright, S., 2012. Politics as Usual? Revolution, Normalization and a New Agenda for Online Deliberation. *New Media & Society*, 14(2), pp. 244–261.

6 One Size Fits All?
British Innovators and American 'Conservatives'

The previous chapters have evidenced how in recent years the use of new media technologies supported important changes in British disability rights advocacy, transforming existing organisations and enabling the formation of new networks. At the same time, however, such digital dynamism was tied indissolubly to the U.K. welfare reform crisis, which acted as a fundamental catalyst for the renewal of grassroots advocacy. In order to gauge the influence of the local context on contemporary forms of digital disability rights advocacy, this chapter compares the British experience to that of American disability organisations. As a country that tends to be regarded as a trendsetter in e-advocacy and online campaigns, the United States makes for a particularly useful comparative case study. Are there any specific differences in the ways in which established disability organisations in the U.K. and the U.S. use online media to pursue their policy objectives? Under what circumstances, if any, do such groups embrace more participatory forms of e-advocacy in each country? And, finally, what are the factors at the root of these patterns?

These questions are tackled here through a comparative inventory of online media use (see Appendix B) and 26 interviews with senior advocates, communication specialists and campaign managers from some of the most prominent groups involved in The Hardest Hit coalition in Britain and their counterparts in America. Furthermore, Web link analysis with IssueCrawler provides additional comparative elements. Given that the main aim of this part of the study is to identify and analyse system-wide differences and similarities, the comparison embraces two heterogeneous sets of established organisations – both professionalised and member-led – that advocate on behalf of disabled people to influence key national policy measures. Each set of organisations includes both groups that focus on specific impairments and organisations that campaign across a pan-disability spectrum (see Table 6.1 for a list of U.S. organisations; see Table 3.2 in Chapter 3 for a list of U.K. organisations). Focusing on established organisations that are fairly similar in scope and structure ensured ideal conditions for uncovering patterns of contextual influence and related differences.

Table 6.1 Overview of American disability organisations

U.S. organisations	Interviews	HQ location	Website
American Association of People with Disabilities (AAPD)*	2	Washington, DC	www.aapd.com
National Federation of the Blind (NFB)	2	Baltimore, MD	www.nfb.org
Learning Disabilities Association of America (LDA)*	1	Pittsburgh, PA	www.ldaamerica.org
National MS Society*	1	New York City, NY Washington, DC (advocacy team)	www.nmss.org
Mental Health America (MHA)*	1	Alexandria, VA	www.nmha.org
National Council on Independent Living (NCIL)*	2	Washington, DC	www.ncil.org
National Disability Rights Network (NDRN)*	1	Washington, DC	www.ndrn.org
The ARC*	1	Washington, DC	www.thearc.org
United Cerebral Palsy (UCP)*	2	Washington, DC	www.ucp.org
Access Living	1	Chicago, IL	www.accessliving.org
Autism Speaks/Autism Votes*	2	Washington, DC	www.autismspeaks.org www.autismvotes.org
ADAPT	1	Denver, CO Austin, TX	www.adapt.org
MS Society, Greater DC-Maryland Chapter	1	Washington, DC	www.nationalmssociety.org/chapters/mdm
Easter Seals*	—	Chicago, IL Washington, DC (govt relations)	www.easterseals.com

Note: *indicates member organisations of the Consortium for Citizens with Disabilities.

Following a brief review of the relevant disability policy agenda in the U.S., the rest of this chapter discusses six key differences that emerged from comparative research. These fall within two broad thematic areas, namely:

a   *Tools and tactics of online advocacy*, including: online coalition vs. fragmentation; email vs. other online communication channels; and the use of personal stories in e-advocacy; and
b   *Perceptions of online participation*, including: the meaning of 'membership' in the digital era; the issue of social media control; and the value of online political action.

Overall, the data revealed a counter-intuitive picture in which British organisations emerged as innovators in online participatory advocacy while their U.S. counterparts unexpectedly constituted a conservative exception in an otherwise forward-thinking e-advocacy landscape. The reasons behind these differences, their implications for user-empowerment and effects on disability rights advocacy as a whole are explored here. The chapter concludes by reflecting on the nature of 'context' in online advocacy and digital campaigning. Most crucially, it discusses the need for researchers in both Internet and disability studies to broaden their analytical horizon and consider the role of volatile circumstantial factors – especially crisis – as fundamental drivers (or inhibitors) of progress in this area.

Policy 'Crisis' in the United States: Medicaid Cuts Proposals

Before delving into discussion, it is useful to reflect on the circumstances under which American groups operated when the data for this study was collected in spring/summer 2011, broadly at the same time as the U.K. welfare reform debate that was discussed previously in this book. In that period, U.S. disability rights organisations focused their efforts first and foremost on opposing 'The Path to Prosperity: Restoring America's Promise'. This was an alternative federal budget plan that Representative Paul Ryan (R-Wisconsin) presented in April 2011, following the electoral success of Tea Party candidates in the 2010 mid-term elections and the establishment of a Republican majority in the House of Representatives. Ryan's counter-budget included a substantial reduction of federal funding for Medicaid,[1] which arguably would have enabled the federal government to save one trillion dollars over a ten-year period. As most disabled Americans rely on Medicaid in order to meet their healthcare costs, this represented a particularly relevant issue for disability advocacy organisations. An intense debate on these proposals ensued both in Congress and on U.S. news media from April 2011 until the budget was finally approved in November of the same year. Eventually, cuts to federal funding for Medicaid were averted as part of a deal to solve the U.S. debt-ceiling crisis.[2]

At first, it could seem tempting to draw a straightforward parallel between these proposals for Medicaid cuts and the U.K. welfare reform crisis. Both these issues erupted on the political agenda fairly suddenly following changes in parliamentary majorities and were underpinned by conservative 'small government' ideologies, as well as by more pragmatic deficit reduction targets. Nevertheless, under these apparent similarities lay a series of fundamental differences that starkly separated these two policy plans. In particular, British organisations were involved in what could be defined as a 'double crisis'. This is because they fought not only against a radical reform of disability welfare, but they were forced to do so also without the support of any major institutional backers, including the parliamentary opposition. Furthermore, as was discussed in previous chapters, the U.K. welfare reform debate focused on issues that have traditionally been integral to the very existence of disability activism in the U.K., as well as the definition of disability in British public discourse. In contrast, Ryan's plan for Medicaid cuts in the U.S. did not question the very principles behind disability welfare provision or insist on a policy area that was central to the very essence of American disability advocacy, which traditionally has organised around civil rights issues (Barnartt & Scotch 2001; Vaughn-Switzer 2003). The debate over U.S. budget plans was intensely politicised. However, American disability groups enjoyed the support of a key institutional ally. That is, their views on Medicaid coincided with those of the White House, to which disability groups have looked rather positively throughout the Obama administration. This was in striking contrast to the political isolation experienced by British disability advocates.

Finally, although U.S. public perceptions of federal welfare programmes tend to be controversial, disability advocates were able to benefit also from the sympathetic frames of 'deservedness' that American news media generally apply to stories involving disabled people (Haller et al. 2006; Haller 2010). This is in contrast to the portrayal of other disadvantaged groups and minorities – particularly African-Americans – who tend to be represented negatively in news coverage of welfare provision (Bell & Entman 2011; Gilens 1999). Conversely, British disability organisations have been confronted with a growing wave of negative public opinion fuelled by controversial media representations of disability benefit claimants as 'scroungers' and 'fraudsters' in recent years (Briant et al. 2013; Garthwaite 2011). For these reasons, what at first may have looked like similar issues generated in fact crucially different circumstances, which were expected to affect the technological choices of disability rights groups.

Same Destination, Separate Ways: Coalition Versus Fragmentation

The first difference to become apparent was that, while British disability organisations had responded to the welfare reform through a joint campaign

(The Hardest Hit), nothing similar had been set up by their American counterparts to oppose proposed cuts to Medicaid. Undoubtedly, stopping Medicaid changes was a top priority for all the U.S. organisations examined here, whose officers repeatedly stated in interviews that:

> [T]he budget stuff caused a lot of controversy – Representative Ryan, when he released his budget with a trillion dollar cut to Medicaid got a lot of [disabled] people very worried and angry.
>
> (Chair, U.S. member-led pan-disability group,
> June 2011)

Although everyone interviewed for this study shared this view, U.S. disability organisations did not set up a collaborative campaign. Instead, they embarked on a series of separate and somewhat redundant efforts, ranging from straightforward email appeals to contact legislators to more organic efforts such as United Cerebral Palsy's (UCP) 'Faces of Medicaid' campaign.[3] This was despite the fact that two-thirds of the American groups examined here were members of the Consortium for Citizens with Disabilities (CCD),[4] a forum of national disability organisations similar to the British Disability Benefits Consortium (DBC) that was behind The Hardest Hit coalition in the U.K. U.S. disability advocates pursued the same objective in a fragmented and arguably inefficient fashion. This constituted a bold reminder of the fact that the Internet *per se* does not constitute a catalyst for the formation of campaigning coalitions among groups with similar interests, including at times of crisis. Potentially, online media can facilitate the emergence of issue-driven collaborative campaigns among different organisations by limiting the investment required from each partner and enabling them to retain their individual brands and identities (Chadwick 2007, pp. 290–1). However, the difference outlined here between U.K. and U.S. cases begged the question of under what circumstances this type of cooperation can effectively flourish.

It emerged from interviews that a combination of multiple offline elements was responsible for the (un-)attractiveness of the Internet as a channel for collaborative action during different policy crises. In particular, the reluctance of American disability organisations to set up a joint online campaign was linked to two main issues. First, the majority of U.S. participants explicitly pointed out the lack of an issue capable of providing sufficiently strong motivation for their respective organisations to join forces. Proposed Medicaid cuts were likely to have a negative impact on the livelihoods of most disabled Americans. In theory, this should have favoured collaboration as in the case of discrimination and civil rights issues in the late 1980s (Barnartt & Scotch 2001, pp. 89–90). However, virtually all the U.S. organisations interviewed for this study stressed that:

> [I]t [Medicaid] never rose to that level [the same level as civil rights for disabled people], Medicaid was part of the whole, you know, it went

into the budget issue and when you get the budget issue you get a lot of other things.

(Head of communications, U.S. disability non-profit,
July 2012)

As another participant from a pan-disability organisation put it:

The passage of the ADA [Americans with Disabilities Act] 20 years ago was really the culmination of a joint effort – I can't really think of any times over the last 20 years where there's been really a need for that kind of grassroots coordination.

(Head of communications, U.S. pan-disability
non-profit, June 2011)

Thus, U.S. disability organisations interpreted the prospect of Medicaid as a purely financial issue rather than a threat to the very principles under-pinning the provision of public resources to meet the needs of disabled citizens. As such, this debate fell short of the 'emergency' character capable of inspiring collaborative online campaigning as it happened instead in the U.K.

In fact, given their nature as a problem of resource re-distribution, plans for Medicaid cuts constituted an inherently divisive issue for American disability groups. This was because it was unclear whether such measures would lead to a general drop in healthcare provision for disabled people or hit some harder than others depending on personal circumstances, con-ditions and impairments. This understandably led impairment-specific organisations in particular to prioritise the interests of their own con-stituents before those of other disabled people. This situation revealed patterns of inter-group competition similar to those that have long been observed by scholars of race-relations and social policy in the U.S., who have documented how resource-related issues can favour conflict between groups that in principle would benefit from joined advocacy initiatives (Giles & Evans 1986).

In light of these considerations, proposed Medicaid cuts insisted upon established rifts in American disability advocacy. As was discussed in Chapter 1, the issue of organisational fragmentation among U.S. dis-ability groups constitutes a central thread in the literature on American disability politics. In particular, the American disability community has been affected traditionally not only by controversies between self-advocacy and 'professionalised' non-profits, but also by strong internal disagreement among different components of the Independent Living Movement itself (Bagenstos 2009, pp. 24–5; Vaughn-Switzer 2003, pp. 76–7). While these tensions were momentarily set aside in the process that led to the adoption of the ADA in 1990 (Jaeger & Bowman 2005, p. 40), they re-surfaced shortly after and have since been boosted by the tendency for advocacy efforts to focus on services and financial benefits for specific sections of the disability community rather than discrimination issues more generally (Barnartt & Scotch 2001, p. 91). The result is a movement that is divided, especially along impairment lines (Bryan 2006, p. 37). In this context, a struggle over public money allocations can easily exacerbate traditional rivalries. Indeed, British disability activism too has been characterised by tension, disagreement and sharp criticism, both between charities and member-led organisations, as well as among the latter. However, in the U.S. the combination of pre-existing splits with a contentious budget issue created an environment that was especially adverse to online collaboration.

Importantly, interview participants from American pan-disability organisations such as the American Association of People with Disabilities (AAPD) and the National Council on Independent Living (NCIL) linked the issue of fragmentation to a loss of efficacy for online action and talked of digital media as channels to connect groups traditionally perceived as 'silo-ed' with other parts of the disability community. Yet, at the same time they also stressed how:

[I]n the U.S. there's so many groups, so many organisations that are very specific to a disability that a lot of times is very hard to organise around 'disability as a whole' [. . .] people still become very segmented when they're organising online [. . .] if we have a common goal of stopping cuts to Medicaid for example everyone has goals specific to what their disability is [. . .], although working together is how we got things accomplished in the past.
(Head of communications, U.S. pan-disability non-profit, July 2011)

These remarks echoed the emphasis placed by American disability literature on the depth of divisions among disability campaigners. Thus, opposition to Medicaid cuts did not evoke a shared past for American disability advocacy groups. Under these circumstances, the tendency for online media to reduce the costs associated with campaign activities may therefore have contributed to a paradoxical exacerbation of existing rifts, rather than promoting *ad hoc*, issue-based collaboration.

These impressions were corroborated by the results of Web link analysis, which showed a divided disability advocacy landscape in the U.S. Connections among the websites of the organisations under examination were retrieved by means of inter-actor mapping on IssueCrawler.[5] On the one hand, the map obtained for American organisations (Figure 6.1) was characterised by weak connections and some missing nodes (The ARC, MS Society). Groups that focused on similar impairments and shared the same organisational ethos (i.e. member-led vs. professionalised) tended to be connected to one another. This was particularly apparent in

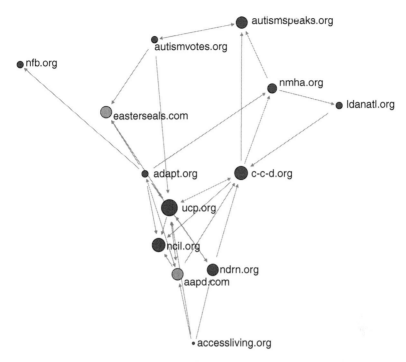

Figure 6.1 Hyperlink network of American formal disability organisations.

the case of groups concerned with intellectual impairments and mental health issues (Mental Health America [MHA], Autism Speaks/Votes, the Learning Disabilities Association of America [LDA]) on one side, and those with a pan-disability outlook (AAPD, NCIL, the National Disability Rights Network [NDRN], Access Living) on the other. These organisations constituted two sub-sets within the U.S. inter-actor network connected to one another only indirectly through their respective links with third, consortium-like organisations (CCD).

On the contrary, U.K. groups were characterised by a relatively greater number of connections (Figure 6.2). Indeed, the strength of these links was limited and comparable to that of connections among U.S. organisations. Yet, inter-actor analysis showed also that the links among British disability groups were distributed more evenly across different types of organisations. Whether this was a by-product of their collaborative campaign against the U.K. welfare reform was of secondary importance here. While in fact hyperlinks should not be assumed to be a sign of endorsement or agreement, their mere existence characterised British organisations as potentially more inclined to dialogue with one another, which provided more fertile ground for collaborative campaigning than in the U.S.

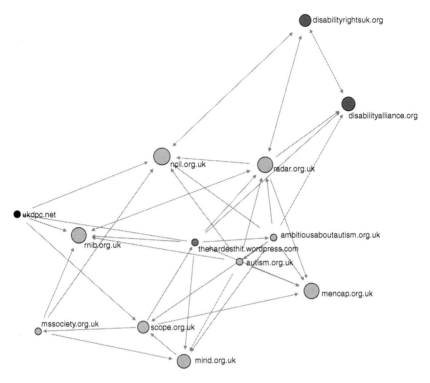

Figure 6.2 Hyperlink network of British formal disability organisations.

Interestingly, if unsurprisingly, the websites of disability groups' consortia constituted focal elements in each network as they were connected to a high number of other nodes. At the same time, however, each of them performed a very different function in their respective networks. The Web pages of Britain's DBC,[6] although well connected, were not pivotal to the very existence of the surrounding network, as organisations tended to link directly to one another, forming a structure that resembled an 'all-channel' network (Arquilla & Ronfeldt 2001, pp. 7–8). Instead, the website of the U.S. CCD constituted a sort of 'hub' that indirectly joined nodes that otherwise would have been completely separate. As such, the shape of the U.S. network was closer to that of a 'star' supported by a central node serving as a facilitator or broker of inter-organisational relationships, albeit not necessarily occupying a hierarchically-dominant position (Mandell 2001, p. 281). Given CCD's very large remit and traditional civil rights focus, it was reasonable to hypothesise that Medicaid cuts did not constitute an issue capable of activating the type of connections typically promoted by that consortium, increasing the likelihood of a fragmented response among American disability organisations.

Conversely, all U.K. organisations stressed that:

> [P]artnering with other organisations at this time [in the wake of welfare reform proposals] is [was] absolutely vital and you need[ed] to be quite creative about it.
>
> (Policy officer, U.K. member-led group, July 2011)

U.K. groups acknowledged that the struggle over disability welfare reform was a key catalyst for setting differences aside and organising a joint campaign, albeit:

> [O]nly in the short term, without a specific strategy to push this into the longer term.
>
> (Communications officer, U.K. charity, July 2011)

Under these circumstances, the Internet enabled a wide range of U.K. disability groups to establish virtual 'headquarters' for their collaborative campaign, while at the same time preserving their individual brands, as is discussed in detail in Chapter 3. U.K. participants pointed at the fact that a joint online campaign dispelled some of the concerns associated with otherwise burdensome formal coalitions and:

> ...showed that if we [disability organisations] work together and all the energies are thrown behind social media, then results happen.
>
> (Head of communications, U.K. charity,
> September 2011)

Overall, this comparison enabled to put the role of the Internet in the emergence of a unitary front against U.K. welfare reform into perspective. In particular, online media facilitated the formation of a flexible, *ad hoc* coalition of established organisations in Britain because the issue at stake was ideological and unifying, requiring a response to controversial government plans rather than a proactive effort to push a new topic on the agenda. In other words, the deeply controversial policy context persuaded British groups that there was more to be gained than to be lost by cooperating online. The Hardest Hit's digital endeavours could be regarded as somewhat of a 'shortcut' to and from collaborative campaigning because they enabled partner organisations to maximise the benefits of working with others while also leaving them free to resume business as usual once the 'storm' was over. Instead, the different nature of the issue at stake in the U.S. inhibited collaboration – online as well as offline – among national disability organisations. Not only did the threat of cuts to Medicaid fail to activate inter-organisational ties, but the relatively low cost of e-advocacy incentivised organisations to proceed independently too. This basic difference influenced the technological preferences of disability rights groups in each country, as is discussed in detail in the next section.

Email is Key, but not Enough for British Organisations

A second theme that emerged from the online media inventory and from interviews was that disability organisations in Britain and America displayed different technological preferences when it came to mobilising supporters and promoting political action. Interviews revealed that seemingly simple technological differences in fact reflected profoundly divergent strategic priorities and the need to adapt e-advocacy to local institutional contexts and cultural norms. While the use of social networking platforms is explored in a dedicated section below, at this point it is useful to reflect on the use of arguably 'old school', one-to-one and traditionally closed digital communication circuits such as email and 'clicktivist' tools (e.g. e-postcards, online petitions, template messages, etc.).

First, U.S. organisations were particularly fond of email, which they saw not only as a channel for communicating with supporters, but also as the primary online vehicle for them to contribute directly to online political action by contacting Congress members. Virtually all the American groups examined here believed that:

> [I]f we didn't have email [action alerts], then a lot of our ability to respond [to unexpected events] would be much more difficult, not impossible but much more difficult, as also making sure that we have our members-input would be much more difficult.
>
> (Chair, U.S. member-led pan-disability group,
> June 2011)

Over two-thirds of the U.S. organisations included in this study used 'action alert networks' (Table 6.2). These invariably took the form of electronic mailing lists that each organisation used to circulate policy updates and targeted 'action calls' whenever it was necessary to demonstrate to policy-makers that the disability community backed its position on a given issue.

Typically, action requests were issued on or around the day of a key Congress vote on legislation likely to affect disabled people and asked supporters to phone or email their elected representatives. These emails provided recipients with an 'action kit' including contact details for elected officials and any relevant government agencies, a brief on the issue or issues at stake and template messages to use as customisable scripts for emailing or phoning politicians. Email constituted an unrivalled e-action channel for U.S. disability rights organisations, most of which had also set up permanent 'email your representative' widgets on their homepages (Table 6.2). Explaining how certain social media platforms can be

Table 6.2 Email and clicktivist tools (U.S. organisations)

Organisation	Action alert network (email)	Other email updates (incl. newsletter)	Find/contact your representative widget	Clicktivist tools (e-petition, e-postcard)	Other activism resources
AAPD	Yes	Yes	Yes	Yes	No
NCIL	Yes	No	Yes	No	No
NDRN	Yes	Yes	Yes	No	No
Access Living	No	Yes	No	No	No
ADAPT	Yes	No	Yes	No	Protest briefings
UCP	Yes	Yes	Yes	No	No
Easter Seals	No	Yes	No	Yes	No
The ARC	Yes	Yes	Yes	No	No
Autism Speaks/ Autism Votes	Yes	Yes	Yes	Yes	No
Mental Health America	Yes	Yes	Yes	No	No
NFB	No	Yes	No	No	No
LDA	Yes	No	No	No	No
MS Society	Yes	Yes	Yes	No	Campaign manual

difficult for disabled people to access independently, particularly people with visual impairments, one participant noted that:

> [P]erhaps we [disability organisations] are a little behind compared to other organisations in that we're still primarily using email, but that has to do with the accessibility of technologies like Facebook.
>
> (Head of communications, U.S. member-led impairment-specific group, May 2011)

The action alerts email system somewhat restricted the scope for direct user input in online political action. Indeed, organisations encouraged supporters to edit and personalise template messages before sending them to policy-makers. However, they also set the topics, timing and modes of interaction with elected representatives. One participant explained that his organisation operated in this way because it was part of its duty to 'keep an eye on Washington' on behalf of members and let them know when something required them to act.

Despite enabling top-down control over both the agenda and the online action repertoire, email alerts paradoxically constituted a rather un-coordinated and un-controlled way of mobilising supporters towards specific policy goals. Virtually all the U.S. organisations interviewed for this project admitted that, in 2011, they were:

> [N]ot monitoring whether then [after members receive an action alert] people do what we [the organisation] asked them for – most alerts we put out to the general membership we have no control over so sometimes we are really surprised by people's responses.
>
> (Head of communications, U.S. non-profit, June 2011)

In other words, after providing the initial input and basic resources, organisations left users to their own devices, contacting them again only when a new action was required. Although participants justified this *vis-à-vis* the relatively high investment required to cover software and staff costs to track e-action uptake rates, this compromised even further the frail 'collective' character of email action alerts.

This was in contrast with the technological choices made by British organisations, which showed them to be keener than their American counterparts on using a variety of online media to mobilise, organise and coordinate supporters around more sophisticated campaign activities. Indeed, half of the U.K. organisations considered here did use email action alerts (Table 6.3).

As a participant from one of these organisations explained, this was mainly because:

> [F]or some people [potential supporters] when it comes to engaging in things like Facebook and Twitter there are still some barriers both in terms of accessibility of those tools and people's confidence in using them [. . .] whereas email is something that most people are very comfortable with.
>
> (Head of digital communications, U.K. charity, May 2011)

Nevertheless, email action alerts were complemented regularly by other online initiatives, including collaborative tasks such as contributing to draft responses to public policy consultations and organising 'spoke' campaigns at the local level. Furthermore, the British disability advocacy organisations that used email networks, interpreted them as channels to:

> [A]dvertise other initiatives and events, for instance tell people about consultations and encourage them to take part, not necessarily going word for word with the organisation [. . .] in a way for us it's a big cultural shift.
>
> (Campaigns officer, U.K. charity, September 2011)

In contrast with U.S. disability organisations, all but one of the British groups examined here had eliminated 'email your MP' widgets from their

Table 6.3 Email and clicktivist tools (U.K. organisations)

Organisation	Action alert network (email)	Other email updates (incl. newsletter)	Find/contact your representative widget	Clicktivist tools (e-petition, e-postcard)	Other activism resources
U.K. Disabled People's Council (UKDPC)	No	No	Yes	No	No
Inclusion London	No	No	No	No	No
National Centre for Independent Living (NCIL)	No	No	No	Yes	No
Disability Alliance	No	No	No	No	No
Royal Association for Disability Rights (RADAR)	Yes	Yes	No	No	No
Leonard Cheshire Disability (LCD)	Yes	Yes	No	No	No
MENCAP	Yes	Yes	No	Yes	Campaign manual
Royal National Institute of Blind People (RNIB)	Yes	Yes	No	Yes	No
SCOPE	Yes	Yes	No	Yes	Campaign manual Event kit/map
MS Society	No	Yes	No	Yes	Campaign manual
MIND	Yes	Yes	No	No	Campaign manual
Ambitious about Autism	No	Yes	No	No	No
National Autistic Society (NAS)	Yes	Yes	No	No	Campaign briefings
Action for ME	No	Yes	No	No	No

websites (Table 6.3) as part of a shift towards other, more sophisticated forms of e-action.

Interestingly, these findings resonated with the results of recent work on major American progressive advocacy groups (Karpf 2010, 2012), which showed that these organisations tended to use action alert emails to introduce supporters to more advanced forms of online participation, encouraging them to climb higher on the 'ladder of engagement'. In broad terms, this tendency was matched by British disability organisations. Instead, the same could not be said of their American counterparts, which from this point of view represented a notable exception in the evolving landscape of U.S. digital advocacy. While in fact a detailed examination of the content of email action requests is beyond the scope of this book, only one interview participant from American organisations defined these messages as a 'stepping stone' towards more complex forms of e-action. The approach of U.K. disability groups to communication technologies, if not quite participatory, was somewhat more innovative than that favoured by U.S. organisations. What, then, led British groups to diversify their online mobilisation tactics, and what instead held back American groups?

While it was reasonable to assume that the acute controversy over welfare reform left British groups with no options but to venture into unchartered online territory, what came to the fore most strongly in interviews on both sides of the Atlantic was the role played by the institutional set-up and political culture of each country. Put simply, technological choices were more likely to be made on the basis of political awareness rather than because of the fashionable appeal of the latest technological innovation. In particular, in Washington email was perceived as a useful vehicle for influencing elected representatives because party discipline and allegiance tend to be less stringent than in London and can be overlooked by politicians in response to specific requests from constituents or, more cynically, as a matter of electoral convenience. This last point is particularly relevant with regard to the U.S. House of Representatives, where most discussions on Medicaid cuts took place and whose short two-year terms afford lobbying groups additional electoral leverage on politicians (Holtz-Bacha & Kaid 2011). As a participant from a pan-disability organisation noted:

> Congressmen wanna know who's voting, who's gonna 'make a stink' in their district if they don't respond to something [...] it's about making sure that legislators know that disabled people vote and even at the Presidential level you get 14.7 million disabled people voting in 2008, so that's a major constituency and it's a swing vote that's not completely liberal.
>
> (Policy officer, U.S. member-led pan-disability organisation, June 2011)

Furthermore, the preference of U.S. disability organisations for email was backed also by a broader trend for which email constitutes the second most popular medium employed by Americans to contact government after the telephone (Smith 2010, p. 13). As Earl and Kimport (2011) noted, the popularity of email campaigns does not come as a surprise given the long history of letter-writing campaigns in the U.S. More specifically, the use of direct emails to elected representatives was in line also with the idea of 'individualism' that is a traditional driver of self-determination and advocacy in the American disability rights movement (Carey 2009, pp. 222–3; Stroman 2003, pp. 213–225).

Having said that, it is legitimate to ask whether email campaigns in the U.S. constituted anything but a mere digital extension of 'phone/write to your Congressman' action calls, which have existed since long before the Internet. From this angle, it could be argued that the fondness of American disability organisations for email as a vehicle for individual and loosely coordinated action truly represented 'politics as usual'. Formal disability groups remained wary of engaging ordinary Internet users in their initiatives beyond a certain threshold for fear of losing control over campaign messages or becoming redundant structures in an era of organisational fluidity and fragmentation. While email remains the most accessible of online media, such lack of experimentation on the part of U.S. organisations prevented disabled Internet users from exploring other potentially viable and more participatory digital tactics.

In Britain, the choice of formal disability organisations to move away from action strategies centred primarily on email was based not only on practical experience with this tactic but also on considerations about the very nature of the U.K.'s political system. This trend reflected the awareness of the fact that British members of parliament (MPs) tend to be under great pressure to adhere to their party's official line and stick to manifesto pledges. In addition, the fact that welfare reform was brought before the Westminster parliament in the initial part of a five-year parliamentary term reduced the potential electoral leverage that constituents might have had on individual politicians even further. Under these circumstances, private email communications made for a poor channel for influencing controversial policy decisions. As one participant explained:

[O]ne of the biggest criticisms we and all other organisations tend to get from MPs is they feel like ignoring the template messages that go into their inbox [...] because there is an impression that people are doing this without really caring, which isn't actually the case, but that's how it is perceived.

(Campaigns officer, U.K. charity, September 2011)

Furthermore, participants confirmed in interviews and correspondence with the author that a growing number of MPs replied to mass email campaigns using template messages that directed petitioners to standardised responses posted on personal or party websites. Importantly, these concerns echoed the conflicting and often inconclusive results of empirical studies on the ability of email campaigns to achieve concrete policy results, which, somewhat ironically, have focused primarily on U.S. case studies (see, for instance, Bergan 2009; Shulman 2006).

Amid these differences, there was one noteworthy similarity between British and American disability organisations. That is, traditional clicktivist tools such as e-petitions and electronic postcards had fallen firmly out of favour with disability rights advocates in both countries. This was apparent from the online media inventory results (see Tables 6.2 and 6.3), as well as from interview accounts. Both American and British participants asserted that:

> [C]licktivism is worth less than any other form of participation [online or offline].
>
> > (Head of government relations, U.S. non-profit, June 2011)

as:

> [I]t may be effective in getting big numbers [of supporters involved] but ultimately decision-makers often don't listen to it.
>
> > (Head of communications, U.S. non-profit, June 2011)

This type of remark resonated with a growing tendency among advocacy professionals, especially in the U.S., to doubt the efficacy of 'push-button' tactics in influencing decision-makers (Earl & Kimport 2011, pp. 93–7). Furthermore, they were complemented by an acknowledgement of the fact that the expectations of those at either end of the policy-making process – citizens on one side and politicians on the other – had evolved in parallel with their familiarity with technology, so that:

> [U]sers want to do more, and decision-makers expect much more than just a template message.
>
> > (Head of public affairs, U.S. non-profit, August 2011)

As one British participant explained:

> [O]ver time people have got more used to this type of communications and therefore as an organisation you [...] start to become more creative, you start almost to lessen your fear of it [...] we now try and encourage people to be, to take more initiative in saying it the way they wanna say it.
>
> > (Campaigns officer, U.K. charity, September 2011)

Overall, participants demonstrated awareness of the growing tendency among their online supporters to look for opportunities for genuine 'entrepreneurial engagement' (Bimber et al. 2012). In response to these expectations, both U.K. and U.S. groups had matured a commitment to avoiding what they described as 'slacktivism', promoting instead the personalisation of campaigns, albeit through different practices. The next section discusses this issue in detail.

Personal Stories as an E-Advocacy Trademark

In both countries, a key way to address expectations for greater user-input was the tendency for e-advocacy initiatives to include personal stories of disability. In particular, interview participants repeatedly stressed that individual narratives were essential to grab the attention of both decision-makers and established news media outlets. Yet, in practice this translated into different ways of incorporating private elements into political messages. As was discussed in detail in Chapter 4, personal stories fulfilled pivotal functions in Facebook discussions among supporters of disability welfare advocacy groups in the U.K. While the increasing personalisation of online activism constitutes a general trend among campaigning organisations (Bennett & Segerberg 2011), the controversial role of disability stories in campaign communications made this an especially crucial part of the comparison. In particular, it was useful to reflect on two issues, including: the consequences of using different types of online media to communicate private narratives; and traditional perceptions of personal stories among disability rights advocates in each country.

In Britain, The Hardest Hit coalition actively encouraged disabled people to share their stories on its Facebook page (see Chapter 4 for details). In addition, half of the U.K. organisations considered in this comparison used their websites to ask supporters to submit stories of disability for inclusion in campaign material (Table 6.4). At the same time, U.S. groups regularly encouraged supporters to mention their own experiences in the emails they sent to policy-makers. In fact, American participants placed such emphasis on the importance of this practice that it seemed appropriate to coin a 'clicktivism plus' category to identify email action alerts that invited users to personalise template messages (Table 6.5).

This marked a clear departure from the obsolete and dubiously effective practice of forwarding fixed messages to policy-makers (Schlosberg et al. 2008). Nevertheless, American organisations did not encourage supporters to share their stories on social networking pages. This was part of a broader tendency for the U.S. organisations examined in this book to refrain from giving complete 'free rein' to supporters on social media, as is discussed below in a dedicated section. Although at first glance these differences between British and American disability organisations may seem merely procedural, they carried substantial implications for disabled Internet users.

Table 6.4 Personalisation features (U.K. disability organisations)

U.K. organisation	Website customisation	Clicktivism plus	'Send us your stories' widget
UKDPC	No	No	No
Inclusion London	No	No	Yes
NCIL	No	No	Yes
Disability Alliance	No	No	No
RADAR	Yes	No	No
LCD	No	No	Yes
MENCAP	Yes	No	No
RNIB	Yes	Yes	Yes
SCOPE	No	No	Yes
MS Society	Yes	Yes	Yes
MIND	Yes	Yes	Yes
Ambitious about Autism	No	No	No
NAS	Yes	Yes	No
Action for ME	Yes	No	No

Table 6.5 Personalisation features (U.S. disability organisations)

U.S. organisation	Website customisation	Clicktivism plus	'Send us your stories' widget
AAPD	No	Yes	Yes
NCIL	No	Yes	No
NDRN	No	Yes	No
Access Living	No	No	No
ADAPT	No	Yes	No
UCP	No	Yes	No
Easter Seals	No	Yes	No
The ARC	Yes	Yes	No
Autism Speaks/Autism Votes	No	Yes	No
Mental Health America	No	Yes	No
NFB	Yes	No	No
LDA	Yes	No	Yes
MS Society	Yes	Yes	Yes

The practice of sharing personal stories of disability on social media had two key benefits. First, it facilitated a collaborative understanding of complex policy issues among those at the receiving end of disability welfare changes, in particular disabled Internet users. Second, it potentially underpinned community building among users, boosting their chances of achieving group agency. Conversely, emails to policy-makers constitute a closed one-to-one communication circuit. For this reason, the 'clicktivism plus' strategy deployed by American disability organisations could only provide an individual lobbying experience that fell short of the positive aspects of social media conversations. As one U.S. participant with previous experience as Congressional staff put it:

> [P]ersonalised communication has a much bigger impact [on law-makers] because people relate to it [...] it's somebody speaking up for themselves and putting a human face on an issue – in advocacy that's the most important thing.
>
> (Head of communications, U.S. non-profit, July 2011)

Yet, at the same time the use of email significantly curtailed the amount of control handed over to supporters, as well as the number of opportunities for them to network with one another. In this framework, the campaign agenda remained firmly in the hands of organisational leaders, favouring a model in which communications tend to flow vertically from top to bottom and users are encouraged to address decision-makers individually.

Despite these reservations, this is not to say that American disability non-profits adopted an approach to personal stories that was inherently inferior to that supported by their British counterparts. It is important to note that U.S. groups encouraged supporters to establish a direct connection with policy-makers, representing their grievances in an unmediated fashion. Thus, it could be argued that this made for a form of lobbying more respectful of individual experiences and personal preferences. Participants from organisations such as AAPD, NCIL and NDRN implicitly acknowledged this in their interviews, remarking that:

> [T]his [supporters contacting policy-makers] is almost beyond our control, because it's out there anyway.
>
> (External relations officer, U.S. non-profit, June 2011)

In contrast, the main aim that British disability organisations had when they elicited personal stories from their online supporters was to acquire compelling accounts to be included in mediated campaign material. In this context, community building and the negotiation of policy meaning among users on platforms such as Facebook represented complementary and possibly inadvertent 'side effects' rather than explicit campaign goals. This was consistent with the tendency for U.K. groups to cast themselves as 'transmission belts' between disabled citizens and representative institutions, as participants repeatedly stated in interviews.

In addition, it should be noted also that personal stories have long occupied a central position in the American disability movement's repertoire. As was mentioned in Chapter 1, U.S. disability groups have pursued the expansion of legislative provisions for disabled people by means of litigation for a long time. This is a common, if lengthy and potentially resource-intensive, strategy among U.S. interest groups active in all sorts of areas (Walker 1991, pp. 181–3). While British disability groups have in fact started to regard court cases as an effective way of promoting policy change only very recently (Vanhala 2011, pp. 146–7, 201–2), U.S. organisations have engaged in legal action for decades, building on a strategy that originated in the civil rights movement (Vaughn-Switzer 2003, pp. 86–9; Zames-Fleischer & Zames 2001, pp. 73–7). Furthermore, individual discrimination cases have provided a compelling background for the introduction of disability legislation to Congress too, the most recent example being Rosa's Law, which was mentioned in interviews by several U.S. participants as an example of effective advocacy work. For this reason, the use of personal stories in email campaigns was in line with the American tradition of arguing for individual cases in order to promote group-wide beneficial changes. Furthermore, as noted by Barnartt and Scotch (2001, pp. 105–6, 223), U.S. disability advocates have applied a 'service provision' frame to their campaigns since the early 1990s. Personal stories of disability lend themselves particularly well to such campaigns, of which electronic messaging represents a contemporary expansion.

Overall, despite some important differences, these findings confirmed that online activism is fostering the personalisation of disability politics in both Britain and America. In fact, it could be argued that the incorporation of private narratives in communications with policy-makers constituted an equal and opposite trend to the one for which in recent decades politicians have tried to appeal to an increasingly disenfranchised citizenry by boosting personal elements in campaign communication (Langer 2010, 2011). Organisations and their online supporters in both countries sought to enrich otherwise 'bland' messages with personal stories in order to catch the eye of potentially inattentive policy-makers. Positive and negative elements co-existed within both forms of this practice examined in this project. Crucially, one could object that emotional appeals and anecdotal evidence make for shaky policy foundations. In light of this, it was not clear whether either of the cases discussed above represented a path to empowerment or rather one towards the fortification of stereotypes and further vilification for disabled people. In this context, a final judgment on the consequences of either of these practices ought to be postponed until additional analysis on the content of personal narratives and the ways in which this is perceived by policy-makers can be carried out.

Moving from these 'tactical' differences, the remainder of this chapter examines the perceptions and beliefs underpinning the technological preferences of disability advocacy organisations in the U.K. and the U.S. In particular, attitudes to the idea of online 'membership', the functions of social media and online political action more generally are discussed *vis-à-vis* social, political and institutional aspects of each national context.

Fluid 'Membership' in the Digital Era

Despite tactical differences and financial constraints, all the organisations examined here confirmed that they were investing to expand their Web presence. In addition to a genuine belief in the potential of new media technologies for making advocacy work more effective, peer-pressure also played a part in this decision. As the chair of one U.K. organisation explained:

> [E]veryone [every disability organisation] is on it [the Internet] so we need to be there too.
>
> (Chair, U.K. member-led pan-disability organization, August 2011)

In this context, it was especially useful to investigate the perceptions of disability groups in both countries with regard to the value of online supporters. While researchers have taken a keen interest in what online participation means to users (Bimber et al. 2012; Lusoli & Ward 2004), less is known about the perspective of formal organisations that are active in specific policy areas. An intuitive way of gauging the importance of online support for a given organisation could be to consider the total number of users who, for example, have subscribed to its email action alerts or 'liked' their pages on Facebook. According to this type of quantitative logic, U.S. disability non-profits looked substantially more successful than their U.K. counterparts at attracting online supporters. At the time of data collection, American organisations counted a disproportionately larger number of Facebook 'fans' compared to British ones, even when the disparity in population between the two countries is taken into account (Table 6.6). It could be tempting to assume that this occurred because American groups placed greater value on their online 'audiences' and invested more than their British counterparts in order to develop their digital support base.

However, this way of measuring the relevance of online support for a given organisation rests on at least two flawed assumptions. First, it presumes that all subscribers participate to the virtual life of these groups in a similar manner. Second, it assumes also that organisations tend to prioritise the acquisition of a large number of online supporters over other aspects of their relationship with Internet users irrespective of their ethos and traditional modes of engagement. Instead, having a large base of online supporters does not necessarily imply that organisations also enable them to be

Table 6.6 Range of Facebook 'fan' numbers (as of 31 March 2012)

	Lowest	*Highest*
U.S. disability organisations	1,500	1,000,000+
U.K. disability organisations	500	27,000

202 *British Innovators, American Conservatives*

meaningful contributors to their initiatives. Furthermore, as demonstrated by the data on Facebook activity discussed in Chapter 4, contribution rates tend to differ greatly among online supporters, of whom only a small minority post new content on a regular basis.

Overall, a somewhat unexpected picture emerged from interviews, which confirmed the 'quantity' of virtual endorsements to be a poor indicator of the 'quality' of user-support as perceived by organisations in both countries. On the one hand, U.S. participants drew a clear distinction between the number of online supporters and their value. On the other hand, conversations with U.K. organisations showed that they were warming up to the notion of 'extended membership'. In particular, American disability organisations found themselves trapped between the formal structure of their:

> ...membership, who pay their dues and in return expect exclusive benefits
>
> (Chair, U.S. member-led pan-disability organisation, June 2011)

on one side and the open nature of social media such as Facebook on the other, which U.S. participants invariably identified as:

> [N]ot quite a problem but certainly a challenge [...] because there are things like for example discussions on developing a position paper that ought to remain members-only.
>
> (Chair, U.S. member-led pan-disability organisation, June 2011)

As a senior representative from a U.S. organisation put it:

> [T]here is no such thing as 'online membership.' Success comes from in-person, active participation.
>
> (Senior VP, U.S. member-led impairment-specific group, June 2011)

While this position was particularly bold, it also signalled a tendency for American disability organisations to cast online support as simply an 'intermediate' step on the path towards full – i.e. paying – membership and not a distinct and intrinsically valuable form of participation. This was consistent with a broader trend for U.S. 'legacy' advocacy organisations to 'maintain a distinction between email "supporters" and dues-paying "members"' (Karpf 2012, p. 37). Indeed, senior leaders and government-relations managers championed this point more frequently in interviews than communication specialists, who seemed more open to a more fluid idea of 'membership'. Yet, as a general trend, this echoed the relative limitedness of the virtual action repertoire offered by U.S. disability groups, hinting at a clear distinction between online and offline participation, which is discussed in detail below.

Conversely, U.K. participants revealed a more appreciative outlook towards online supporters, who they consistently cast as something more than just 'future member material'. Not only did British groups greatly value the contribution made by online supporters to their initiatives, but they also demonstrated a certain degree of vision in:

> . . . providing different interaction options for different people depending on what their interests and their time-constraints are – there are different levels of engagement so for example opening an email would be a level one engagement, clicking through an email would be a level two and so on, but physical presence is not any more valuable than online engagement.
>
> (Head of digital communications,
> U.K. charity, May 2011)

As one participant noted:

> [T]here are quite a few people who don't want to be formally associated with a large national organisation, especially people who have had bad experiences with a charity before, but social media gives them very much a kind of 'arms reach' contact and opportunities to criticise as well.
>
> (Campaigns officer, U.K. charity, September 2011)

This approach resonated with a general tendency for campaigning organisations to carry out a 'reassessment of what it means to be a "member" or a "supporter"' (Chadwick 2007, p. 288) for which 'new cohorts of "affiliate" members [now] sit alongside traditional dues-paying members' (ibid.). As such, British formal disability organisations focused on the benefits afforded by a flexible understanding of 'membership' in the digital era that were first championed by non-conventional activist groups and have since made inroads into the way of thinking of more traditional advocacy organisations (Brainard & Siplon 2004; Ward 2011, p. 932).

Indeed, the idea that political organisations rank supporters as more or less valuable according to their perceived contribution to common goals is not particularly new. However, the advent of digital politics has complicated these matters, effectively forcing advocacy groups to deal with new types of supporters and unconventional modes of engagement. In recent years, this trend has attracted the attention of political communication scholars, who hypothesised the existence of a 'ladder of political loyalty' (Lilleker 2012) inspired by key concepts drawn from marketing theory (Christopher et al. 1991). Furthermore, it is also logical that groups operating within different national contexts categorise supporters according to different criteria. Yet, the views of British and American disability organisations on the issue of online membership were so distant from each other that it was crucial to understand what led the former to attach considerable value to a group that the latter regarded instead as less valuable.

Interview data suggested that the main factor behind this sharp divide was, yet again, the difference in nature and severity between the policy crises surrounding each set of organisations. Most British participants made direct references to the welfare reform controversy as the key reason for re-evaluating the importance of online supporters. This is not to say that such a shift would have failed to happen if the debate over disability benefits had not turned into a contentious issue. In the longer run, U.K. disability groups might certainly have come under pressure to experiment with 'online membership' as a way to remedy the decline of traditional member numbers, as already experienced by other advocacy organisations (Bimber et al. 2012; Lusoli & Ward 2006). Yet, participants suggested that this policy crisis had added a crucial sense of urgency to their plans, requiring them to attract new energies quickly and accelerating the move towards a more fluid type of membership. In other words, events pushed British organisations to:

> [F]ocus on the short term, not thinking of what would happen more than a few months down the line.
>
> (Head of digital communications,
> U.K. charity, May 2011)

In turn, this ushered in a fresh perspective on the value of online participation, which challenged established organisational norms.

In contrast, the different nature of Medicaid events did not require American disability organisations to re-consider their preference for formal membership. It could be argued that their views still represented an outdated conceptualisation of the relationship between digital media and organisational structures. Yet, it also ought to be noted that this idea is connected to two factors that could make it potentially detrimental for American disability non-profits to embrace the idea of informal online membership unreservedly. First and foremost are financial reasons. Unlike most of their British counterparts, American disability non-profits rely on donations and generally do not run services that generate revenue to re-invest in advocacy work (Walker 1991, p. 107). Therefore, the choice to base their social media approach on the belief that:

> Facebook, Twitter and YouTube will increase [formal] membership
> (Chair, U.S. member-led pan-disability
> organisation, June 2011)

can be understood *vis-à-vis* the need for donations money. In this context, online media provide a powerful extension for 'marketing membership' practices whose ultimate goal is to sign up as many supporters as possible as full paying members (Jordan & Maloney 1997, pp. 148–165). Second, the main purpose of these organisations remains to build a movement operating over the long term in a specific policy niche, and as such their preference is clearly oriented towards what they perceive to be solidly committed supporters.

It is probably too early to say whether such divergent perspectives on the idea of 'online membership' will have a lasting impact on either set of organisations. Yet, these observations provided further confirmation of the fact that, on their own, new media technologies are insufficient to generate meaningful organisational change. Instead, change is more likely to occur if the use of technology is simultaneously underpinned by circumstances that effectively force otherwise reluctant leaders to consider novel paths. These results reaffirmed the centrality of external catalysts – in particular acute policy crises – in pushing the boundaries of e-advocacy. Inevitably, key ideas on the value of online support resonated also with the approach of these groups to social media and online political action more generally.

Social Media: *'Mildly Terrifying'* or a *'Force for Change'*?

An in-depth comparative assessment of the use of social media by British and American formal disability organisations could probably take up an entire book. However, given the increasing centrality of these platforms to online politics, it is useful to reflect here on what was revealed in interviews with regard to the approach of these groups to the likes of Twitter and Facebook. On balance, a number of important similarities emerged. First, the vast majority of organisations in both countries showed awareness of social media's ambivalence for disability rights advocacy. All but one of the participants spontaneously offered to discuss issues of social media accessibility, demonstrating attention for how these can constitute exclusionary barriers for supporters with specific impairments. Thus, everyone outlined how his or her organisation was trying to address accessibility problems by consistently complementing its social media presence with more accessible digital channels – chiefly email – and continued to distribute printed material for the benefit of older supporters despite the considerable financial costs involved. Having said that, British and American disability organisations held divergent views on the function of social media within their respective communication and action repertoires. While in fact the vast majority of interview participants in both countries interpreted social media's bottom-up nature as a potential challenge to the consolidated position that their respective organisations held in the realm of disability politics, British groups tended to emphasise this as a positive chance for 'renewal', albeit one that was complex for them to navigate. In contrast, their U.S. counterparts overwhelmingly withdrew into a more conservative approach that sought to blend traditional control patterns with two-way communications.

Once again, it was reasonable to assume that the climate of profound emergency connected to U.K. disability welfare reform underpinned the emergence of a more positive perspective on social media among British organisations. As was discussed earlier in this chapter in relation to the personalisation of email content, British disability groups thought that, given the circumstances, it was necessary to entrust online supporters with a certain degree of freedom and in a way accepted that some changes in their organisational dynamics were beyond their control. This gave the impression of a set of groups that sought to 'manage' a complicated but necessary transition instead of blatantly trying to ignore the new circumstances under which it had to work. In particular, British participants frequently mentioned The Hardest Hit as an example of a campaign enriched by user-generated suggestions collected through social media. They also outlined the value of social media as:

> [E]ssential tools for online protest for those who otherwise would not make the [Hardest Hit] march [on 26 March 2011], whether because of financial or physical barriers, or because they don't deal well with crowd situations.
>
> (Campaigns officer, U.K. charity, August 2011)

As a campaigns officer from one of Britain's biggest impairment-specific charities noted:

> [T]here is an audience who are younger who maybe wouldn't engage with 'Victorian' organisations like ours who now can do so on their own platform [Facebook].
>
> (Campaigns officer, U.K. charity, September 2011)

Although further research is needed to establish whether the social media presence of these groups actually stood up to the principles discussed in interviews, these comments corroborated the impression of a refreshing departure from the suspicious attitude to these platforms encountered among Scottish disability in a previous study (Trevisan 2014). It is useful to point out that, while participants in previous research had cast social media as channels for marketing and fundraising (ibid.), the representatives of U.K. organisations interviewed for this project demonstrated a more sophisticated understanding of these platforms as geared towards dialogue with users.

This was in stark contrast to the rhetoric that participants from American disability organisations deployed when they discussed the function of social media in interviews. Overall, these groups came to social networking platforms from a more sceptical angle, explaining that:

> [S]ocial media can facilitate a conversation, but online advocacy is an entirely different thing.
>
> (Head of communications, U.S. non-profit,
> August 2011)

This attitude was exemplified by the choice of some U.S. groups to prevent ordinary Internet users from starting their own conversation threads on Facebook pages (Table 6.7). This clearly distinguished American organisations from British ones, all of which enabled supporters to post starter contributions on their Facebook pages and influence the agenda for online discussion instead (Table 6.8). As one participant from a pan-disability organisation explained, the approach of U.S. disability rights groups reflected a determination to:

> [K]eep it [Facebook] somewhat superficial unless we know that everybody's gonna agree [...] we don't wanna give our supporters an opportunity to get into a 'dog-fight' on our Facebook page.
>
> (Head of communications, U.S. pan-disability
> non-profit, June 2011)

Furthermore, in accordance with the financial model discussed above, most U.S. groups had integrated a fundraising element in their Facebook pages by adopting *Causes* (an app that enables supporters to make donations through Facebook; see Table 6.5). This was again in opposition to the experience of their British counterparts, none of which were using this tool at the time of data collection (Table 6.6).

Table 6.7 Facebook key features (U.S. groups)

U.S. organisation	Anyone can start a Facebook thread	Facebook Causes App
AAPD	No	Yes
NCIL	Yes	No
NDRN	No	No
Access Living	Yes	Yes
ADAPT	No	Yes
UCP	Yes	Yes
Easter Seals	Yes	Yes
The ARC	Yes	Yes
Autism Speaks/Autism Votes	No	Yes
Mental Health America	Yes	Yes
NFB	n/a	n/a
LDA	Yes	No
MS Society	Yes	Yes

Table 6.8 Facebook key features (U.K. groups)

U.K. organisation	Anyone can start a Facebook thread	Facebook Causes App
UKDPC	Yes	No
Inclusion London	n/a	n/a
NCIL	n/a	n/a
Disability Alliance	Yes	No
RADAR	Yes	No
LCD	Yes	No
MENCAP	Yes	No
RNIB	Yes	No
SCOPE	Yes	No
MS Society	Yes	No
MIND	Yes	No
Ambitious about Autism	Yes	No
NAS	Yes	No
Action for ME	Yes	No

As shown in previous research (Kenix 2007, 2008a, 2008b), it is natural for advocacy organisations that operate in any area to assume that handing control over to users might deprive their leaders of authority and endanger their position as intermediaries in policy-making. Yet, in reality most groups have little choice but to measure themselves with new forms of online engagement. In this context, future successes depend on the ability to understand and embrace both the challenges and opportunities offered by new media (Brainard & Siplon 2002, 2004). Most American participants were aware that they took a risk by sticking to a traditional approach. In particular, U.S. communication specialists interviewed for this study sought to place responsibility for this choice with:

> [P]ublic policy team[s, who] are resistant to the openness of social media.
>
> (Head of communications, U.S. impairment-specific non-profit, June 2011)

Although this is not the place to discuss the impact of internal organisational structures on technological preferences, these types of comments hinted at a detrimental disconnect between those in charge of government relations and those responsible for communications within American disability organisations. Furthermore, participants expressed wider views on online action and on how this compares to its offline counterpart. The next section focuses specifically on this point, which bears crucial connections to the local institutional architecture of each country and the position that disability non-profits occupy in their respective governance structures.

'Showing up on Capitol Hill is Equivalent to 10,000 Emails': Does Online Action Really Matter?

The quote in the heading above is drawn from an interview carried out with a participant from a large impairment-specific American non-profit. While it expresses a uniquely bold view, it also encapsulates the perspective shared by the vast majority of the American disability organisations examined here. U.S. groups, irrespective of their structure and ethos, drew a clear distinction between in-person and online participation. Put simply, these groups had established a 'hierarchy of value' between offline and online political action for which the former was considered superior to the latter. This was exemplified not only by their hesitant approach to social media, but also by the fact that none of them had set up a 'virtual participation' page in connection with their main policy objectives. Although it may seem obvious for these types of assertions to come from a group of 'Washington-insiders' who liaise with decision-makers on a regular basis, such offline/online dichotomy still prompted some important reflections. In particular, the perspective of U.S. organisations was in direct contrast with that of U.K. groups, which interpreted online participation as more than a mere supplement to offline action. As one British participant explained:

> [T]hey [online and offline action] are of equal value because they matter in different ways to different people – for example, they allow people who would be excluded from direct action to also voice their concerns as through Twitter we can reach politicians and the [news] media directly.
> (Head of communications, U.K. charity, August 2011)

In this context, online action was seen as complementary to offline initiatives, but not in a subordinate way. What, then, lay at the root of such divergent evaluations of online action?

Participants linked these trends to important differences in the institutional architecture and political culture of the two countries. This not only constituted further evidence in support of the idea that online politics is deeply interwoven with offline events, but it also showed that opportunities for disabled Internet users to become engaged in online collective action are strongly dependent upon local constraints. American participants explained that:

> [T]he best way to have influence on Capitol Hill is relationships, personal relationships: who knows who, who has the ability to talk to whom, because personal relationships influence people, [...] of course you can see a video or whatever, but it's not gonna have the same effect on you.
> (Chair, U.S. member-led pan-disability organisation, June 2011)

As another participant put it, e-advocacy alone was unlikely to be effective because:

> [Y]ou're not gonna beat an in-person presence on the Hill, you're not gonna beat a real conversation with a legislator [. . .] so virtual action alone would probably not get you anywhere.
>
> (Policy officer, U.S. member-led pan-disability organisation, June 2011)

These were widely held beliefs that resonated with the function traditionally assigned to formal interest groups in U.S. federal policy-making processes (Walker 1991, p. 49). As such, disability non-profits participate in one of the core pillars of American democracy, which *de facto* enshrines them in the Washington law-making apparatus and bestows upon them an 'official' representative role. While this system may appear somewhat discomforting to foreign eyes not versed in the U.S. pressure group system, in American terms this more plainly provides an institutionalised path for the citizenry's grievances to reach elected representatives (Kernell & Jacobson 2006, pp. 515–27). Both professionalised and member-led American disability non-profits implicitly acknowledged the validity of this structure by pointing out in interviews that they needed to ensure what they called 'the Washington balance', which required them to build a constructive liaison with decision-makers while at the same time letting them know if their constituents disagreed with any aspect of a particular policy proposal.

Although participants praised this system for 'getting things done', at the same time this also restricted the action repertoire available to American disability organisations. Most notably, virtually all the groups under scrutiny refrained from organising protests and public demonstrations, which they described as tactics better suited to more 'militant' groups such as ADAPT (Zames-Fleischer & Zames 2001, pp. 82–3). Instead, their actions included Capitol Hill rallies and briefing days, which can be managed more effectively as attendance is restricted to invitees. In this context, online action was subjected to many of the same restrictions as its offline counterpart. This not only explained the absence of 'virtual protest pages' from the repertoire of American disability non-profits, but also provided a justification for their reluctance to experiment with forms of online collective action that:

> [L]et just anyone take part, including those who may send out the wrong message.
>
> (Head of communications, U.S. non-profit, July 2011)

One participant from an American pan-disability organisation explained that:

> [C]onstituents are unrestrained and don't see social media as places to be nice or polite, it's more like for policy-makers to get a flavor of the 'fury' but we also need to ensure that we're seen as responsible negotiators.
>
> (Policy officer, U.S. pan-disability member-led organisation, June 2011)

Conversely, in Britain the role of non-profits as intermediaries in policy-making has tended to be less institutionalised, although ironically more dependent on public funding. Indeed, attempts have been made in recent years to co-opt willing organisations into closer relationships with decision-makers, especially during New Labour's tenure in government between 1997 and 2010 (Barnes et al. 2003; Craig & Taylor 2002). Yet, it would be fair to say that this set-up still lacks the formality of the American system. As a result, and despite some of the British groups examined here being no strangers to the process of institutionalisation of disability advocacy promoted in recent years (Barnes 2007; Oliver & Barnes 2012), British formal disability organisations tended to rely on a richer variety of tactics for reaching policy-makers than that of their U.S. counterparts. Among its most high-profile components were mass gatherings, marches and demonstrations, including those that took place throughout 2011 as part of the mobilisation against the welfare reform. In this context, online action came to occupy a very valuable position. As one participant put it:

> [O]nline and offline complement each other – some voices can be heard online that would not be offline; for instance some of our members would find it difficult to attend a protest in person but can participate virtually.
>
> (Communications officer, U.K. charity, September 2011)

At the same time, British organisations also stressed that meetings with policy-makers constituted very valuable opportunities to 'get things done'. In all fairness, some of them admitted to using social media as a means to an end, namely to gain visibility on the Internet in order to be invited to face-to-face meetings with ministers and MPs. However, in interviews the rhetoric of complementariness between different forms of participation consistently outweighed that of hierarchy between online and in-person action. Thus, the points made by British participants echoed the arguments put forward by Internet scholars who regard the distinction between 'virtual' and 'real' to be artificial, and the boundaries between the two, if they exist, to be entirely permeable (Rogers 2009). In this framework, it makes little sense for activists and campaigners to rank online action against its offline counterpart. Rather, these constitute two profoundly interwoven components of the same advocacy process.

Context in Online Campaigning: The '4-Cs' Matrix

Overall, formal British disability organisations were relatively more comfortable with online interactivity, innovation and experimentation compared to their U.S. counterparts. British groups built virtual 'headquarters' for their impromptu coalition against the government's welfare reform, used email to publicise a variety of other online engagement options, interpreted social media as platforms for 'online protest' and were open to negotiating the challenges and opportunities presented by flexible forms of online membership. Conversely, U.S. organisations were reluctant to join forces online towards a common goal, saw email as the only really valuable Internet channel for political action and tried to apply traditional control tactics to interactive Web platforms.

These findings were counter-intuitive as previous research identified American political groups as trendsetters in e-advocacy. As such, U.S. formal disability organisations constituted a noticeable exception in an otherwise innovation-rich context. However, this is not to say that the groups examined in this study were naïve about digital politics, but rather that the development of online tactics for influencing policy-making is deeply affected by contextual factors. Indeed, this supports one of the original assumptions made in this book that e-advocacy never starts as a blank canvas, but that it is always necessary to adapt the use of new media technologies to suit external circumstances. Hence, while the idea that established organisations have been blending their repertoires with participatory elements derived from networked and social movement activist tactics holds as a general trend, the extent to which this on-going transformation is taking place is likely to differ from one country to another, as well as between different policy areas within the same country.

In light of these considerations, a truly useful conceptualisation of the 'context' in which contemporary e-advocacy takes place is one that combines systemic factors with more volatile elements. The traditional focus on national norms and institutions that was adopted in previous comparative Internet research needs to be reviewed to pay greater attention to circumstantial factors, particularly in relation to crisis situations. Four key elements emerged from this chapter that invite further reflection, including two circumstantial and two systemic factors.

Circumstantial factors include:

- Controversy type (Is the campaign merely targeted at policy objectives, or are there wider political implications?)
- Catalyst nature (Does the issue at stake focus on resources re-distribution with potentially divisive consequences, or is it rather an ideological and potentially unifying one?)

Table 6.9 Key factors influencing disability rights e-advocacy in Britain and America

	Circumstantial factors		Systemic factors	Community ties	E-activism features
	Controversy type	Catalyst nature	Constitutional arrangement		
U.K.	Double (policy & political)	Ideological (unifying)	• Strong parties • Westminster centralism • Parliament as key legislator • Civil society groups 'outside the tent'	• Pre-existing coalition on welfare issues • Internet as useful space for temporary unity	• High interaction (two-way communication) • High innovation (social media for campaigning; online membership) • High coordination (online coalition) • High integration (online/offline of equal value)
U.S.	Single (policy only)	Resource-focused (divisive)	• Loose parties • Federal system • Congress, state legislatures and courts as key legislators • Interest groups 'inside the tent'	• Pre-existing collaboration on civil rights issues • Deep rifts among impairment-specific groups • Individualism	• Low interaction (top-down communication) • Low innovation (email; online supporters vs. paying members divide) • Low coordination (separate campaigns) • Low integration (offline/online hierarchy)

Systemic factors include:

- Constitutional arrangement (How strong are political parties? Are institutions highly centralised or organised in a more localised federal system? What position do civil society groups occupy within the policy-making apparatus?)
- Community ties (Are there any collaboration and/or internal conflict precedents? Is advocacy in that particular policy domain inspired by individualism or group agency?)

Undoubtedly, future research is poised to refine and expand this list of factors. However, Controversy type, Catalysts nature, Constitutional arrangement and Community ties constitute key contextual elements that can be reasonably assumed to influence e-advocacy in any given democratic context. As such, this '4-Cs' matrix (Table 6.9) provides researchers, campaigners and policy-makers alike with a useful starting point for studying, planning or indeed responding to online advocacy. While systemic factors can be fairly predictable, circumstantial ones are by definition difficult to anticipate. Yet, as shown by the case studies discussed in this chapter, circumstantial factors can constitute particularly effective innovation drivers in online campaigning. In particular, both the nature and magnitude of the U.K. welfare reform crisis crucially pushed British disability organisations towards a more sophisticated repertoire of online action in recent years, whereas previously these groups held rather conservative views on digital media. Although pre-existent institutional and cultural factors were responsible for shaping the detail of online disability rights advocacy in Britain and America, it was the specific crisis context that provided a catalyst for change in one case and somewhat inhibited innovation in the other. This calls for a fundamental re-think of the way in which context is understood, conceptualised and captured in studies of online political participation to which the next and final chapter in this book seeks to make an initial contribution.

Notes

1 Medicaid is a means-tested assistance programme aimed primarily at supporting the healthcare needs of people on low incomes. It is funded jointly by the federal and state governments and managed by the States. 'The Path to Prosperity' plan included measures for a radical reform of Medicaid's funding mechanism that would gradually reduce the federal government's share of funding as part of an ambitious deficit reduction plan.
2 After months of stalemate, in November 2011 Congress reached a debt-limiting deal for which the ability of the federal government to borrow could be increased as long as $1.5 trillion worth of savings were found over the following decade. This agreement stated that a cuts plan should be in place by December 2011. Otherwise, $100 billion a year would be cut automatically

from the federal budget starting in January 2013. Crucially, Medicaid and other social security programmes were exempted from automatic cuts.
3 See: http://ucp.org/tag/faces-of-medicaid/ (accessed 10 June 2016).
4 CCD includes over 100 American national disability groups. It provides a forum for member organisations to discuss a wide variety of topics, from education to health, and from transport to technology, with a particular emphasis on civil rights issues. More information can be found at: www.c-c-d.org (accessed 10 March 2016).
5 Differently from 'snowball' and 'co-link' crawls used in previous chapters in relation to U.K. disability organisations, 'inter-actor' analysis with Issue-Crawler focuses solely on the connections among the websites entered as seed URLs.
6 In 2011, DBC Web pages were hosted on the Disability Alliance's website (www.disabilityalliance.org; accessed 21 September 2011).

References

Arquilla, J. & Ronfeldt, D., 2001. *Networks and Netwar: The Future of Terror, Crime and Militancy*, Santa Monica, CA: RAND.

Bagenstos, S.R., 2009. *Law and the Contradictions of the Disability Rights Movement*, New Haven, CT: Yale University Press.

Barnartt, S.N. & Scotch, R.K., 2001. *Disability Protests: Contentious Politics 1970–1999*, Washington, DC: Gallaudet University Press.

Barnes, C., 2007. Disability Activism and the Struggle for Change Disability, Policy and Politics in the UK. *Education, Citizenship and Social Justice*, 2(3), pp. 203–221.

Barnes, M., Newman, J., Knops, A. & Sullivan, H., 2003. Constituting 'the Public' in Public Participation. *Public Administration*, 81(2), pp. 379–399.

Bell, C.V. & Entman, R.M., 2011. The Media's Role in America's Exceptional Politics of Inequality Framing the Bush Tax Cuts of 2001 and 2003. *The International Journal of Press/Politics*, 16(4), pp. 548–572.

Bennett, W.L. & Segerberg, A., 2011. Digital Media and the Personalization of Collective Action. *Information, Communication & Society*, 14(6), pp. 770–799.

Bergan, D.E., 2009. Does Grassroots Lobbying Work? A Field Experiment Measuring the Effects of an e-Mail Lobbying Campaign on Legislative Behavior. *American Politics Research*, 37(2), pp. 327–352.

Bimber, B., Flanagin, A.J. & Stohl, C., 2012. *Collective Action in Organizations: Interaction and Engagement in an Era of Technological Change*, Cambridge: Cambridge University Press.

Brainard, L.A. & Siplon, P.D., 2002. Cyberspace Challenges to Mainstream Nonprofit Health Organizations. *Administration & Society*, 34(2), pp. 141–175.

——— 2004. Toward Nonprofit Organization Reform in the Voluntary Spirit: Lessons from the Internet. *Nonprofit and Voluntary Sector Quarterly*, 33(3), pp. 435–457.

Briant, E., Watson, N. & Philo, G., 2013. Reporting Disability in the Age of Austerity: The Changing Face of Media Representation of Disability and Disabled People in the United Kingdom and the Creation of New 'Folk Devils'. *Disability & Society*, 28(6), pp. 874–889.

Bryan, W.V., 2006. *In Search of Freedom*, Springfield, IL: Charles C Thomas Publisher.

Carey, A.C., 2009. *On the Margins of Citizenship: Intellectual Disability and Civil Rights in Twentieth-Century America*, Philadelphia, PA: Temple University Press.

Chadwick, A., 2007. Digital Network Repertoires and Organizational Hybridity. *Political Communication*, 24(3), pp. 283–301.

Christopher, M., Payne, A. & Ballantyne, D., 1991. *Relationship Marketing: Bringing Quality Customer Service and Marketing Together*, Oxford: Butterworth-Heinemann.

Craig, G. & Taylor, M., 2002. Dangerous Liaisons: Local Government and the Voluntary and Community Sector. In C. Glendinning, C. Powell, & K. Rummery, eds. *Partnerships, New Labour and the Governance of Welfare*. Bristol: The Policy Press, pp. 131–148.

Earl, J. & Kimport, K., 2011. *Digitally Enabled Social Change: Activism in the Internet Age*, Cambridge, MA: The MIT Press.

Garthwaite, G., 2011. The Language of Shirkers and Scroungers: Talking about Illness, Disability and Coalition Welfare Reform. *Disability and Society*, 26(3), pp. 369–372.

Gilens, M., 1999. *Why Americans Hate Welfare: Race, Media, and the Politics of Antipoverty Policy*, Chicago: The University of Chicago Press.

Giles, M.W. & Evans, A., 1986. The Power Approach to Intergroup Hostility. *Journal of Conflict Resolution*, 30(3), pp. 469–486.

Haller, B.A., 2010. *Representing Disability in an Ableist World*, Louisville, KY: The Avocado Press.

Haller, B.A., Dorries, B. & Rahn, J., 2006. Media Labeling Versus the US Disability Community Identity: A Study of Shifting Cultural Language. *Disability & Society*, 21(1), pp. 61–75.

Holtz-Bacha, C. & Kaid, L.L., 2011. Political Communication Across the World. In E. P. Bucy & R. L. Holbert, eds. *The Sourcebook for Political Communication Research. Methodological Issues Involved in International Comparisons*. New York/London: Routledge, pp. 395–416.

Jaeger, P.T. & Bowman, C.A., 2005. *Understanding Disability: Inclusion, Access, Diversity, and Civil Rights*, Westport, CT/London: Praeger Publishers.

Jordan, G. & Maloney, W., 1997. *The Protest Business? Mobilizing Campaign Groups*, Manchester/New York: Manchester University Press.

Karpf, D., 2010. Online Political Mobilization from the Advocacy Group's Perspective: Looking Beyond Clicktivism. *Policy & Internet*, 2(4), pp. 7–41.

————— 2012. *The MoveOn Effect: The Unexpected Transformation of American Political Advocacy*, New York: Oxford University Press.

Kenix, L.J., 2007. In Search of Utopia: An Analysis of Non-Profit Web Pages. *Information, Community and Society*, 10(1), pp. 69–94.

————— 2008a. Nonprofit Organizations' Perceptions and Uses of the Internet. *Television & New Media*, 9(5), pp. 407–428.

————— 2008b. The Internet as a Tool for Democracy? A Survey of Non-Profit Internet Decision-Makers and Web Users. *First Monday*, 13(7).

Kernell, S. & Jacobson, G.C., 2006. *The Logic of American Politics* Third Edition, Washington, DC: CQ Press.

Langer, A.I., 2010. The Politicization of Private Persona: Exceptional Leaders or the New Rule? The Case of the United Kingdom and the Blair Effect. *The International Journal of Press/Politics*, 15(1), pp. 60–76.

—— 2011. *The Personalisation of Politics in the UK: Mediated Leadership from Attlee to Cameron*, Manchester: Manchester University Press.

Lilleker, D., 2012. *Getting Them Involved: Attracting and Empowering Supporters. In 10th e-Campaigning Forum*, 21–22 March, Oxford.

Lusoli, W. & Ward, S., 2004. Digital Rank-and-File: Party Activists' Perceptions and Use of the Internet. *The British Journal of Politics & International Relations*, 6(4), pp. 453–470.

—— 2006. Hunting Protestors: Mobilisation, Participation and Protest Online in the Countryside Alliance. In S. Oates, D. Owen, & R. Gibson, eds. *The Internet and Politics: Citizens, Voters and Activists*. London: Routledge, pp. 52–71.

Mandell, M.P., 2001. Collaboration Through Network Structures for Community Building Efforts. *National Civic Review*, 90(3), pp. 279–288.

Oliver, M. & Barnes, C., 2012. *The New Politics of Disablement*, Basingstoke: Palgrave Macmillan.

Rogers, R., 2009. *The End of the Virtual: Digital Methods*, Amsterdam: Vossiuspers UVA.

Schlosberg, D., Zavestoski, S. & Shulman, D.S.W., 2008. Democracy and E-Rulemaking: Web-Based Technologies, Participation, and the Potential for Deliberation. *Journal of Information Technology & Politics*, 4(1), pp. 37–55.

Shulman, S.W., 2006. Whither Deliberation? Mass E-Mail Campaigns and U.S. Regulatory Rulemaking. *Journal of E-Government*, 3(3), pp. 41–64.

Smith, A., 2010. *Government Online: The Internet Gives Citizens New Paths to Government Services and Information*, Washington, DC: Pew Internet and American Life Project.

Stroman, D.F., 2003. *The Disability Rights Movement: From De-Institutionalization to Self-Determination*, Lanham, MD: University Press of America.

Trevisan, F., 2014. Scottish Disability Organizations and Online Media: A Path to Empowerment or 'Business as Usual?' *Disability Studies Quarterly*, 34(3).

Vanhala, L., 2011. *Making Rights a Reality? Disability Rights Activists and Legal Mobilization*, Cambridge: Cambridge University Press.

Vaughn-Switzer, J., 2003. *Disabled Rights: American Disability Policy and the Fight for Equality*, Washington, DC: Georgetown University Press.

Walker, J.L., 1991. *Mobilizing Interest Groups in America: Patrons, Professions, and Social Movements*, Ann Arbor, MI: The University of Michigan Press.

Ward, J., 2011. Reaching Citizens Online. *Information, Communication & Society*, 14(6), pp. 917–936.

Zames-Fleischer, D. & Zames, F., 2001. *The Disability Rights Movement: From Charity to Confrontation*, Philadelphia, PA: Temple University Press.

7 New Directions in Disability Rights Advocacy

In March 2014, the information technology (IT) outsourcing firm Atos Origin settled with the U.K. government to terminate early its multi-year multi-million pound contract to carry out the controversial Work Capability Assessment (WCA) tests on Employment and Support Allowance (ESA) claimants. Although the exact impact of disability rights activism on this decision cannot be measured, the high-profile protests that a range of advocacy groups organised against Atos are likely to have played a role in this process. As a senior Atos executive explained during a Westminster select committee hearing in 2014, for the previous few years disability rights advocates successfully publicised episodes that showed Atos's misconduct in WCA tests and contributed to tarnishing its reputation. The early termination of this contract was an important victory for U.K. disability advocates and was underpinned by a substantial amount of change and revitalisation in the disability rights movement. As the research discussed in this book has shown, new media technologies played an important role in this process of reform and renewal. In the U.K., the sense of urgency sparked by the government's decision to bring forward a radical reform of disability welfare in 2010, coupled with the opportunities for participatory campaigning offered by social media, re-shaped disability advocacy significantly. In the U.S. too, e-advocacy has become ubiquitous among disability rights organisations, although so far it has not fostered the kind of profound changes seen in Britain with regard to structure, tactics and leadership.

It was particularly interesting to see digital media make such an impression in an area of advocacy that before 2010 seemed very sceptical about the opportunities offered by online communications (Trevisan 2014). In just a few years, Internet-based media went from being an irrelevant civic resource for disabled people, to important platforms for public participation. This book explored this new advocacy landscape and discussed its inherent opportunities, challenges and potential contradictions. Although the case study approach displayed in this work requires caution in trying to generalise its findings, several trends emerged here that transcended individual cases, inviting reflections on the transformations underway in the realm of citizen-initiated politics, as well as the direct impact of these changes on disabled people's political inclusion. Three main issues came to the fore in this book, including:

1   Changes in the ecology of British disability advocacy, including the emergence of new types of groups and the transformation of existing organisational forms;
2   A new model of 'peer-mediated' yet democratically ambiguous citizenship supported by the emergence of a young, technology-savvy disabled leadership; and, finally,
3   The centrality of circumstantial factors – in particular crisis – in the evolution of e-advocacy.

The rest of this chapter discusses each of these issues in detail and concludes by sketching an agenda for future research on disability, politics and new media.

Towards a New Ecology of British Disability Advocacy

The e-advocacy and online protest initiatives that flourished in the wake of the U.K. Conservative–Liberal Democrat coalition government's welfare reform led to some substantial changes in the ecology of British disability advocacy. First, both existing disability organisations and informal networks of experienced disabled activists overcame some of their reservations with regard to participatory online media. As discussed in this book, in particular in Chapter 5, the way in which these groups approached online media – Facebook in particular – were influenced by a range of factors including their traditional action repertoires, founding principles and relationship with the broader political landscape (see Table 7.1). That said, it is important to note that they all engaged with new media on an unprecedented scale. Second, digital media supported the emergence of an entirely new, online-only type of disability rights group defined here as 'digital action network'. This was characterised by a young and technology-savvy disabled leadership that favoured a pragmatic issue-focused approach and devised a distinctive online-only action repertoire. Through their work, these bloggers-cum-activists distinguished themselves from both 'professionalised' advocacy organisations and dissent groups focused on street protest, and promoted arguably more effective ways to influence public decision-making.

The 'digital switch' implemented both by formal disability organisations such as those participating in The Hardest Hit coalition and experienced disabled activists such as Disabled People Against Cuts (DPAC) constituted a source of innovation in a context that until recently was lagging behind most other areas of citizen-initiated politics. The decision of these groups to use social media to catalyse dissent against the U.K. welfare reform showed

Table 7.1 The new ecology of British disability rights advocacy

	Structure	Outlook on representative democracy and the political system	Intended purpose of Facebook and other social media
Digital action networks (e.g. The Broken of Britain)	Strong core group: new, technology-savvy generation of disabled self-advocates.	Sees the representative system as legitimate, but politicians as morally corrupt. Considers direct representation essential, but avoids contentious tactics.	• Space for peers and supporters to talk and vent frustration • Provide new activist generation with legitimacy/ support
Digitised disabled activists (e.g. DPAC)	Social movement-style group; founding members linked to 1980s and 1990s disabled people's movement.	Sees representative institutions as inherently exclusionary. Street protest is its primary type of action.	• Support the organisation of offline mobilisation (esp. street protests) • Facilitate remote participation in protests
Coalition of formal organisations (e.g. The Hardest Hit)	Formal leadership (bureaucratised) and membership structure, but open to 'online membership'.	Sees the representative system as legitimate, but considers the use of 'extraordinary' measures such as street rallies if circumstances require it.	• Replicate mediated participation • Multiply endorsements • Support specific events • Micro-empowerment • Crowd-sourcing of ideas to inspire new initiatives

that existing disability groups engage with digital media when the circumstances require them to mobilise a mass of supporters quickly and online advocacy is the most effective way to do so. At the same time, however, their approach to Internet-based media could be described as incremental rather than outright transformational, as both The Hardest Hit and DPAC sought to blend online tactics within their existing communicative and political action repertoires. On the one hand, experienced activists in DPAC remained anchored to traditional protest tactics, limiting online protest to a support role that reaffirmed the centrality of offline contentious initiatives. On the other hand, the formal organisations that took part in The Hardest Hit sought the input of online supporters in crafting their message, at least in part. Thus, they adopted a more 'receptive' advocacy style, while at the same time trying to preserve their role as legitimate brokers and mediators of the disability community's interests *vis-à-vis* democratic institutions.

In contrast, the emergence of a digital action network such as The Broken of Britain constituted a moment of profound rupture with the past of disability advocacy. The founders of this campaign were a group of disabled bloggers who used online media to overcome the traditional dichotomy between 'professional' charity-like organisations and social-movement-type protest groups. The Broken of Britain substituted existing action repertoires with an innovative, online-only organisational paradigm that had the potential to attract a different kind of supporter. This initiative filled the gap between co-optation and street protest in disability activism by using digital media to devise less contentious and arguably more effective ways of expressing dissent at a time when disabled people's pleas were finding little support from political parties, including historical allies such as Labour.

In a way, the emergence of different types of groups could be interpreted as a sign of division in British disability advocacy. Undoubtedly, a fragmented response to controversial policy proposals was likely to be less effective. In particular, the case of The Broken of Britain seemed to demonstrate that politically-minded disabled Internet users unhappy with the existing options for expressing dissent could use new media technologies to bypass established groups and set up a different campaign. Nevertheless, this also injected more choice into the disability movement, providing disabled Internet users with new ways to join the debate on disability welfare and, possibly, participate in online activities to contrast the government's agenda. In particular, The Broken of Britain's Facebook page – as also The Hardest Hit's, albeit in a more directed fashion – facilitated the sharing of personal disability stories on Facebook as a way for Internet users unfamiliar with political debates to articulate their concerns in 'everyday' terms and better understand complex policy measures. Importantly, this trend was in line with a more general personalisation of the online political discourse, as well as previous work that praised interactive online platforms for hosting unmediated and alternative representations of disability (Goggin & Noonan 2007; Thoreau 2006). In addition, it also showed the value of sharing personal narratives in promoting political citizenship and agency among disabled people (Watson 1998) and highlighted the 'political' nature of seemingly 'private' experiences that previously had been pointed out by feminist disability scholars (Crow 1996; Fawcett 2000; French 1993; Morris 1991, 1992).

Overall, the picture of British disability advocacy that emerged from these findings was one that had shifted towards the model of 'connective action' proposed by Bennett and Segerberg (2012, p. 756), albeit somewhat selectively. The groups examined here, including emerging ones such as

The Broken of Britain, continued to be characterised by certain organising practices that tend to be associated with traditional collective action. First, 'digitised' activist groups such as DPAC remained strongly opposed to the use of personalised action frames. While this possibly contributed to this group's difficulty in generating a substantial amount of conversation on their Facebook page, as discussed in Chapter 4, it also showed that consolidated activist practices can still shape the use of digital media for campaigning purposes (Kavada 2010). Second, formal disability organisations assumed a background role to create a digitally-enabled and loosely connected coalition, The Hardest Hit. However, this unity was only temporary and issue-focused, while the organisations that took part in this joint campaign closely guarded their independence and individual identities throughout the process. Third, the joint examination of Facebook conversations and interviews with core organisers revealed that The Broken of Britain was in fact much more centrally coordinated than one would assume.

These considerations raised two main questions. First, there was the issue of whether this new ecology of British disability advocacy can be sustainable in the long term. The digital age is characterised by high organisational fluidity, as shown by the fact that The Broken of Britain ceased to operate as a group after little more than a year from its foundation. However, what about its original organising practices and action repertoire? Are those here to stay and be adopted by other groups? As Castells (2012) noted, networked movements 'will continue to fight and debate, evolve and eventually fade away in their current states of being' (p. 244). Thus, technological development, evolving uses of new media and external circumstances can be expected to nurture further changes in the future of disability advocacy and networked activism more generally (Rainie & Wellman 2012, p. 276).

Having said that, there are signs that The Broken of Britain left behind an important legacy, both in organisational and tactical terms. The fact that some of the original founders of The Broken of Britain established the Spartacus Network at the beginning of 2012 echoed the idea of sedimentary networks (Chadwick 2007, 2012; Flanagin et al. 2006, p. 42). This suggests that digital action networks are not a temporary oddity in the ecology of British disability advocacy. However, as in the case of 'headline chasing' organisations such as MoveOn.org (Karpf 2010, 2012), the future sustainability of this form of advocacy will depend on the ability of core organisers to ensure continuous membership turnover by regularly updating the agenda and repertoire to attract new supporters to compensate for those who lapse once a given issue has lost its original thrust. This can be more challenging for organisations that operate within a restricted niche such as disability rights groups compared to 'generalist' ones such as MoveOn.org, Avaaz and GetUp!, which can take on virtually any issue. Furthermore, some of the tactics developed by The Broken of

Britain have been adopted by other groups in recent years. For example, DPAC started to include personal stories of disability in its most recent campaigns, as is discussed in Chapter 3.

Second, there was the issue of whether any of the new forms of digital disability advocacy in Britain had enhanced the sense of citizenship for the ordinary Internet users who were involved in them. In other words, did the newly reinvigorated British disability movement foster meaningful participation for its online supporters, in particular disabled Internet users? This point is closely connected to the structure of each group and the relationship between core organisers and ordinary online supporters as determined by communication flows. The next section focuses on these issues.

Inclusive Citizenship: Work in Progress

Although it was clear from the onset of this study that the technology-enabled mass empowerment of disabled citizens theorised by scholars such as Finkelstein (1980) and Nelson (1994) was simply utopian, the picture that emerged from empirical research was not one of 'politics as usual' either, at least not entirely. Instead, the unprecedented use of online media by British disability rights advocates in the wake of the most severe policy crisis in recent years affected the citizenship levels of those involved in two main ways. Once again, the formal disability organisations involved in The Hardest Hit and the experienced self-advocates in DPAC supported a partially updated version of their traditional participation schemes. In contrast, The Broken of Britain embarked on a more ambitious plan to make interactive e-advocacy work better for disabled Internet users, enhancing their ability to participate in politics, albeit with some important limits. Most notably, the structure of this group was far from being perfectly democratic. Nevertheless, it promoted a new way for disabled Internet users to perform political citizenship through the brokerage of politically driven and tech-savvy disabled peers who had been propelled to a position of leadership by their visibility on online media.

Greater Engagement but Within Clear Boundaries

Both the formal disability organisations that sponsored The Hardest Hit campaign and the experienced disabled activists that launched DPAC provided ordinary Internet users with opportunities to become genuinely engaged in their initiatives. Most of these opportunities, however, were firmly anchored to traditional tactics and established mobilisation practices. New media technologies helped to make the activities of these groups – from 'write to your MP' campaigns to street protest – more easily accessible to Internet users. However, they did not fundamentally change the nature of their action repertoire or complement it with new types of action. In other words, the Web presence of these groups, including their Facebook pages, made disability rights advocacy available to a greater number of potential supporters, but at the same time did not foster a qualitative shift in the way in which people could become engaged.

For example, DPAC's practice of linking its virtual protest pages to street protests and other disruptive events at the peak of the welfare reform debate had the potential to address the issue of distance and other physical barriers for those interested in participating. However, this type of approach to new media technologies did not increase the range of options available to potential supporters. The traditional repertoire of contention became digitised, but did not branch out in new directions. This was problematic, as it limited the ability of an important group like DPAC, to attract new, possibly younger supporters by providing suitable alternatives for those who were unconvinced by or uncomfortable with protest to become engaged in other ways. To draw a parallel with institutionalised forms of e-participation, this approach functioned in much the same way as government sponsored e-democracy initiatives, which tend to attract people who have a strong interest in politics, as well as the knowledge, time and confidence needed to take part in high-threshold political activities (Chadwick 2012, p. 50).

By expanding, but not re-designing, the space for engagement, digitised disability activists risked preaching to the converted. Those who are typically disengaged from politics were not afforded new opportunities to become fuller citizens. Indeed, protest continues to have a role to play in influencing policy-making, but it is other, possibly less contentious and less demanding forms of online participation that are more likely to attract disenfranchised people. Engaging with new forms of action does not mean forgetting about more established ones. DPAC took some tentative steps towards blending innovative and traditional tactics in some of its most recent initiatives such as the 'Save the Independent Living Fund (ILF)' campaign mentioned in Chapter 3. However, whether or not these attempts can reach beyond the 'usual suspects' and involve new types of supporters remains to be demonstrated. Having said that, it is important to note that DPAC was also the only group among those examined in this book that continued to operate in 2016, six years after its foundation. This was a testament to both the strengths and vulnerabilities of a traditional activist group based on strong principles and centred on a set of committed organisers.

In contrast, the formal disability organisations that joined forces to form The Hardest Hit coalition in 2010 went beyond groups such as DPAC in terms of personalisation and user-engagement. Indeed, it was interesting to note that The Hardest Hit organised several street demonstrations in London and other cities across the U.K. between May and October 2011. This was a highly unusual move for many of the non-profits involved in this collaborative campaign and reaffirmed the importance of physical space and street protest in times of crisis, which in recent years has been displayed also by much larger contemporary movements such as Occupy and the Spanish *Indignados* (Gerbaudo 2012, p. 155). This demonstrated also that moderate and somewhat 'institutionalised' advocacy organisations are willing to resort to more contentious tactics when the stakes are particularly high. Besides protest rallies, The Hardest Hit promoted both mediated (e.g. the 'Your Stories' section of the website) and un-mediated (e.g. personalised messages to policy-makers, individual stories shared on Facebook) forms of online action. Although these types of action lacked the coordination that typically characterises in-person protest, they also gave online supporters the freedom to craft their own campaign content and choose from a range of ways to participate, albeit not a very extensive one. While it is difficult to imagine that these forms of online action could boost collective agency in the disability community, they still had the potential to generate micro-empowerment at the individual level.

As was pointed out in Chapter 3, The Hardest Hit's online infrastructure was designed to mobilise a strong response to government policy quickly rather than organising the disability community for years to come. As a result, the enthusiasm for this type of collaborative advocacy faded after the Welfare Reform Act was passed in 2012. Despite this limit, which was associated in part with the need to negotiate different advocacy styles and different priorities among a very wide range of organisations, the way in which The Hardest Hit approached online media was nevertheless remarkable for two main reasons. First, it showed that many established disability organisations in the U.K. were open to embracing an expanded idea of membership, recognising that many people want to participate in advocacy initiatives without necessarily becoming 'members' of an organisation. Second, it offered online supporters opportunities to channel their anger into something more than just plain talk. Overall, this was disability advocacy re-configured to be more readily available and in some ways also more inclusive, although within some clear boundaries. Arguably, these boundaries had been designed not necessarily to retain tight organisational control, but to prevent fragmentation.

Digital Networks, De Facto *Leadership and 'Peer-Mediated' Citizenship*

Digital action networks stood out in the new ecology of British disability advocacy in many ways. The example examined in this book, The Broken of Britain, seemed to come from nowhere to gain near instant visibility in late 2010. Its founding members, all young disabled bloggers, were able to capitalise on their experience with new media technologies to quickly coalesce a number of Internet users around their group's social media presence. They were also pragmatically open to assessing the initiatives organised by other groups and collaborating with them if appropriate. That said, this group focused exclusively on e-advocacy and shunned mass in-person events. Social media were instrumental in helping The Broken of Britain's founders to build an image of this group as a legitimate representative of the disability community. The analysis of conversations drawn from this group's Facebook page showed that its supporters welcomed opportunities to participate in the welfare reform debate that were different from traditional protest and established advocacy methods, seen respectively as too far 'outside' and 'inside' the tent of representative democracy to be truly effective. At the same time, however, The Broken of Britain's founders were determined also to project a coherent message and overall 'brand' towards policy-makers and the news media. This encouraged a level of centralisation that was somewhat at odds with the idea of online networks as horizontal structures in which power is distributed more or less equally among a broad range of actors.

While the consequences of The Broken of Britain's structure for the levels of citizenship of those associated with it – in particular disabled Internet users – are discussed in detail in Chapter 5, it is useful to reflect here on two factors that set this group apart from the others examined in this book. On the one hand, its core organisers demonstrated themselves to be particularly attentive to the needs of other disabled Internet users. Their inventiveness and experience as disabled users of new media technologies enabled them to mix and match ready-made platforms to devise new ways for other disabled Internet users to take part in activities such as '#TwitterStories' and a blog swarm. This marked a qualitative shift in collective action as it not only aimed at making e-advocacy more accessible to disabled Internet users, but also went beyond the mere expansion of established protest tactics. On the other hand, the fact that The Broken of Britain's founders were all young disabled people set this group apart from formal disability organisations, many of which continue to be controlled by a non-disabled leadership. Indeed, the small group of core organisers at the centre of The Broken of Britain was firmly in control of decision-making. The online-only character of this group helped its founders cement their role as *de facto* leaders, while supporters were confined to seemingly lesser roles as informants ('monitorial citizens') and observers ('latent citizens'). However, this system enabled those in the last two groups to be represented by a set of technology-savvy peers instead of a non-disabled leadership. This process was described here as 'peer-mediated citizenship'. New media technologies were the enablers of this system as they created connections that otherwise would not have existed between geographically dispersed aspiring self-advocates and potential supporters.

Intuitively, this system provided an important opportunity for disabled Internet users to enhance their stake in citizenship. However, it is less clear whether it contributed to the realisation of truly inclusive citizenship.

One of the cornerstones of inclusive citizenship is participatory parity, which implies that everyone enjoys fair and equal opportunities to participate in public life. The initiatives set up by The Broken of Britain's founders provided ordinary disabled Internet users with new ways to participate in democratic politics not only by taking part in online actions, but also by interacting with core organisers through conversations on social media platforms such as Facebook. Yet, this group also limited opportunities for supporters to act more spontaneously in order to protect its image from the backlash generated by potentially inappropriate actions. In addition, its structure made it difficult for ordinary supporters to join the ranks of core organisers. This generated a power imbalance and lack of internal accountability that was at odds with the ideal of participatory parity. The reasons that led The Broken of Britain's founders to favour this model are easily understandable: balancing the benefits of participatory advocacy with those of a strong leadership capable of projecting a coherent message and engaging directly with policy-makers when needed. This demonstrated that, in digital action networks, the tension between full equality of participation and the need for efficiency remains unresolved. Thus, 'peer-mediated' citizenship is not entirely democratic, but nonetheless preferable to delegating disabled people's voice to third party organisations.

Given that the emergence of other digital disability action networks after The Broken of Britain suggested that this type of advocacy group is likely here to stay, it is important to consider its implications for disabled people who still do not use the Internet. While the other types of British disability groups examined in this book sought to reach out to their stakeholders – in particular disabled people – using both online and offline channels, The Broken of Britain focused exclusively on online communications. Undoubtedly, the visibility that this self-advocacy group was able to acquire by operating online defied the popular assumption that, due to digital divide issues, the Internet cannot represent an important civic resource for disadvantaged groups, including disabled citizens. In particular, core organisers showed a strong commitment to making e-advocacy accessible by capitalising on their experience as disabled users to combine readily available interactive media in innovative ways. Yet, the decision not to engage in any forms of offline communication, whether because of resource implications or deeper strategic reasons, constituted a serious barrier to participation for those – especially older disabled people – who are not able to use the Internet independently or, to this day, continue to be completely unconnected. Although only a minority of disabled Britons is now in this situation (Dutton & Blank 2013), it is still a sizeable number of people.

Disabled non-users are not necessarily cut out from the work of digital action networks such as The Broken of Britain and its successors. It is still possible for non-users to come into contact with these types of initiatives through proxy Internet use, i.e. by having someone else access the Internet for them. In addition, word of mouth can provide another option for non-users to receive updates about digital action networks through friends and acquaintances in a similar fashion to the 'cascading' model employed by recent online election campaigns to reach unconnected voters, particularly in the U.S. (Gibson 2009; Kreiss 2012). That said, the online-only nature of digital action networks prevents disabled non-users from contributing directly and independently to their advocacy efforts, forcing them to depend on others to participate. This highlights an implicit paradox in digital disability action networks, which provide disabled Internet users with new ways to exercise their political rights, but at the same time risk excluding those who cannot afford technology or for whom it remains inaccessible. While more accessible new media platforms and more affordable connection options continue to be developed, those at the centre of future digital disability action networks should urgently consider ways to extend this new way of organising to disabled non-users. This is not only an equal opportunities issue, but also one that has to do with strategy and political efficacy. Ultimately, the decision to operate exclusively online to defend the rights of a social group in which more than four in ten people remain unconnected restricts the number of supporters that can be reached and mobilised. As supporter numbers continue to matter in today's political game (Chadwick 2012, p. 54), this is likely to represent an important limit for any new disability rights group wishing to take the same approach.

Crisis and the Context of E-Advocacy

The comparison between British and American formal disability organisations showed that the broader political context plays a fundamental role in fostering or inhibiting the development of innovative forms of e-advocacy. While the influence of systemic factors such as governance structures, constitutional arrangements and ties between advocacy organisations and their primary constituents has been researched extensively in previous work on Internet politics, it is particularly useful to reflect here on the role of circumstantial factors such as the events that trigger e-advocacy and online protest. Indeed, the link between disruptive events and citizen mobilisation pre-dates the Internet era (Woliver 1993). However, as an increasingly diverse range of actors is using new media technologies to express dissent, it is important to distinguish between the events that can and those that cannot ignite innovation in e-advocacy and collective action. The case studies discussed in this book suggested that the more 'intense' a controversy is, the more likely advocacy groups are to experiment with participatory media. Two complementary dimensions determined the 'intensity' of the controversies examined here.

The first dimension was the nature of the issues at stake. Issues with deep ideological ramifications prompted a different response compared to those that dealt more simply with the re-distribution of public funds.

Deep crises that involve the re-definition of fundamental rights can be assumed to encourage advocates to adopt new and bolder tactics. This was the case for British disability organisations, which joined forces to experiment with an unprecedented mix of participatory media and street rallies in the wake of the welfare reform, which represented a fundamental setback in disability policy. Instead, re-distribution issues tend to provide advocates with comparatively fewer incentives to go beyond tried and tested online tactics, and develop new repertoires. In addition, these types of issues can foster divisions among groups that compete for the same resources. The Medicaid cuts controversy in the U.S. offered a classic example of the dilemma that advocates face under these circumstances. Although the cuts were poised to affect the vast majority of disabled Americans, they also fuelled intra-group competition. Ultimately, this led to a fragmented response and curbed opportunities for high-profile action, including street rallies, given that no one wanted to be seen as a potential troublemaker while budget allocations were being discussed.

The second dimension of intensity was provided by the political climate that surrounded the issues at stake. Did advocacy groups receive any backing from representative institutions, including opposition parties, or were they left to 'fight their corner' on their own? In 2011, U.S. disability advocates benefited from the support of the Obama administration in their opposition to Republican budget plans that included deep cuts to Medicaid. This not only boosted their success chances, but also mitigated the sense of urgency associated with that issue, suggesting that ordinary advocacy tactics may be sufficient in that case. In contrast, British disability rights advocates faced what could be described as a 'double crisis'. Not only did they need to fend off plans to 'roll back' disability benefits, but they also did not receive support from any major institutional ally. In particular, the Labour Party – the main opposition party and a traditional ally of disabled people – was slow at mounting a decisive attack against the planned overhaul of disability benefits. This created a representation 'void' around the interests of disabled citizens, which British disability advocates sought to fill by adopting innovative online repertoires and launching wholly new forms of organisation such as digital action networks.

In light of these considerations, both the nature of the issues at stake and the availability of institutional backing for grassroots groups constitute fundamental components of the context in which e-advocacy takes place (Figure 7.1). Although the case study approach adopted in this study invites caution in trying to generalise its findings, the evidence presented in this book suggests that these two circumstantial factors can favour or disfavour innovation and growth in e-advocacy depending on how they are combined.

Flexibility should be adopted in assessing the 'intensity' of a given crisis, as issues that appear similar can take on very different nuances in different countries. Furthermore, given that this project focused on clear-cut case studies in which circumstantial factors were combined in ways that were

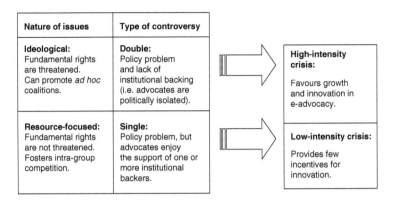

Nature of issues	Type of controversy
Ideological: Fundamental rights are threatened. Can promote *ad hoc* coalitions.	**Double:** Policy problem and lack of institutional backing (i.e. advocates are politically isolated).
Resource-focused: Fundamental rights are not threatened. Fosters intra-group competition.	**Single:** Policy problem, but advocates enjoy the support of one or more institutional backers.

High-intensity crisis:

Favours growth and innovation in e-advocacy.

Low-intensity crisis:

Provides few incentives for innovation.

Figure 7.1 Circumstantial influences on e-advocacy.

mutually reinforcing, it is important to ask whether this model can be applied also to situations in which circumstantial factors are oriented in opposite directions, making the distinction between 'high' and 'low' intensity crises less straightforward and open to interpretation. This is a question that requires more empirical research. That said, the evidence collected for this project revealed that, in spite of the apparent uniqueness of the events that surround online advocacy at any one time, keeping a close eye on both the nature of the issues at stake and the surrounding political climate can help scholars understand better whether growth and innovation in online advocacy can be expected.

Circumstantial factors did not replace, but rather complemented, systemic elements in generating a more sophisticated understanding of the 'context' in which e-advocacy takes places. For example, the decline of mass-email campaigns in Britain was explained by the relative ineffectiveness of this tactic in a governance system in which political party allegiance is tightly enforced. This and other systemic factors contributed, together with the intense policy crisis, to pushing British groups towards the adoption of an innovative online repertoire. Similarly, the absence of a unified online response to Medicaid cuts in the U.S. derived from the fact that this policy issue failed to strike the chords that would have re-activated old connections among disability advocates. In the past, American disability organisations cooperated on civil rights issues for disabled citizens (Vaughn-Switzer 2003). However, the Medicaid issue fostered division, as every organisation was preoccupied with protecting the interests of their own constituents. This meant that, while the U.S. context is not in itself unsuited to online collaboration, joint efforts are more or less likely depending on the issues at stake. Overall, the study of e-advocacy greatly benefits from a clear understanding of the context that surrounds it. While different systemic factors are likely to come to the fore in different regimes, the two dimensions of crisis discussed here transcend geo-political boundaries.

Looking Ahead: What Next for Disability, Politics and New Media Studies?

This book has shed light on several aspects of the relationship between disability and new media technologies that so far have been disregarded. In doing so, it exposed the centrality of the Internet in the recent evolution of disability rights advocacy, particularly in the U.K. However, this is a very complex issue and many other aspects remain to be explored. As this book went to print, particularly after Britain's vote to leave the European Union in June 2016, the spectre of financial instability once again loomed large over the global economy with the potential for a new crisis and more austerity in the years to come. At the same time, different types of disability advocacy groups continued to experiment with new online tools and tactics. This fluid context provides a number of opportunities for further work that builds directly on the findings of this study and expands this research to examine the significance of online media for mobilising and organising among other disadvantaged groups in addition to disabled people. There are at least four main strands of research to consider.

First, how will the relationship between disability rights advocacy and new media develop in the longer term? As was noted throughout this book, disability advocacy groups, despite being latecomers to the digital arena, constantly refine their online tactics and learn from each other, as well as from more or less formalised organisations active in other areas. Once more daring groups have experimented with new tactics, others tend to adopt them too as shown by the increasingly frequent use of personal stories of disability as channels for articulating complex policy issues in everyday terms and strategic communication tools to influence the news media and policy-makers. Also, a string of new groups has emerged since 2011 and, given the political and economic uncertainty of current times, as well as fast-paced technological evolution, electronic organising around disabled people's rights is likely to see further transformation in the years ahead. While the exploratory nature of this book called for a 'small data' approach to investigate the use of social media at the height of the U.K. welfare reform debate, further work could benefit from big data approaches to identify key trends in this emerging area of electronic advocacy.

Second, it is important to gain a better understanding of how new media technologies influence the participation of disabled citizens in 'formal' political processes that constitute the heart of representative democracy. This book focused on the efforts of grassroots advocacy groups and civil society organisations. That is where fundamental citizenship skills are practised, dissent is exercised and political agency strengthened. However, public decision-making is ultimately located in representative systems and institutionalised politics that have historically discriminated against disabled people. Is the Internet re-configuring 'formal' political processes in ways likely to affect disabled citizens, either positively or negatively? A useful place to start could be to explore the significance of online election campaigns for disabled people. As was noted in Chapter 1, in countries such as the U.K. and the U.S. disabled people continue to face a range of exclusionary barriers that prevent them from being able to participate fully in elections as voters, campaigners and candidates. Given that election campaigns are becoming increasingly digitised, it is important to ask whether this shift can help disabled citizens overcome some barriers or if this instead constitutes a new source of exclusion.

Third, one ought to ask also why the innovative e-advocacy tactics used by U.K. groups generated only limited tangible policy outcomes. Except for Atos's decision to withdraw from its ESA contract in 2014, British disability advocates have not scored other significant policy victories in recent years. There were no substantial modifications to the Welfare Reform Bill before it was passed into law in March 2012. More recently, campaigns to prevent the closure of the ILF did not stop this benefit from being discontinued in summer 2015. Atos remains in charge of the controversial new points-based tests associated with Personal Independent Payments (PIPs) and in March 2016 the U.K. Conservative government announced further cuts to this benefit worth over £1 billion. In order to understand the reasons behind these limited policy results, it is important to consider e-advocacy in the broader context of policy-making.

In particular, it would be useful to explore the relationship between grassroots advocacy groups and the news media, which continue to play a central role in policy-formation processes (Koch-Baumgartner & Voltmer 2010, p. 223). It is clear that the rhetoric and arguments used by British disability rights advocates at the peak of the welfare reform debate clashed with the negative frames that painted Disability Living Allowance (DLA) claimants as 'benefit scroungers' in a large part of the British press (Briant et al. 2013). More broadly, representations of disability in the news continue to be tied to a set of distinctive frames that tend to restrict the debate and often skew public opinion towards negative assumptions. Although new representations of disability have started to emerge in areas such as sports reporting and TV entertainment, news coverage in general tends to lag behind these trends and the 'benefit fraudster' frame outlined above is arguably part of a set of 'new, crippling [news reporting] norms that are evident' (Ellis & Goggin 2015, p. 76). This suggests that it may be difficult or even impossible for online advocacy initiatives to establish successful counter-narratives in contested policy areas such as that of disability welfare, especially when government spin is aligned with both the negative stereotypes used in news media and public opinion sentiments more broadly.

These issues speak to a current debate in communication and media studies. As Hoskins (2013) pointed out, 'the influences and impact of any medium cannot be understood in isolation from other media' (p. 4). In recent years there have been some useful attempts to conceptualise contemporary news production and event mediatisation processes through emergent paradigms such as those of 'new media ecology' (Awan et al. 2011) and the 'hybrid media system' (Chadwick 2013). Despite different terminologies, this literature has in common a renewed focus on the interaction between online actors on one side – both groups and individuals – and traditional news outlets on the other. Some have argued that 'the hybridised ways in which important political news events are now mediated presents new opportunities for nonelite actors to enter news production assemblages through timely interventions' (Chadwick 2011, p. 19). This could benefit grassroots advocates greatly. At the same time, it is possible also that social media contribute to the diffusion and reinforcement of dominant news media frames, including negative stereotypes. For these reasons, getting to the root of the limited policy outcomes achieved by British disability advocacy groups requires an in-depth investigation of the ways in which competing narratives of disability welfare were produced, shared and re-framed across different media.

Finally, it would be useful to expand the type of research that focused here on disabled people to other groups that traditionally have been marginalised or altogether excluded from democratic politics in order to better understand whether the Internet can be a civic resource for them too. As the experience of British disability advocacy groups has shown, extraordinary circumstances such as profound policy controversies can lead to unexpected changes in online participation patterns for a group such as disabled people. What about other groups such as immigrants, refugees, minority ethnic groups, people on low incomes or unemployed, social tenants and others? The current economic situation and future policy controversies that might ensue, as well as their impact on living standards and social relations, provide researchers with an opportunity to better understand the use of online media for disadvantaged groups that so far have incautiously and simplistically been relegated to the raw end of the digital divide.

This is a broad research agenda that could be approached from several different angles and with multiple methods. It is nevertheless essential that anyone wanting to delve into these topics, whatever strategy they may wish to adopt, remains open to any possible outcome and lets the data do the talking. Compelling theories such as the digital divide can serve as inspiration for research in these areas. Yet, they also restrict our perspective on emerging social trends by encouraging us to over-simplify what instead are complex and nuanced phenomena. Hopefully, this book showed that it pays off to challenge established paradigms and popular assumptions in relation to online citizenship, and ask whether what we can see is the entire picture or in fact there are important details that are still waiting to be discovered.

References

Awan, A.N., Hoskins, A. & O'Loughlin, B., 2011. *Radicalisation and Media: Connectivity and Terrorism in the New Media Ecology*, London: Routledge.

Bennett, W.L. & Segerberg, A., 2012. The Logic of Connective Action: Digital Media and the Personalization of Contentious Politics. *Information, Communication & Society*, 15(5), pp. 739–768.

Briant, E., Watson, N. & Philo, G., 2013. Reporting Disability in the Age of Austerity: The Changing Face of Media Representation of Disability and Disabled People in the United Kingdom and the Creation of New 'Folk Devils'. *Disability & Society*, 28(6), pp. 874–889.

Castells, M., 2012. *Networks of Outrage and Hope: Social Movements in the Internet Age*, Cambridge: Polity Press.

Chadwick, A., 2007. Digital Network Repertoires and Organizational Hybridity. *Political Communication*, 24(3), pp. 283–301.

———— 2011. The Political Information Cycle in a Hybrid News System: The British Prime Minister and the 'Bullygate' Affair. *The International Journal of Press/Politics*, 16(1), pp. 3–29.

———— 2012. Recent Shifts in the Relationship Between the Internet and Democratic Engagement in Britain and the United States: Granularity, Informational Exuberance, and Political Learning. In E. Anduiza, M. Jensen, & L. Jorba, eds. *Digital Media and Political Engagement Worldwide: A Comparative Study*. Cambridge: Cambridge University Press, pp. 39–55.

———— 2013. *The Hybrid Media System: Politics and Power*, New York: Oxford University Press.

Crow, L., 1996. Including All of Our Lives: Renewing the Social Model of Disability. In C. Barnes & G. Mercer, eds. *Exploring the Divide: Illness and Disability*. Leeds: The Disability Press, pp. 55–72.

Dutton, W.H. & Blank, G., 2013. *Cultures of the Internet: The Internet in Britain*, Oxford: Oxford Internet Institute.

Ellis, K. & Goggin, G., 2015. *Disability and the Media*, London: Palgrave.

Fawcett, B., 2000. *Feminist Perspectives on Disability*, Harlow: Pearson Education Limited.

Finkelstein, V., 1980. *Attitudes and Disabled People*, New York: World Rehabilitation Fund.

Flanagin, A.J., Stohl, C. & Bimber, B., 2006. Modeling the Structure of Collective Action. *Communication Monographs*, 73(1), pp. 29–54.

French, S., 1993. Disability, Impairment, or Something in Between. In C. Barnes, J. Swain, S. French & C. Thomas, eds. *Disabling Barriers, Enabling Environments*. London: SAGE, pp. 17–25.

Gerbaudo, P., 2012. *Tweet and the Streets: Social Media and Contemporary Activism*, London: Pluto Press.

Gibson, R.K., 2009. New Media and the Revitalisation of Politics. *Representation*, 45(3), pp. 289–299.

Goggin, G. & Noonan, T., 2007. Blogging Disability: The Interface Between New Cultural Movements and Internet Technology. In A. Bruns & J. Jacobs, eds. *Uses of Blogs*. New York: Peter Lang Publishing, pp. 161–172.

Hoskins, A., 2013. Death of a Single Medium. *Media, War & Conflict*, 6(1), pp. 3–6.

Karpf, D., 2010. Advocacy Group Communications in the New Media Environment. In *8th APSA Political Communication Pre-conference meeting*, Washington, DC, 1 September.

—— 2012. *The MoveOn Effect: The Unexpected Transformation of American Political Advocacy*, New York: Oxford University Press.

Kavada, A., 2010. Activism Transforms Digital: The Social Movement Perspective. In M. Joyce, ed. *Digital Activism Decoded: The New Mechanics of Change*. New York: International Debate Education Association, pp. 101–118.

Koch-Baumgartner, S. & Voltmer, K., 2010. Conclusion: The Interplay of Mass Communication and Political Decision Making – Policy Matters! In S. Koch-Baumgartner & K. Voltmer, eds. *Public Policy and the Mass Media: The Interplay of Mass Communication and Political Decision Making*. London: Routledge, pp. 215–227.

Kreiss, D., 2012. *Taking Our Country Back: The Crafting of Networked Politics from Howard Dean to Barack Obama*, Oxford: Oxford University Press.

Morris, J., 1991. *Pride Against Prejudice: Transforming Attitudes to Disability*, London: The Women's Press.

—— 1992. Personal and Political: A Feminist Perspective on Researching Physical Disability. *Disability, Handicap & Society*, 7(2), pp. 157–166.

Nelson, J.A., 1994. Virtual Reality: The Promise of a Brave New World for Those with Disability. In J. A. Nelson, ed. *The Disabled, the Media, and the Information Age*. Westport, CT: Greenwood Press, pp. 197–209.

Rainie, L. & Wellman, B., 2012. *Networked: The New Social Operating System*, Cambridge, MA: The MIT Press.

Thoreau, E., 2006. Ouch!: An Examination of the Self-Representation of Disabled People on the Internet. *Journal of Computer-Mediated Communication*, 11(2), pp. 442–468.

Trevisan, F., 2014. Scottish Disability Organizations and Online Media: A Path to Empowerment or 'Business as Usual?' *Disability Studies Quarterly*, 34(3).

Vaughn-Switzer, J., 2003. *Disabled Rights: American Disability Policy and the Fight for Equality*, Washington, DC: Georgetown University Press.

Watson, N., 1998. Enabling Identity: Disability, Self and Citizenship. In T. Shakespeare, ed. *The Disability Reader*. London: Continuum, pp. 147–162.

Woliver, L., 1993. *From Outrage to Action: The Politics of Grassroot Dissent*, Urbana & Chigago: The University of Illinois Press.

Appendix A
Semi-Structured Interview Guide

Introduction:

- Can you describe briefly your organisation/group/campaign? How is it organised, who are its members, what does it stand for?
- Are you a staff member/trustee/volunteer/activist/all of the above, other?
- How would you describe your role and responsibilities? To what extent are these formalised?
- How/why did you become involved in this organisation/group/campaign?

Advocacy and campaigning in the Internet age:

- What makes the Internet useful for your advocacy work?
- Has the Internet changed campaigning/lobbying/advocacy as you knew it?
- What are the most significant changes that have occurred in the past five years?
- Have new media technologies brought with them any challenges for advocates like you?

Digital media strategy:

- Whom are you trying to reach online? Are there any particular groups or types of people you are trying to target?
- What position do new media technologies occupy in your overall communications strategy (if any)? Are they a priority?
- How does online advocacy compare to in-person events such as rallies and protests?
- How far ahead do you plan your online operations?
- If something unforeseen happens, are you able to react quickly?
- You use a number of online platforms, how do you co-ordinate among them?
- Give me an example of something you think you have achieved through the use of digital media.

User preferences:

- From your point of view, what are the most useful online platforms and why?
- From the point of view of your members/supporters, which do you think are the most useful platforms to them?
- (As a disabled advocate) what is your personal experience with social media?

- Have you developed any specific strategies for reaching as many disabled Internet users as possible?

Participation catalysts:

- Tell me a little bit about your current advocacy campaigns; what prompted them?
- Where do you see your Web presence in 12 months from now?
- How do you measure the success of your e-advocacy initiatives?

Appendix B
Online Media Inventory Matrix

Strategic function	Interactive feature	Code
Personalisation & user-input	Audience segmentation (customisable website)	Present (1); Absent (0)
	Share your stories page	Present (1); Absent (0)
	Polls & surveys	Present (1); Absent (0)
	Clicktivism 'plus'	Present (1); Absent (0)
Broadcast information (top-down communication)	Email action network	Present (1); Absent (0)
	Other email lists and/or discussion groups	Present (1); Absent (0)
	RSS feed	Present (1); Absent (0)
	Regular newsletter	Both online and offline (1); Online only (2); Offline only (3); Absent (0)
	Events calendar	Present – customisable (1); Present – not customisable (2); Absent (0)
	Personal contact details for officers	Present (1); Absent (0)
	Generic contact details	Present (1); Absent (0)
Develop community (horizontal communication)	Discussion forum	Present (1); Absent (0)
	Official blogs	Present – comments enabled (1); Present – comments disabled (2); Absent (0)
	Members-only area	Present (1); Absent (0)
	Twitter account	Present (1); Absent (0)
	Facebook page	'Fan' page (1); Group page (2); Absent (0)

(Continued)

Strategic function	Interactive feature	Code
Develop community (horizontal communication) – *continued*	YouTube	Dedicated channel (1); Individual videos (2); Absent (0)
	Flickr account	Present (1); Absent (0)
	Join button on homepage	Present (1); Absent (0)
	Donate button on homepage	Present (1); Absent (0)
	Share button on homepage	Present (1); Absent (0)
Action resources	E-petitions	Present (1); Absent (0)
	E-postcards/letters	Present (1); Absent (0)
	Dedicated campaigns/ advocacy website section	Present (1); Absent (0)
	Event maps	Present (1); Absent (0)
	Virtual protest pages	Present (1); Absent (0)
	Other resources	Please specify

Appendix C
Facebook Content Coding Frame

Section A: Apply to each entire Facebook conversation thread as coding unit

Box	Variable	Categories
A	Thread ID	T001; T002; T003; etc.
B	Sponsor/owner of page/ content	HHIT – The Hardest Hit DPAC – Disabled People Against Cuts BOB – The Broken of Britain
C	Date coded	DD/MM/YYY
D	Coder ID	Initials
E	Thread length	Nr of posts (including starter post)
F	Date of first post	DD/MM/YYYY
G	Date of most recent post	DD/MM/YYYY
H	Nr of unique contributors	Nr
I	Structural focus	1- Politics 2- Policy 3- Both 4- Other 5- Not classifiable
J	Structural topic	1 – On primary topic (Welfare reform and public expenditure cuts) 0 – On other topic

Section B: Apply to each individual Facebook post as coding unit

Box	Variable	Categories
K	Post ID	P0001; P0002; P0003; etc.
L	Date posted	DD/MM/YYYY
M	Time posted	24hr
N	Function of post	1 – Starter 2 – Comment
O	Post's length	Nr of words
P	Primary medium used in post	1 – Text 2 – Photo (original) 3 – Video (original) 4 – Link to news media site (traditional) 5 – Link to news media site (emergent/activist) 6 – Link to sponsor/owner's own site 7 – Link to blog (organisation's own) 8 – Link to blog (other) 9 – Link to other disability organisation/group/campaign 10 – Other 11 – Not classifiable
Q	User ID	User0001; User0002; etc.
R	User type	1 – Page owner (using group's name) 2 – Administrator/main blogger (posting using personal screen name) 3 – Individual user/supporter 4 – Other campaign/organisation 5 – Other (specify)
S	Personal story of disability	1 – Yes 0 – No
T	Personal story's authorship (source of story)	1 – Direct account in the 1st person 2 – Friend/family member 3 – Carer (un-related) 4 – Professional help (medical, legal, etc.) 5 – Other (specify) 6 – Not classifiable 0 – Not applicable

(*Continued*)

(Continued)

Box	Variable	Categories
U	Key topics covered in post (enter all that apply)	1 – Welfare reform plans and public expenditure cuts 2 – Other issues with the welfare/benefits system 3 – Current government plans in other policy area (please specify) 4 – Opposition policy/plans 5 – Sponsor organisation's own event/initiative 6 – Other organisation's event/initiative 7 – Political process more generally (elections/legislative process/decision-making) 8 – Politicians' attitudes to social inequalities/discrimination 9 – Other disabling barriers (including societal attitudes) 10 – Other (issues not connected to disability and/or politics) 11 – Not classifiable 0 – Not applicable
V	Problem framing	1 – Collective 2 – Individual 3 – Not classifiable 0 – Not applicable
W	Main argument framing (if in doubt, indicate more than one)	1 – Socio-economic citizenship 2 – Political citizenship 3 – Civil (legal) rights/Human rights 4 – Moral panic 5 – Tragedy 6 – Media propaganda 7 – Irony 8 – Other 9 – Not classifiable 0 – Not applicable
X	Institutions mentioned (enter all that apply)	1 – Prime minister (by name or role) 2 – Department for Work and Pensions 3 – Minister for Disabled People (by name or role) 4 – Other government member/-s (by name or role) 5 – Government (generic) 6 – Parliament (and parliamentary committees, MPs – generic)

(Continued)

Box	Variable	Categories
		7 – Leader of the opposition (by name or role)
		8 – Conservative Party
		9 – Liberal Democrats
		10 – Labour Party
		11 – National Health Service (NHS)
		12 – Private contractors for DWP/NHS (e.g. Atos)
		13 – Traditional news media organisations
		14 – Other (please specify)
		0 – Not applicable
Y	Political action mentioned (enter all that apply)	1 – Individual online/offline action (e.g. email/phone/write to government officials; contribute to consultation process)
		2 – Endorse leaders/organisers to represent disabled people and other supporters (e.g. meeting with politicians, contributing to public consultations, etc.)
		3 – Collective online action (e.g. sign e-petition; contribute to e-protest page; use personal social networking profile as part of innovative collective action such as #TwitterStories, etc.)
		4 – Collective in-person protest (e.g. street march, rally, demonstration, occupation)
		5 – Contact news media organisations
		6 – Contact other online locations (spread the word)
		7 – Oust politicians at the next election
		8 – Unspecified need to influence decision-makers
		9 – Other (please specify)
		0 – Not applicable (no action)

Index

Note: Tables are indicated in bold; figures and illustrations in italics.